P9-DEI-896

American Foreign Policy

Cases and Choices

FOREIGN AFFAIRS BOOKS

American Foreign Policy: Cases and Choices *(2003)*

The War on Terror (Updated and Expanded *2003)*

America and the World: Debating the New Shape of International Politics *(2002)*

Globalization: Challenge and Opportunity *(2002)*

The Middle East in Crisis *(2002)*

The Rise of China *(2002)*

How Did This Happen? Terrorism and the New War *(2002) Public Affairs*

The American Encounter:
The United States and the Making of the Modern World *(1997) BasicBooks*

Clash of Civilizations? The Debate *(1996)*

To order, call W.W. Norton & Company at 800-233-4830 or
visit www.wwnorton.com

COUNCIL ON FOREIGN RELATIONS

Emergency Responders: Drastically Underfunded,
Dangerously Unprepared *(2003)*

Iraq: The Day After *(2003)*

Meeting the North Korean Nuclear Challenge *(2003)*

Chinese Military Power *(2003)*

Burma: Time for Change *(2003)*

Indonesia Commission: Peace and Progress in Papua *(2003)*

To order, call the Brookings Institution at 800-275-1447 or
visit www.brookings.edu

American Foreign Policy

Cases and Choices

A Foreign Affairs Book

FOREIGN AFFAIRS / Council on Foreign Relations

NEW YORK

Distributed by
W.W. Norton & Company
500 Fifth Avenue
New York, New York 10110

The Council on Foreign Relations is dedicated to increasing America's
understanding of the world and contributing ideas to U.S. foreign policy.
The Council accomplishes this mainly by promoting constructive debates,
clarifying world issues, producing reports, and publishing
Foreign Affairs, the leading journal on global issues.

**The Council takes no institutional position on policy issues and has no
affiliation with the U.S. government. All statements of fact and expressions of
opinion contained in all its publications are the sole responsibility of the author or authors.**

The Council's bimonthly magazine, *Foreign Affairs*, has been America's leading
publication on international affairs and foreign policy for over 80 years.
With a circulation of 130,000 worldwide, Foreign Affairs has long been
the most influential forum for important new ideas, analysis, and debate on significant
global issues. To subscribe, or for more information, visit www.foreignaffairs.org.

Foreign Affairs books are distributed by W.W. Norton (www.wwnorton.com).

Copyright © 2003 by the Council on Foreign Relations®, Inc.
All rights reserved. Printed in the United States of America.

This book may not be reproduced in whole or in part, in any form
(beyond copying permitted by Sections 107 and 108 of the U.S. Copyright Law
and excerpts by reviewers for the public press), without written permission
from the publisher. For information, write Licensing and Permissions,
Foreign Affairs, 58 East 68th Street, New York, NY 10021. www.foreignaffairs.org

Contents

Introduction

Gideon Rose

It is not the critic who counts; not the man who points out how the strong man stumbles, or where the doer of deeds could have done them better. The credit belongs to the man who is actually in the arena, whose face is marred by dust and sweat and blood; who strives valiantly; who errs, and comes short again and again, because there is no effort without error and shortcoming; but who does actually strive to do the deeds. . . .

THEODORE ROOSEVELT, "Citizenship in a Republic"

WHAT TEDDY KNEW

IN 1910, THEODORE ROOSEVELT spoke at the Sorbonne in Paris on the topic of what democratic republics required of their citizenry. In other kinds of polities, he noted, the attributes of the rulers are all-important. In a democracy, however, it is the attributes of ordinary citizens that matter, since ultimately it is they who are responsible for the quality of the policies followed. It was thus vital, he felt, for people in general, and the educated classes in particular, to develop an appropriately serious attitude toward policymakers and policymaking. If they could not go into public service themselves, they could at least avoid the occasional tendency of intellectuals to sneer at those who did, taking cheap shots from the sidelines at the dirty hands and difficult compromises that officials had to live with. As one approaches the challenges of American foreign policy nearly a century later, his words remain worth bearing in mind.

Most media debates about foreign policy start from the assumption that every question has a relatively obvious correct answer. Pundits

---

GIDEON ROSE is Managing Editor of *Foreign Affairs*.

imply that those who agree with them are wise and good, while those who disagree are fools or knaves. Most academic treatments of the subject, meanwhile, start from the assumption that government decision-making doesn't really matter much, because foreign policy choices are driven by broad structural forces such as the distribution of power in the international system or the nature of a country's domestic political institutions.

In fact, both of these perspectives are wrong, or rather seriously incomplete. Despite what talking heads might argue, knowledgeable people of good character and similar politics often disagree about what to do in a particular situation. And despite what social scientists might think, officials often have enough freedom of action to send history down any of several different tracks. Foreign policy professionals, accordingly, tend to view the subject in a different light, as an arena of constrained choice. They try to figure out just how much room for maneuver they actually have, and how they can use it best to advance national (and other) interests.

What the academics think of as "independent variables," the professionals think of as practical constraints—things that rule out one or another hypothetical course of action. They know that policy X, for example, might be an excellent substantive response to a certain problem, but also know that if it is anathema to a powerful ally, bureaucratic faction, or special interest group, it won't be adopted. So they pass over it quickly, spending their time debating the relative merits of policies Y and Z, which promise fewer benefits but also fewer costs.

And where amateurs see issues as black or white, professionals know that the choice is almost always between shades of gray—or more precisely, between separate bundles of black and white elements packaged together in different ways. The hallmark of the serious professionals' approach to foreign policy is thus not certainty but doubt; they live in a world with no free lunches, only an endless series of competing goods and unpleasant tradeoffs.

This collection is intended as an introduction to that world. Originally published in the pages of *Foreign Affairs*, the essays gathered here lay out a broad range of opinion on a variety of pressing questions in American foreign policy. The authors all know what they are talking about and all have the best interests of the country and the world at heart. Yet they come at the issues from different perspectives and often passionately disagree with each other's conclusions and recommendations. Fair-minded readers will conclude that they all score at least some points and must be taken seriously, which only sharpens the dilemma about what should be done in each case. Accepting that there are no good answers is the easy part; trying to decide which answer is the least bad, and why, is where things get interesting.

THE CHINA SYNDROME

THE FIRST FOUR ESSAYS deal with China, offering a variety of perspectives on how the United States should deal with a state rapidly pushing its way into the top ranks of international politics. Since power transitions have led to much of the trouble in world history, many consider this the single greatest long–term challenge for American foreign policy.

Richard Bernstein and Ross H. Munro see China's rise as a threat to important U.S. interests, and argue that Washington must prevent China from becoming a regional bully. Robert S. Ross, in contrast, argues that "the United States needs a policy to contend with China's potential for destabilizing [Asia], not a policy to deal with a future hegemon." He emphasizes China's efforts to cooperate with its neighbors and favors a response of engagement rather than containment.

Gerald Segal claims that both the China hawks and the China doves are misguided, entranced by visions of Chinese power that vastly exceed the mundane reality. China is "a country that has promised to deliver for much of the last 150 years but has consistently disappointed"—and may well again. Once the China problem is placed in proper perspective, he argues, sensible answers to it become much clearer.

Minxin Pei, finally, assesses the current status of China's political development, arguing that its rapid rise has been real but has left it confronting a variety of difficult domestic challenges. Figuring out how to solve the country's domestic governance crisis, he writes, is the real problem of the day, one that grand geopolitical perspectives rarely engage.

WAR—WHAT IS IT GOOD FOR?

THE NEXT FOUR PIECES deal with the question of humanitarian intervention—what the United States should do about terrible tragedies abroad that engage its compassion but not necessarily its strategic interests. Given the human suffering at issue, this question tends to generate strong emotions among analysts, and the pair of exchanges gathered here are no exceptions.

Michael Mandelbaum offers a scathing critique of the Clinton administration's intervention in Kosovo, arguing that it was a "perfect failure." Rather than helping the people of the Balkans, he claims, it hurt them; rather than establishing a model for future operations, it served as an object lesson in how not to fight a war; and rather than advancing American interests, it set them back.

James B. Steinberg, deputy national security adviser during the conflict, shoots right back, accusing Mandelbaum of "a breakdown of logic so elemental that it boggles the mind." The Clinton administration "worked to build a Europe undivided, democratic, and at peace," he writes, and in Kosovo it "did the right thing in the right way."

Alan J. Kuperman, meanwhile, argues that despite much retrospective hand-wringing, no American actions could have saved most of the victims of the 1994 Rwandan genocide. Facile assumptions about the possibilities of humanitarian intervention do little to help anyone, he claims, and can even divert attention from other sorts of policies—such as preventive diplomacy—that might help stave off tragedies in the first place.

Alison L. Des Forges, however, argues that Kuperman is far too quick to absolve Washington of indirect culpability through malign neglect, and that timely measures to thwart the unfolding nightmare in Rwanda were ready at hand and should have been tried. That they were not, she feels, is a lasting reproach to the United States and the international community at large. A response by Kuperman, countering some of Des Forges' points, concludes the exchange.

Introduction

SOME OF THE MOST IMPORTANT and contentious foreign policy issues involve economic questions such as trade with other countries. Thus sanctions—the denial of trade or other kinds of relations with a country as punishment for some sort of misbehavior—have become a commonly used foreign policy tool in recent years, and a controversial one.

Richard N. Haass argues that "the growing use of economic sanctions to promote foreign policy objectives is deplorable" because "they frequently contribute little to American foreign policy goals while being costly and even counterproductive." He sees many impositions of sanctions as sops to domestic audiences that backfire on policymakers, getting them into unpleasant situations from which extrication is difficult.

Jesse Helms, however, writing as a senator, claims that the supposed domination of American foreign policy by congressionally mandated sanctions is a canard. Not only are they imposed less frequently than often asserted, he writes, but they are also usually more sensibly conceived. What critics are really opposed to, he believes, are the substantive policies which lie behind the sanctions—policies that put moral values over business as usual, to the chagrin of many companies and the diplomatic establishment.

Sanctions are not the only impediments to free trade, however; domestic protectionism is also common, and a subject that sparks much debate. The George W. Bush administration has claimed that, like its predecessors, it is trying to maximize trade with other countries. C. Fred Bergsten agrees, arguing that the administration's concessions to domestic interest groups such as farmers and steel producers are not simply politically inspired backtracking from free trade—as critics charge—but the price the administration had to pay for the renewal of "fast track" negotiating authority, which was itself a precondition for a new global round of universal trade liberalization.

Bernard K. Gordon, however, is reluctant to give the administration such credit, arguing that its trade policies are counterproductive. Rather than press hard for broad new trade cuts, he claims, the administration has pursued the low-hanging fruit of bilateral and regional trade agreements. Despite what the administration avers, says Gordon, these are likely to slow rather than speed up progress on a new global trade round, and thus hurt the very cause the administration claims to support.

THE TROUBLE WITH ROGUES

HOW TO DEAL with the problem states often referred to as "rogues" is a perennial foreign policy issue, one that has emerged with even greater force than usual recently thanks to the Bush administration's singling out of Iraq, Iran, and North Korea—the "axis of evil"—for special attention.

Writing before the recent war in Iraq, Fouad Ajami laid out the case for it by pointing to the benefits to be gained from "spearheading a reformist project that seeks to modernize and transform the Arab landscape." U.S. efforts to try to manage the situation and avoid confronting the dysfunctional internal politics of the Middle East had failed, he argued, and massive external intervention was thus an unfortunate necessity—both to protect American interests and to help Iraqis and others in the region climb out of their morass.

Richard K. Betts disagreed, however, arguing that there was insufficient provocation to justify embarking on a preventive war, something Bismarck had aptly characterized as "suicide from fear of death." "By mistakenly conflating the immediate and longterm risks of Iraqi attack and by exaggerating the dangers in alternatives to war," he claimed, "the advocates of a preventive war against Saddam have miscast a modest probability of catastrophe as an acceptable risk."

Writing in the wake of the Iraq conflict, Kenneth M. Pollack notes that with Saddam gone, in some ways the security problems of the Persian Gulf might get more challenging rather than less. "Any Iraq strong enough to balance and contain Iran," he argues, "will inevitably be capable of overrunning Kuwait and Saudi Arabia." Actively countering Iran's nuclear weapons program, meanwhile, could strengthen hard-liners and thus actually increase the risks the program poses—and pulling back to lessen domestic political pressure on the brittle oil-rich states of the Gulf Cooperation Council could decrease rather than increase their incentives to reform. So no matter what course Washington chooses, Pollack says, it should not be surprised if it gets dragged into yet another regional crisis some years down the road.

Turning to North Korea, Victor Cha argues that the Bush administration's policies there are not as confused as they sometimes appear. There is a logic to "hawk engagement," he claims, that can shape events on the Korean Peninsula "in a way that best suits America's larger strategic interests—both during unification and beyond." Former U.S. ambassador to Korea, James T. Laney, and Jason T. Shaplen disagree, making the case that a return to less confrontational policies is necessary in order to move beyond the current impasse. Sustained negotiations toward a broader and deeper settlement than the 1994 Agreed Framework, they argue, should be Washington's objective.

Ray Takeyh, finally, offers an intriguing update on the doings of one of yesterday's villains, Libyan strongman Mu'ammar Qaddafi. The gradual evolution of Libyan policies to meet Washington's demands, Takeyh argues, poses the question of how the United States should handle a rogue regime that begins to come in from the cold. The continuation of this trend after the publication of Takeyh's piece, with the recent finalization of an agreement between Libya and the families of the Lockerbie bombing victims, only underscores his point.

AMERICA AND THE WORLD

THE DIPLOMATIC DUSTUP preceding the Iraq war has raised the issue of what the relation between the United States and the chief international organization is and should be. Analyzing that fracas, Michael J. Glennon argues that the UN Security Council has been just as disabled by American unipolarity as it was by the bipolarity that characterized the Cold War. The UN founders' "grand attempt to subject the use of force to the rule of law" thus lies in ruins, he claims, and can be revived only by some future attempt to create a new international institutional framework more suited to an era of American preeminence.

Picking up the gauntlet, Edward C. Luck, Anne-Marie Slaughter, and Ian Hurd challenge Glennon's analysis on practically every point.

Far from revealing the Security Council's obsolescence, they claim, the prewar diplomatic maneuvers demonstrated not only the institution's continued relevance, but also the necessity of multilateral consultation in transforming raw material power into international legitimacy.

Such views are held in little regard by the foreign policy gurus of the Bush administration, who favor robust American leadership rather than deference to the opinions of others. Setting out in 1996 what would later become the administration's game plan, William Kristol and Robert Kagan called for a "benevolent global hegemony" that would put America's exceptional power behind its exceptional values. A policy of "military supremacy and moral confidence," they argued, would lock in and extend a global system favorable not only to U.S. interests but also to international order and justice.

Joseph S. Nye, writing in the wake of the Iraq war, argues that in following such advice the Bush administration has neglected its "soft power" resources and unnecessarily ruffled feathers abroad. "The problem for U.S. power in the twenty-first century," Nye writes, "is that more and more continues to fall outside the control of even the most powerful state." From terrorism to global warming, nuclear proliferation to international financial stability, the United States will thus have little choice but to mobilize international coalitions to address shared threats and common challenges.

And in closing the volume, Andrew Moravcsik calls for a new transatlantic bargain that gives each side of the Western alliance its due. "The Iraq crisis offers two basic lessons," he notes. "The first, for Europeans, is that American hawks were right. Unilateral intervention to coerce regime change can be a cost-effective way to deal with rogue states. In military matters, there is only one superpower—the United States—and it can go it alone if it has to." But the second lesson, "for Americans, is that moderate skeptics on both sides of the Atlantic were also right. Winning a peace is much harder than winning a war. Intervention is cheap in the short run but expensive in the long run. And when it comes to the essential instruments for avoiding chaos or quagmire once the fighting stops— trade, aid, peacekeeping, international monitoring, and multilateral legitimacy—Europe remains indispensable."

Introduction

BEWARE OF WHAT YOU WISH FOR

FOR YEARS TO COME, American foreign policy decision-makers will have greater freedom from external constraint than any of their predecessors could ever dream of. In guiding the actions of the greatest power in the international system—in fact, the greatest power in modern history—they will have an unprecedented opportunity to shape the future of the world itself. But despite appearances, that power is actually something of a mixed blessing, since with great power comes great responsibility. As the essays above amply demonstrate, moreover, the freedom to choose does not make the choices themselves any clearer or more obvious.

How Should the United States Deal with a Rising Power?

The Coming Conflict with America

Richard Bernstein and Ross H. Munro

THE RISING ASIAN HEGEMON

FOR A quarter-century—indeed, almost since Richard Nixon signed the Shanghai Communiqué in 1972—a comforting, even heart-warming notion has prevailed among many policymakers and experts on American policy toward the People's Republic of China. They believe that China will inevitably become more like the West—non-ideological, pragmatic, materialistic, and progressively freer in its culture and politics. According to them, China is militarily weak and unthreatening; while Beijing tends toward rhetorical excess, its actual behavior has been far more cautious, aimed at the overriding goals of economic growth and regional stability.

While this vision of China, and especially its diplomatic and economic behavior, was largely true until the middle to late 1980s, it is now obsolete, as it ignores many Chinese statements and actions that suggest the country is emerging as a great power rival of the United States in the Pacific. True, China is more open and internationally engaged than at any time since the communist revolution of 1949. Nevertheless, since the late 1980s Beijing's leaders,

RICHARD BERNSTEIN is a *New York Times* book critic and was *Time* magazine's first Beijing Bureau Chief. ROSS H. MUNRO is Director of Asian studies at the Center for Security Studies and Conflict Research. This article originally appeared in the March/April 1997 issue of *Foreign Affairs*.

especially those who have taken over national policy in the wake of Deng Xiaoping's enfeeblement, have set goals that are contrary to American interests. Driven by nationalist sentiment, a yearning to redeem the humiliations of the past, and the simple urge for international power, China is seeking to replace the United States as the dominant power in Asia.

Since the late 1980s, Beijing has come to see the United States not as a strategic partner but as the chief obstacle to its own strategic ambitions. It has, therefore, worked to reduce American influence in Asia, to prevent Japan and the United States from creating a "contain China" front, to build up a military with force projection capability, and to expand its presence in the South China and East China Seas so that it controls the region's essential sea-lanes. China's sheer size and inherent strength, its conception of itself as a center of global civilization, and its eagerness to redeem centuries of humiliating weakness are propelling it toward Asian hegemony. Its goal is to ensure that no country in the region—whether Japan seeking oil exploration rights in the East China Sea, Taiwan inviting the Dalai Lama for an official visit, or Thailand allowing American naval vessels to dock in its ports—will act without taking China's interests into prime consideration.

TACTICALLY TACTFUL

CHINA AND the United States have, to be sure, been through phases of friendship and tension, with some of the latter unrelated to China's hegemonic goals. At times relations have soured because of inconsistent American policies, especially on human rights and trade matters, that have irritated China's leaders and produced a nationalistic reaction among intellectuals and ordinary Chinese alike. China's current leaders understand the value of stable relations with Washington and under the right terms will accept, as President Jiang Zemin recently did, a resumption of the ceremonies of high-level exchanges.

But China's willingness, even eagerness, to improve the Sino-American mood represents a tactical gesture rather than a strategic one. Since its setback in the Taiwan crisis of early 1996—when China's decision to stage large-scale military exercises in the Straits of Taiwan during Taiwan's presidential election drew harsh criticism from the international community and led the United States to deploy two aircraft carrier task forces to the region—Beijing has tempered its confrontational rhetoric and retreated from some of the actions that most annoyed Washington. China's deference reflects its continued interest in the burgeoning trade and technology transfer relationship with the United States and its hope of quelling anti-Chinese sentiment in Congress and among the American public. When Jiang Zemin comes to Washington in the next year or two, many Americans will likely regard the visit as a sign of a restored sense of common interests. Influential Chinese planners like General Mi Zhenyu, vice-commandant of the Academy of Military Sciences in Beijing, on the other hand, will see it as the next step in bringing China's strength and influence up to par with the United States. "For a relatively long time it will be absolutely necessary that we quietly nurse our sense of vengeance," Mi wrote last year. "We must conceal our abilities and bide our time."[1]

China's goal of achieving paramount status in Asia conflicts with an established American objective: preventing any single country from gaining overwhelming power in Asia. The United States, after all, has been in major wars in Asia three times in the past half-century, always to prevent a single power from gaining ascendancy. It seems almost indisputable that over the next decade or two China will seek to become the dominant power on its side of the Pacific. Actual military conflict between the United States and China, provoked, for example, by a Chinese attempt to seize Taiwan by force or to resolve by military means its territorial claims in the South China Sea, is always possible, particularly as China's military strength continues to grow.

Even without actual war, China and the United States will be adversaries in the major global rivalry of the first decades of the century. Competition between them will force other countries to take sides and will involve all the standard elements of international

---

[1]*Megatrends China*, Beijing: Hualing Publishing House, May 1996.

competition: military strength, economic well-being, influence among other nations and over the values and practices that are accepted as international norms. Moreover, the Chinese-American rivalry of the future could fit into a broader new global arrangement that will increasingly challenge Western, and especially American, global supremacy. China's close military cooperation with the former Soviet Union, particularly its purchase of advanced weapons in the almost unrestricted Russian arms bazaar, its technological and political help to the Islamic countries of Central Asia and North Africa, and its looming dominance in East Asia put it at the center of an informal network of states, many of which have goals and philosophies inimical to those of the United States, and many of which share China's sense of grievance at the long global domination of the West. Samuel Huntington of Harvard University has argued that this emerging world order will be dominated by what he calls the clash of civilizations. We see matters more in the old-fashioned terms of political alliance and the balance of power. Either way, China, rapidly becoming the globe's second most powerful nation, will be a predominant force as the world takes shape in the new millennium. As such, it is bound to be no strategic friend of the United States, but a long-term adversary.

MIGHT LEANS RIGHT

ONE COMMON view of China holds that its integration into the world economy will make it more moderate and cautious in its foreign policy and more open and democratic at home. But the alternative view sees China's more aggressive behavior of the last five years as a consequence of its growing economic and military strength and as linked to its intensifying xenophobic impulses. China's more modern economy and its greater economic influence are already giving it the power to enhance its authoritarianism at home, resist international dissatisfaction with its policies and practices, and expand its power and prestige abroad in ways hostile to American interests.

China's ability to resist and ultimately beat back efforts by the Clinton administration to protest Chinese human rights abuses by withholding most-favored-nation status is a case in point. While complaining bitterly about the American use of economic pressure for political goals, the Chinese applied powerful economic and political pressure on both the United States and elsewhere—notably in Europe and the United Nations—to force President Clinton to retreat from his earlier position. The irony in Sino-American relations is that when China was in the grip of ideological Maoism and displayed such ideological ferocity that Americans believed it to be dangerous and menacing, it was actually a paper tiger, weak and virtually without global influence. Now that China has shed the trappings of Maoism and embarked on a pragmatic course of economic development and global trade, it appears less threatening but is in fact acquiring the wherewithal to back its global ambitions and interests with real power.

Many factors contribute to China's more assertive stance, not least its sense of being Asia's naturally dominant power—an attitude that has not been lost on some regional leaders. As former Singaporean Prime Minister Lee Kuan Yew recently put it, "Many medium and small countries in Asia are uneasy that China may want to resume the imperial status it had in earlier centuries and have misgivings about being treated as vassal states having to send tribute to China as they used to in past centuries." More immediate and concrete shifts in China's strategic attitude can be traced to major events of the late 1980s and early 1990s that increased the power and prestige of China's conservative nationalists and the military, a power shift exacerbated by the incapacitation of paramount leader Deng Xiaoping, who tended to exert a pro-American and moderating influence.

The first of those events was the Tiananmen Square demonstrations of May and June 1989. The rise of a powerful anti-party movement convinced Chinese Communist Party conservatives of the need to maintain stricter control over the country's intellectuals and to "strike hard" (in the current anticrime campaign parlance) against dissenters. Concurrently, the collapse of the Soviet Union removed China's main regional security threat and increased, virtually overnight, China's comparative power in Asia. More important for the conservative-nationalist faction, Mikhail

Gorbachev's attempted reform program was taken in Beijing as a powerful negative example, an illustration of the mortal danger to party authority posed by piecemeal liberal political reforms. The third event, the Gulf War, had, as David Shambaugh of George Washington University put it, a "jarring effect" on the People's Liberation Army, whose power and prestige had increased dramatically in the wake of Tiananmen and Deng's enfeeblement. The war demonstrated in the most graphic terms imaginable just how far behind the country was in terms of military technology. "This was the PLA's first exposure to a high-tech war, and they were stunned," Shambaugh has written. Their shock led them to press for a rapid and expensive modernization of China's armed forces, including further nuclear testing and long-range-missile development. The Chinese understood that they would have to master the techniques demonstrated by the Americans if they were to pose a credible threat of their own, whether in the disputed areas of the South China Sea or in any eventual expedition to "liberate" Taiwan.

THE NUMBERS GAME

NOTHING COULD be more important in understanding China's goals and self-image than its military modernization program. China's official position, which is given credence in many Western analyses, is that its primary goal is to develop a world-class economy while maintaining a defensive military force. The official annual defense budget of $8.7 billion—compared to the $265 billion spent annually by the United States or even the $50 billion spent by Japan—seems to support that claim. In reality, almost every major study of Chinese military spending, whether conducted by the U.S. Government Information Office or the International Institute for Strategic Studies, has concluded that actual spending is at least several times Beijing's official figure.

The official budget, for example, does not include the cost of the People's Armed Police, even though it consists mostly of former soldiers demobilized to reduce the size of the army and serves as a reserve available for use in an international conflict. The official budget also excludes nuclear weapons development and soldiers' pensions. When the Chinese purchased 72 su-27 fighter jets from Russia in 1995 for about $2.8 billion, the entire amount was covered by the State Council and was not deemed a defense expenditure.[2] The official numbers also exclude the cost of research and development. Part of the funding for the development of nuclear weapons, for example, comes from the Ministry of Energy budget, and part of the money for aircraft development comes from the Ministry of Aeronautics and Astronautics Industry. Beijing also excludes proceeds from arms sales, which totaled nearly $8 billion between 1987 and 1991 alone, as well as income from businesses and industries owned and operated by the army, which, with unknown and largely unaccounted-for resources, has quietly become a major player in the global economy.[3]

Realistic analyses of China's defense budget (or those of any other country's, for that matter) must also take into account purchasing power parity—the difference between what something would cost in China and what it would cost elsewhere. As much as 68 percent of Chinese expenditures, from soldiers' salaries and pensions to weapons systems and supplies, which the PLA purchases at artificially low state-set prices, cost a fraction of their equivalent American value. Taking all these factors into account, a conservative estimate of China's actual military expenditures would be at least ten times the officially announced level. In other words, China's real annual defense budget amounts to a minimum of $87 billion per year, roughly one-third that of the United States and 75 percent more than Japan's. Moreover, the figure was 11.3 percent higher in 1996 than in 1995, and 14.6 percent higher in 1995 than in 1994. Even adjusting for inflation, that is still an exceptionally high rate of growth. No other part of the Chinese government budget has increased at a rate anywhere near that, whether adjusting for inflation or not.

---

[2]June Teufel Dreyer, "Chinese Strategy in Asia and the World," paper prepared for the First Annual Strategy Forum Conference on China, U.S. Naval Academy, Annapolis, Maryland, April 27-28, 1996.

[3]Chong-Pin Lin, "Chinese Military Modernization: Perceptions, Progress, and Prospects," paper given at the American Enterprise Institute Conference on the People's Liberation Army, Staunton Hill, Virginia, June 17-19, 1994, p. 11.

Richard Bernstein and Ross H. Munro

It is true, as the more optimistic analysts point out, that China poses little direct military threat to the United States. But comparing the two countries to highlight Chinese shortcomings is a pointless and misleading exercise, and not only because China's actual military expenditures are a moving target. Whatever the exact figures, China is now engaged in one of the most extensive and rapid military buildups in the world, one that has accelerated in recent months even as China's rhetoric has softened and Beijing has moved to improve its ties with the United States. Driven by its setback in the Taiwan crisis last year and disturbed by the awesome power of the two American aircraft carrier task forces dispatched to the waters near the Straits of Taiwan, China has stepped up its efforts to acquire two capabilities: a credible Taiwan invasion force and the capacity to sink American aircraft carriers should the United States interfere militarily in the China-Taiwan issue.

Even before the Straits of Taiwan incident, China was acquiring airborne early warning technology in Europe and Israel and developing its own in-flight refueling techniques to extend the range of its warplanes. Since the incident, it has sealed a deal with Russia to acquire two destroyers equipped with modern cruise missiles. In the past several years, China has acquired SU-27 fighter-bombers and Russian Kilo-class submarines. In the last three years, China has built 34 modern warships on its own and developed a fleet of M-9 and M-11 mobile-launched missiles of the sort fired near Taiwan during the crisis. It has also expanded its rapid reaction force from 15,000 to 200,000 men and built an airfield in the Paracel Islands and an early warning radar installation on Fiery Cross Reef in the Spratlys. China is the only Asian country to deploy nuclear weapons and the world's third-largest nuclear power in terms of the number of delivery vehicles in service, having surpassed Britain and France by the late 1970s.[4]

As time passes, in other words, it will become far riskier for Washington to preempt Chinese aggression with the kind of overwhelming show of force made during the Straits of Taiwan crisis. With the largest army, navy, and air force in Asia, China spends

[4]Ibid., p. 11.

more both relatively and absolutely than any of its neighbors, with the possible exception of Japan, whose modern forces are untested and whose operations could be severely hampered by pacifist leanings at home. In short, China's relative strength gives it the ability to intimidate regional foes and win wars against them. If it continues its rapid military modernization, China will soon become the only country capable of challenging American power in East Asia—and only the United States will have the influence to counterbalance China's regional ascendancy. Moreover, China's goals go a long way toward explaining its tactical attitude toward its relations with the United States, where an annual trade imbalance approaching $40 billion has helped China finance its arms acquisitions. China's mercantilist policies, which include large-scale technology transfers from American sources and the purchase of dual-use technologies in the American market, are likely to become a major source of Sino-American conflict as Beijing grows stronger.

A DEMOCRATIC PEACE?

OF COURSE, if China became a democracy its military build-up would be far less threatening than if it remained a dictatorship. But while the forces pushing toward global democracy are probably too powerful for China to remain unaffected by them forever, there is no reason to believe that China will become democratic in the near future. In the first place, that would be contrary to Chinese political culture. In its entire 3,000-year history, China has developed no concept of limited government, no protections of individual rights, no independence for the judiciary and the media. The country has never operated on any notion of the consent of the governed or the will of the majority. Whether under the emperors or the party general secretaries, China has always been ruled by a self-selected and self-perpetuating clique that operates in secret and treats opposition as treason.

For there to be real democratic reform, the bureaucrats in and near that clique would have to relinquish some of their power, and there is no sign that they are ready to do so. Receiving personal benefits from political power is a Chinese tradition, whether the

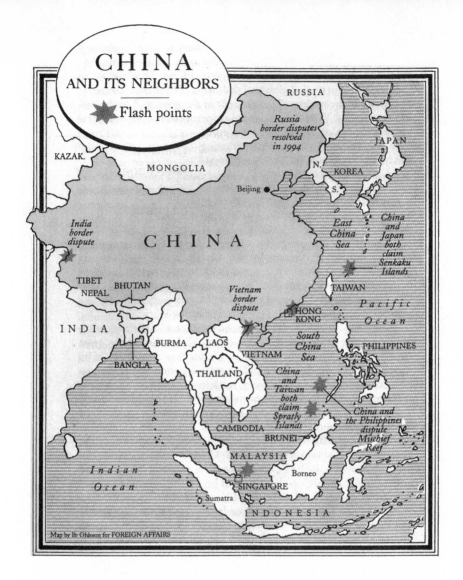

CHINA
AND ITS NEIGHBORS

⭑ Flash points

RUSSIA

KAZAK.

MONGOLIA

Russia border disputes resolved in 1994

JAPAN

N. KOREA

Beijing ●

S.

India border dispute

CHINA

TIBET

NEPAL BHUTAN

Vietnam border dispute

East China Sea

China and Japan both claim Senkaku Islands

TAIWAN

INDIA

HONG KONG

Pacific Ocean

BURMA LAOS

VIETNAM

South China Sea

PHILIPPINES

BANGLA

THAILAND

China and Taiwan both claim Spratly Islands

CAMBODIA

BRUNEI

China and the Philippines dispute Mischief Reef

MALAYSIA

Indian Ocean

Borneo

SINGAPORE

Sumatra

INDONESIA

Map by Ib Ohlsson for FOREIGN AFFAIRS

benefits involve a state-maintained harem, servants provided by the state, or a Mercedes-Benz donated by a Japanese or overseas Chinese businessman in exchange for an import license. The bureaucracy will not voluntarily relinquish such perks for the sake of democratic principles imported from the West.

Moreover, China's leaders are probably sincere in their equation of democratic reform with social chaos. China has made great strides in creating a more prosperous life for tens of millions of its people, but it remains a potentially unstable nation where the gap between rich and poor is growing, restlessness and unemployment are rampant, and rising expectations have turned the minds of many. The population seems to be at once happy with rising standards of living and discontented with corruption, crime, petty abuses of power by local officials, and the precariousness of life without the guarantees the state once provided. China's leaders, facing the prospect of social uprisings, are sure to stress patriotic solidarity and unquestioned leadership. They cannot be counted on to relinquish their monopolistic hold on power.

Finally, for China's government, subjecting itself to the popular will would mean abdicating its control in areas where it feels the national interest allows no such loss. If, for example, Tibet were to be governed by democratic principles rather than diktat from Beijing, the Tibetan people would create an independence movement that would challenge Chinese control. Similarly, democracy in China would force China's leaders to acknowledge the right of the people of Taiwan to decide the shape of their own future. But granting any such power to the Taiwanese would sabotage China's nonnegotiable insistence on reunification. It would also provide an unwanted precedent for the people of the mainland: if the Taiwanese are consulted on the issue of their political identity, why not the rest of the people of China? China's ruling clique shows no willingness to suffer the loss of power and prestige that a move toward real democracy would entail.

The most likely form for China to assume is a kind of corporatist, militarized, nationalist state, one with some similarity to the fascist states of Mussolini or Francisco Franco. China already has a cult of the state as the highest form of human organization, the entity for whose benefit the individual is expected to sacrifice his or her own interests and welfare. The army is emerging as the single most powerful institution in the country. It has ultimate political authority and has created a large number of influential business enterprises. Unlike the Soviet Union, China is not becoming a powerful military power founded on a pitifully weak economy, but a powerful economy creating a credible military force. It promises to be a state based on the continued rule of a disciplined party that controls information and demands political obedience.

Completing this picture of China is a wounded nationalism, a sense of unredeemed historical suffering, and a powerful suspicion of foreigners. Given the decline of ideology and the passing of the country's charismatic leaders, the government encourages and exploits such sentiments in an effort to enhance its legitimacy and control. When those sentiments prove insufficient to maintain order, the army and the leaders can turn to a vast, intrusive security and police system operating in close cooperation with a compliant judiciary to maintain their undisputed power.

TAIWAN'S DIRE STRAITS

THE GENERAL conditions for Sino-American conflict spring from China's desire to replace the United States as Asia's great power. But there is another, more immediate potential flashpoint: the complex and intractable problem of Taiwan. The Taiwan situation comprises two irreconcilable elements: the people of Taiwan do not want to be ruled by the current Beijing regime, but Beijing has made reunification too important a goal to relinquish. As China grows militarily and the regime runs out of patience, the possibility of an invasion increases. As one Chinese foreign affairs specialist in Beijing told us, "Historically, Chinese leaders have believed in force. Force worked in Tiananmen. It intimidated the intellectuals, and that paved the way for economic growth and political stability. It is realpolitik. And in the Chinese value system, sovereignty, national unification, and preserving the regime have always been higher than peace."

If China invades Taiwan, the United States will be under enormous pressure to prevent a military takeover—or else lose forever its claim to be the great-power guarantor of stability in the Asia-Pacific region. Taiwan thus epitomizes the challenge that China's greater assertiveness and determination to dominate Asia pose for the United States. But there are other places where China's actions and the United States' interests could conflict, the South China Sea being the most obvious. China's buildup of naval, air, and amphibious forces will enable it to seize and hold control of almost the entire South China Sea, now divided between Vietnam, Malaysia, Brunei, and the Philippines. Indeed, China's stated goal is to occupy islands and outcroppings so far to the south that Chinese forces would almost be in sight of Singapore and Indonesia. That would place China astride the only viable international sealane connecting the Pacific with the Indian Ocean. If China succeeded in extending its control over Taiwan, it would simultaneously gain control of the two southern approaches to Japan, the Taiwan and Luzon Straits. There are signs in articles and statements from Beijing that China increasingly views Taiwan as a strategic prize as well as a renegade province.

Conflict is possible even in areas where China and the United States share interests, as with preventing trouble on the Korean peninsula. When Korea is finally reunified, as it almost surely will be, China will likely press for a withdrawal of American forces from northeast Asia, save for troops in Japan to inhibit remilitarization. As long as Korea remains divided, China will accept the American military presence there to avoid a peninsula-wide war. But once that danger has passed, China will use its influence in northeast Asia for two purposes, both of them inimical to American interests: to bring about a pro-Chinese, anti-American, and anti-Japanese stance in Korea, and to perpetuate Japan's status as a non-normal country, one without the right to assume primary responsibility for its own defense. China could thus assure its predominance in Asia vis-à-vis the only country in the region with the size and strength to challenge it.

THE NEW STRATEGIC TRIANGLE

THE PRIMARY American objective in Asia must be to prevent China's size, power, and ambition from making it a regional hegemon. Achieving that goal requires maintaining the American military presence in Asia and keeping it vastly more powerful and effective than China's armed forces. Furthermore, preventing China from expanding its nuclear weapons arsenal should clearly be an American goal. In the worst-case scenario, Sino-American relations would witness the reappearance of a nuclear standoff reminiscent of the Cold War, with each side relying on the doctrine of mutually assured destruction to prevent an attack from the other. In fact, China has numerous incentives to avoid a nuclear arms race. The United States should play a quiet but effective role in building international pressure to persuade China to make its current moratorium on nuclear weapons testing permanent. Washington should also actively fight against nuclear proliferation in China and elsewhere. The third element in maintaining a balance of power involves Taiwan—specifically, ensuring that it maintains a credible defensive deterrent such that reunification, should it occur, would be voluntary.

The growth of Chinese power has made America's overarching attitude toward Japan obsolete. The United States can no longer operate on the assumption that a weak Japan is a good Japan. If that was once true, it was only because China was poor and weak. In the post-Cold War world, it is Japan's weakness that threatens peace and stability by creating a power vacuum that the United States alone can no longer fill. A strong Japan, in genuine partnership with the United States, is vital to a new balance of power in Asia. A weak Japan benefits only China, which wants no stabilizing balance of power but Chinese hegemony, under which Japan would be little more than Beijing's most useful tributary state.

The difficulties here are considerable. The United States cannot block Chinese hegemony in Asia unless Japan is an equal and willing partner in the process. But if it pushes Japan, the result could well be an anti-American reaction there. Resolving that dilemma might be the single most important task of American diplomacy in the near future. The United States must demonstrate that it is a reliable ally—as it did last spring in the waters near Taiwan—while waiting for Japan to come to grips with an increasingly threatening security environment. China's determination to achieve hegemonic status in Asia will probably facilitate this. But the United States and Japan must realize they need each other. ❷

China's military budget indicate that China's defense spending remains relatively low, both as a share of gross national product and compared with the spending of other great powers.

THE LUXURY TO ENGAGE

THUS FAR, post-Cold War international relations have not hardened into opposing blocs. The opportunity still exists to establish a stable international order. But the sine qua non of such an order is Chinese participation in its creation. Chinese leaders remain committed to seeking constructive relations with all their neighbors. Given the costs that China can impose on America and its allies, U.S. policy should take advantage of that posture to reinforce China's interest in regional stability and strengthen its commitment to global stability. Engagement, not isolation, is the appropriate policy.

Engagement must mean more than simply offering China the opportunity to follow the rules. It requires acknowledging Chinese interests and negotiating solutions that accommodate both American and Chinese objectives. In bilateral relations, this will entail compromise approaches over the future of Taiwan. It will require mutual accommodation to prevent nuclear proliferation on the Korean peninsula and accommodation of Chinese interests in Sino-Pakistani security ties. Washington must acknowledge the economic sources of trade imbalances and the Chinese government's limited ability to enforce its domestic laws and international commitments.

Engagement also requires multilateral collaboration with Chinese interests. The United States and the other major powers must invite China to participate in international rule-making. This includes encouraging Chinese membership as well as leadership responsibilities in various arms control regimes, including the Missile Technology Control Regime, the Zangger Committee, and the Nuclear Suppliers Group, which regulate nuclear-related exports, the Australia Group on chemical precursors and biological agents, and the Wassenaar Arrangement, the successor to the Coordinating Committee on Multilateral Export Controls, which tracks trade in conventional weapons and technologies. It also entails admitting China into the World Trade Organization on terms that reflect both U.S. concern for China's significant influence in the international economic system and the less-developed conditions of China's domestic economy.

Engagement will not be easy. For it to succeed, China must be willing to accommodate important U.S. interests in controlling proliferation of all kinds of weapons, whether or not proscribed by international regimes, in regions where the United States has vital interests, including the Middle East. China will have to make a formal commitment to reform its economic system and sustained efforts to enforce its international economic commitments. It will also have to make allowances for American domestic conditions and political values, especially as they affect U.S. economic policy and human rights diplomacy. Finally, China will have to use its leadership responsibilities wisely, seeking to consolidate a broadly beneficial international society, rather than striving for unilateral gains at the expense of international stability.

There is no guarantee that engagement will work. It will often involve acrimonious negotiations as the two sides make difficult policy adjustments and seek compromise solutions. At times, Washington will have to protect its interests unilaterally. It will also have to maintain its current military deployments in Asia. U.S. strategic retrenchment would do far more to alter the Sino-American bilateral balance of power and the regional balance of power than any combination of Chinese military and economic policies. But it is also clear that reliance on purely coercive measures will not elicit Chinese cooperation. Rather, it would almost guarantee renewed tension in Sino-American relations and heightened instability in East Asia. Given the strategic head start the United States and its allies enjoy, Washington has the luxury of observing Chinese modernization before adopting a more assertive posture.@

Does China Matter?

Gerald Segal

MIDDLE KINGDOM, MIDDLE POWER

DOES CHINA MATTER? No, it is not a silly question—merely one that is not asked often enough. Odd as it may seem, the country that is home to a fifth of humankind is overrated as a market, a power, and a source of ideas. At best, China is a second-rank middle power that has mastered the art of diplomatic theater: it has us willingly suspending our disbelief in its strength. In fact, China is better understood as a theoretical power—a country that has promised to deliver for much of the last 150 years but has consistently disappointed. After 50 years of Mao's revolution and 20 years of reform, it is time to leave the theater and see China for what it is. Only when we finally understand how little China matters will we be able to craft a sensible policy toward it.

DOES CHINA MATTER ECONOMICALLY?

CHINA, UNLIKE Russia or the Soviet Union before it, is supposed to matter because it is already an economic powerhouse. Or is it that China is on the verge of becoming an economic powerhouse, and you must be in the engine room helping the Chinese to enjoy the benefits to come? Whatever the spin, you know the argument: China is a huge market, and you cannot afford to miss it (although few say the same about India). The recently voiced "Kodak version" of this argument is that if only each Chinese will buy one full roll

The late GERALD SEGAL was Director of Studies at the International Institute for Strategic Studies in London. This article originally appeared in the September/October 1999 issue of *Foreign Affairs*.

of film instead of the average half-roll that each currently buys, the West will be rich. Of course, nineteenth-century Manchester mill owners said much the same about their cotton, and in the early 1980s Japanese multinationals said much the same about their television sets. The Kodak version is just as hollow. In truth, China is a small market that matters relatively little to the world, especially outside Asia.

If this judgment seems harsh, let us begin with some harsh realities about the size and growth of the Chinese economy. In 1800 China accounted for 33 percent of world manufacturing output; by way of comparison, Europe as a whole was 28 percent, and the United States was 0.8 percent. By 1900 China was down to 6.2 percent (Europe was 62 percent, and the United States was 23.6 percent). In 1997 China accounted for 3.5 percent of world GNP (in 1997 constant dollars, the United States was 25.6 percent). China ranked seventh in the world, ahead of Brazil and behind Italy. Its per capita GDP ranking was 81st, just ahead of Georgia and behind Papua New Guinea. Taking the most favorable of the now-dubious purchasing-power-parity calculations, in 1997 China accounted for 11.8 percent of world GNP, and its per capita ranking was 65th, ahead of Jamaica and behind Latvia. Using the U.N. Human Development Index, China is 107th, bracketed by Albania and Namibia—not an impressive story.

Yes, you may say, but China has had a hard 200 years and is now rising swiftly. China has undoubtedly done better in the past generation than it did in the previous ten, but let's still keep matters in perspective—especially about Chinese growth rates. China claimed that its average annual industrial growth between 1951 and 1980 was 12.5 percent. Japan's comparable figure was 11.5 percent. One can reach one's own judgment about whose figures turned out to be more accurate.

Few economists trust modern Chinese economic data; even Chinese Prime Minister Zhu Rongji distrusts it. The Asian Development Bank routinely deducts some two percent from China's official GDP figures, including notional current GDP growth rates of eight percent. Some two or three percent of what might be a more accurate GDP growth rate of six percent is useless goods produced to rust in warehouses. About one percent of China's growth in 1998 was due to massive government spending on infrastructure. Some three percent of GDP is accounted for by the one-time gain that occurs when one takes peasants off the land and brings them to cities, where productivity is higher. Taking all these qualifications into account, China's economy is effectively in recession. Even Zhu calls the situation grim.

China's ability to recover is hampered by problems that the current leadership understands well but finds just too scary to tackle seriously—at least so long as East Asia's economy is weak. By conservative estimates, at least a quarter of Chinese loans are nonperforming—a rate that Southeast Asians would have found frightening before the crash. Some 45 percent of state industries are losing money, but bank lending was up 25 percent in 1998—in part, to bail out the living dead. China has a high savings rate (40 percent of GDP), but ordinary Chinese would be alarmed to learn that their money is clearly being wasted.

Some put their hope in economic decentralization, but this has already gone so far that the center cannot reform increasingly wasteful and corrupt practices in the regions and in specific institutions. Central investment—20 percent of total investment in China—is falling. Interprovincial trade as a percentage of total provincial trade is also down, having dropped a staggering 18 percent between 1985 and 1992. Despite some positive changes during the past 20 years of reform, China's economy has clearly run into huge structural impediments. Even if double-digit growth rates ever really existed, they are hard to imagine in the near future.

In terms of international trade and investment, the story is much the same: Beijing is a seriously overrated power. China made up a mere 3 percent of total world trade in 1997, about the same as South Korea and less than the Netherlands. China now accounts for only 11 percent of total Asian trade. Despite the hype about the importance of the China market, exports to China are tiny. Only 1.8 percent of U.S. exports go to China (this could, generously, be perhaps 2.4 percent if re-exports through Hong Kong were counted)—about the same level as U.S. exports to Australia or Belgium and about a third less than U.S. exports to Taiwan. The same is true of major

European traders. China accounts for 0.5 percent of U.K. exports, about the same level as exports to Sri Lanka and less than those to Malaysia. China takes 1.1 percent of French and German exports, which is the highest in Asia apart from Japan but about par with exports to Portugal.

China matters a bit more to other Asian countries. Some 3.2 percent of Singapore's exports go to China, less than to Taiwan but on par with South Korea. China accounts for 4.6 percent of Australian exports, about the same as to Singapore. Japan sends only 5.1 percent of its exports to China, about a quarter less than to Taiwan. Only South Korea sends China an impressive share of its exports—some 9.9 percent, nudging ahead of exports to Japan.

Foreign direct investment (FDI) is even harder to measure than trade but sheds more light on long-term trends. China's massive FDI boom, especially in the past decade, is often trumpeted as evidence of how much China does and will matter for the global economy. But the reality is far less clear. Even in 1997, China's peak year for FDI, some 80 percent of the $45 billion inflow came from ethnic Chinese, mostly in East Asia. This was also a year of record capital flight from China—by some reckonings, an outflow of $35 billion. Much so-called investment from East Asia makes a round-trip from China via some place like Hong Kong and then comes back in as FDI to attract tax concessions.

Even a more trusting view of official FDI figures suggests that China does not much matter. FDI into China is about 10 percent of global FDI, with 60 percent of all FDI transfers taking place among developed countries. Given that less than 20 percent of FDI into China comes from non-ethnic Chinese, it is no surprise that U.S. or European Union investment in China averages out to something less than their investment in a major Latin American country such as Brazil. China has never accounted for more than 10 percent of U.S. FDI outflows—usually much less. In recent years China has taken around 5 percent of major EU countries' FDI outflow—and these are the glory years for FDI in China. The Chinese economy is clearly contracting, and FDI into China is dropping with it. In 1998 the United Nations reported that FDI into China may be cut in half, and figures for 1998–99 suggest that this was not too gloomy a guess. Japanese FDI into China has been halved from its peak in 1995. Ericsson, a multinational telecommunications firm, says that China accounts for 13 percent of its global sales but will not claim that it is making any profits there. Similar experiences by Japanese technology firms a decade ago led to today's rapid disinvestment from China. Some insist that FDI flows demonstrate just how much China matters and will matter for the global economy, but the true picture is far more modest. China remains a classic case of hope over experience, reminiscent of de Gaulle's famous comment about Brazil: It has great potential, and always will.

It does not take a statistical genius to see the sharp reality: China is at best a minor (as opposed to inconsequential) part of the global economy. It has merely managed to project and sustain an image of far greater importance. This theatrical power was displayed with great brio during Asia's recent economic crisis. China received lavish praise from the West, especially the United States, for not devaluing its currency as it did in 1995. Japan, by contrast, was held responsible for the crisis. Of course, Tokyo's failure to reform since 1990 helped cause the meltdown, but this is testimony to how much Tokyo matters and how little Beijing does. China's total financial aid to the crisis-stricken economies was less than 10 percent of Japan's contribution.

The Asian crisis and the exaggerated fears that it would bring the economies of the Atlantic world to their knees help explain the overblown view of China's importance. In fact, the debacle demonstrated just how little impact Asia, except for Japan, has on the global economy. China—a small part of a much less important part of the global system than is widely believed—was never going to matter terribly much to the developed world. Exaggerating China is part of exaggerating Asia. As a result of the crisis, the West has learned the lesson for the region as a whole, but it has not yet learned it about China.

DOES CHINA MATTER MILITARILY?

CHINA IS a second-rate military power—not first-rate, because it is far from capable of taking on America, but not as third-rate as most of its Asian neighbors. China accounts for only 4.5 percent of global defense spending (the United States makes up 33.9 percent) and 25.8 percent of defense spending in East Asia and Australasia. China poses a formidable threat to the likes of the Philippines and can take islands such as Mischief Reef in the South China Sea at will. But sell the Philippines a couple of cruise missiles and the much-discussed Chinese threat will be easily erased. China is in no military shape to take the disputed Senkaku Islands from Japan, which is decently armed. Beijing clearly is a serious menace to Taiwan, but even Taiwanese defense planners do not believe China can successfully invade. The Chinese missile threat to Taiwan is much exaggerated, especially considering the very limited success of the far more massive and modern NATO missile strikes on Serbia. If the Taiwanese have as much will to resist as did the Serbs, China will not be able to easily cow Taiwan.

Thus China matters militarily to a certain extent simply because it is not a status quo power, but it does not matter so much that it cannot be constrained. Much the same pattern is evident in the challenge China poses to U.S. security. It certainly matters that

China is the only country whose nuclear weapons target the United States. It matters, as the recent Cox report on Chinese espionage plainly shows, that China steals U.S. secrets about missile guidance and modern nuclear warheads. It also matters that Chinese military exercises simulate attacks on U.S. troops in South Korea and Japan. But the fact that a country can directly threaten the United States is not normally taken as a reason to be anything except robust in defending U.S. interests. It is certainly not a reason to pretend that China is a strategic partner of the United States.

The extent to which China matters militarily is evident in the discussions about deploying U.S. theater missile defenses (TMD) in the western Pacific and creating a U.S. national missile defense shield (NMD). Theoretically, the adversary is North Korea. In practice, the Pentagon fears that the U.S. ability to defend South Korea, Japan, and even Taiwan depends in the long term on the ability to defend the United States' home territory and U.S. troops abroad from Chinese missiles. Given the $10 billion price tag for NMD and the so-far unknowable costs of TMD, defense planners clearly think that China matters.

But before strategic paranoia sets in, the West should note that the Chinese challenge is nothing like the Soviet one. China is less like the Soviet Union in the 1950s than like Iraq in the 1990s: a regional threat to Western interests, not a global ideological rival. Such regional threats can be constrained. China, like Iraq, does not matter so much that the United States needs to suspend its normal strategies for dealing with unfriendly powers. Threats can be deterred, and unwanted action can be constrained by a country that claims to be the sole superpower and to dominate the revolution in military affairs.

A similarly moderated sense of how much China matters can be applied to the question of Chinese arms transfers. China accounted for 2.2 percent of arms deliveries in 1997, ahead of Germany but behind Israel (the United States had 45 percent of the market, and the United Kingdom had 18 percent). The $1 billion or so worth of arms that Beijing exports annually is not buying vast influence, though in certain markets Beijing does have real heft. Pakistan is easily the most important recipient of Chinese arms, helping precipitate a nuclear arms race with India. Major deals with Sudan, Sri Lanka, and Burma have had far less strategic impact. On the other hand, arms transfers to Iran have been worrying; as with Pakistan, U.S. threats of sanctions give China rather good leverage. China's ability to make mischief therefore matters somewhat—primarily because it reveals that Chinese influence is fundamentally based on its ability to oppose or thwart Western interests. France and Britain each sell far more arms than China, but they are by and large not creating strategic problems for the West.

Hence, it is ludicrous to claim, as Western and especially American officials constantly do, that China matters because the West needs it as a strategic partner. The discourse of "strategic partnership" really means that China is an adversary that could become a serious nuisance. Still, many in the Clinton administration and elsewhere do not want to call a spade a spade and admit that China is a strategic foe. Perhaps they think that stressing the potential for partnership may eventually, in best Disney style, help make dreams come true.

On no single significant strategic issue are China and the West on the same side. In most cases, including Kosovo, China's opposition does not matter. True, the U.N. Security Council could not be used to build a powerful coalition against Serbia, but as in most cases, the real obstacle was Russia, not China. Beijing almost always plays second fiddle to Moscow or even Paris in obstructing Western interests in the Security Council. (The exceptions to this rule always concern cases where countries such as Haiti or Macedonia have developed relations with Taiwan.) After all, the Russian prime minister turned his plane to the United States around when he heard of the imminent NATO attack on Serbia, but the Chinese premier turned up in Washington as scheduled two weeks later.

NATO's accidental May bombing of the Chinese embassy elicited a clear demonstration of China's theatrical power. Beijing threatened to block any peace efforts in the United Nations (not that any were pending), but all it wanted was to shame the West into concessions on World Trade Organization membership, human rights, or arms control. China grandiosely threatened to rewrite the Security Council resolution that eventually gave NATO an indefinite mandate to keep the peace in Kosovo, but in the end it meekly abstained. So much for China taking a global perspective as one of the five permanent members of the Security Council. Beijing's temper tantrum merely highlighted the fact that, unlike the other veto-bearing Security Council members, it was not a power in Europe.

In the field of arms control, the pattern is the same. China does not block major arms control accords, but it makes sure to be among the last to sign on and tries to milk every diplomatic advantage from having to be dragged to the finish line. China's reluctance to sign the Nuclear Nonproliferation Treaty (NPT), for instance, was outdone in its theatricality only by the palaver in getting China to join the Comprehensive Test Ban Treaty. China's participation in the Association of Southeast Asian Nations Regional Forum—Asia's premier, albeit limited, security structure—is less a commitment to surrender some sovereignty to an international arrangement than a way to ensure that nothing is done to limit China's ability to pursue its own national security objectives. China matters in arms control mainly because it effectively blocks accords until doing so ends up damaging China's international reputation.

Only on the Korean Peninsula do China's capacities seriously affect U.S. policy. One often hears that China matters because it is so helpful in dealing with North Korea. This is flatly wrong. Only once this decade did Beijing join with Washington and pressure Pyongyang—in bringing the rogue into compliance with its NPT obligations in the early phases of the 1994 North Korean crisis. On every other occasion, China has either done nothing to help America or actively helped North Korea resist U.S. pressure—most notoriously later in the 1994 crisis, when the United States was seeking support for sanctions and other coercive action against North Korea. Thus the pattern is the same. China matters in the same way any middle-power adversary matters: it is a problem to be circumvented or moved. But China does not matter because it is a potential strategic partner for the West. In that sense, China is more like Russia than either cares to admit.

DOES CHINA MATTER POLITICALLY?

THE EASIEST category to assess—although the one with the fewest statistics—is how much China matters in international political terms. To be fair to the Chinese, their recent struggle to define who they are and what they stand for is merely the latest stage of at least 150 years of soul-searching. Ever since the coming of Western power demonstrated that China's ancient civilization was not up to the challenges of modernity, China has struggled to understand its place in the wider world. The past century in particular has been riddled with deep Chinese resistance to the essential logic of international interdependence. It has also been marked by failed attempts to produce a China strong enough to resist the Western-dominated international system—consider the Boxer movement, the Kuomintang, or the Chinese Communist Party (CCP). Fifty years after the Chinese communist revolution, the party that gave the Chinese people the Great Leap Forward (and 30 million dead of famine) and the Cultural Revolution (and perhaps another million dead as well as a generation destroyed) is devoid of ideological power and authority. In the absence of any other political ideals, religions and cults such as the Falun Gong (target of a government crackdown this summer) will continue to flourish.

China's latest attempt to strengthen itself has been the past 20 years of economic reforms, stimulated by other East Asians' success in transforming their place in the world. But the discourse on prosperity that elicited praise for the order-sustaining "Asian values" or Confucian fundamentals was burned in the bonfire of certainties that was the Asian economic crisis. China was left in another phase of shock and self-doubt; hence, economic reforms stalled.

Under these circumstances, China is in no position to matter much as a source of international political power. Bizarre as old-style Maoism was, at least it was a beacon for many in the developing world. China now is a beacon to no one—and, indeed, an ally to no one. No other supposedly great power is as bereft of friends. This is not just because China, once prominent on the map of aid suppliers, has become the largest recipient of international aid. Rather, China is alone because it abhors the very notion of genuine international interdependence. No country relishes having to surrender sovereignty and power to the Western-dominated global system, but China is particularly wedded to the belief that it is big enough to merely learn what it must from the outside world and still retain control of its destiny. So China's neighbors understand the need to get on with China but have no illusions that China feels the same way.

China does not even matter in terms of global culture. Compare the cultural (not economic) role that India plays for ethnic Indians around the world to the pull exerted by China on ethnic Chinese, and one sees just how closed China remains. Of course, India's cultural ties with the Atlantic world have always been greater than China's, and India's wildly heterogeneous society has always been more accessible to the West. But measured in terms of films, literature, or the arts in general, Taiwan, Hong Kong, and even Singapore are more important global influences than a China still under the authoritarian grip of a ruling Leninist party. Chinese cities fighting over who should get the next Asian Disneyland, Chinese cultural commissars squabbling over how many American films can be shown in Chinese cinemas, and CCP bosses setting wildly fluctuating Internet-access policies are all evidence of just how mightily China is struggling to manage the power of Western culture.

In fact, the human-rights question best illustrates the extent to which China is a political pariah. Chinese authorities correctly note that life for the average citizen has become much more free in the past generation. But as Zhu admitted on his recent trip to the United States, China's treatment of dissenters remains inhuman and indecent.

Still, China deserves credit for having stepped back on some issues. That China did not demand the right to intervene to help Indonesia's ethnic Chinese during the 1998–99 unrest was correctly applauded as a sign of maturity. But it was also a sign of how little international leadership China could claim. With a human-rights record that made Indonesia seem a paragon of virtue, China was in no position to seize the moral high ground.

Measuring global political power is difficult, but China's influence and authority are clearly puny—not merely compared to the dominant

West, but also compared to Japan before the economic crisis. Among the reasons for China's weakness is its continuing ambiguity about how to manage the consequences of modernity and interdependence. China's great past and the resultant hubris make up much of the problem. A China that believes the world naturally owes it recognition as a great power—even when it so patently is not—is not really ready to achieve greatness.

DOES IT MATTER IF CHINA DOESN'T MATTER?

THE MIDDLE KINGDOM, then, is merely a middle power. It is not that China does not matter at all, but that it matters far less than it and most of the West think. China matters about as much as Brazil for the global economy. It is a medium-rank military power, and it exerts no political pull at all. China matters most for the West because it can make mischief, either by threatening its neighbors or assisting anti-Western forces further afield. Although these are problems, they will be more manageable if the West retains some sense of proportion about China's importance. If you believe that China is a major player in the global economy and a near-peer competitor of America's, you might be reluctant to constrain its undesired activities. You might also indulge in the "pander complex"—the tendency to bend over backward to accommodate every Chinese definition of what insults the Chinese people's feelings. But if you believe that China is not much different from any middle power, you will be more willing to treat it normally.

This notion of approaching China as a normal, medium power is one way to avoid the sterile debates about the virtues of engaging or containing China. Of course, one must engage a middle power, but one should also not be shy about constraining its unwanted actions. Such a strategy of "constrainment" would lead to a new and very different Western approach to China. One would expect robust deterrence of threats to Taiwan, but not pusillanimous efforts to ease Chinese concerns about TMD. One would expect a tough negotiating stand on the terms of China's WTO entry, but not Western concessions merely because China made limited progress toward international transparency standards or made us feel guilty about bombing its embassy in Belgrade. One would expect Western leaders to tell Chinese leaders that their authoritarianism puts them on the wrong side of history, but one would not expect Western countries to stop trying to censure human rights abuses in the United Nations or to fall over themselves to compete for the right to lose money in the China market.

To some extent, we are stuck with a degree of exaggeration of China's influence. It has a permanent U.N. Security Council seat even though it matters about as much as the United Kingdom and France, who hold their seats only because of their pre–World War II power. Unlike London and Paris, however, Beijing contributes little to international society via peacekeeping or funding for international bodies. China still has a hold on the imagination of CEOs, as it has for 150 years—all the more remarkable after the past 20 years, in which Western companies were bamboozled into believing that staying for the long haul meant eventually making money in China. Pentagon planners, a pessimistic breed if ever there was one, might be forgiven for believing that China could eventually become a peer competitor of the United States, even though the military gap, especially in high-technology arms, is, if anything, actually growing wider.

Nevertheless, until China is cut down to size in Western imaginations and treated more like a Brazil or an India, the West stands little chance of sustaining a coherent and long-term policy toward it. Until we stop suspending our disbelief and recognize the theatrical power of China, we will continue to constrain ourselves from pursuing our own interests and fail to constrain China's excesses. And perhaps most important, until we treat China as a normal middle power, we will make it harder for the Chinese people to understand their own failings and limitations and get on with the serious reforms that need to come.☯

China's Governance Crisis

Minxin Pei

MORE THAN MUSICAL CHAIRS

PREDICTING THE OUTCOME of China's upcoming leadership succession has become a popular parlor game in certain Washington circles. The curiosity aroused by the transition is understandable, given the huge stakes involved for the world's largest country. If all goes well, the Chinese Communist Party (CCP) is scheduled to select a new and younger leadership at its Sixteenth Party Congress this fall. The incumbent CCP general secretary, 76-year-old Jiang Zemin, may step down and be replaced by China's Vice President Hu Jintao, who is 59. The all-powerful Politburo Standing Committee will see most of its members retire, as will the important Central Committee. In addition, Chinese Premier Zhu Rongji is to step down in March, and Li Peng, the leader of the National People's Congress (the country's legislature), may be heading for the exit as well.

In a country ruled largely by man, not law, succession creates rare opportunities for political intrigue and policy change. Thus, speculation is rife about the composition, internal rivalries, and policy implications of a post-Jiang leadership. The backgrounds of those expected to ascend to the top unfortunately reveal little. By and large, the majority of new faces are technocrats. Some have stellar résumés but thin records; other front-runners boast solid experience as provincial party bosses but carry little national clout.

In any case, conjectures about the immediate policy impact of the pending leadership change are an exercise in futility, because

MINXIN PEI is Senior Associate at the Carnegie Endowment for International Peace. This article originally appeared in the September/October 2002 issue of *Foreign Affairs*.

Jiang will likely wield considerable influence even after his semi-retirement. A truly dominant new leader may not emerge in Beijing for another three to five years. And regardless of the drama that the succession process might provide, a single-minded focus on power plays in Beijing misses the real story: China is facing a hidden crisis of governance. This fact ought to preoccupy those who believe that much more is at stake in Beijing than a game of musical chairs.

The idea of an impending governance crisis in Beijing may sound unduly alarmist. To the outside world, China is a picture of dynamism and promise. Its potential market size, consistently high growth rates, and recent accession to the World Trade Organization have made the Middle Kingdom a top destination of foreign direct investment ($46 billion in 2001), and multinational corporations salivate at the thought of its future growth. But beneath this giddy image of progress and prosperity lies a different reality—one that is concealed by the glitzy skylines of Shanghai, Beijing, and other coastal cities. The future of China, and the West's interests there, depends critically on how Beijing's new leaders deal with this somber reality.

DOT COMMUNISM AND ITS DISCONTENTS

CHINA'S CURRENT CRISIS results from fundamental contradictions in the reforms that it has pursued over the past two decades—a period that has seen the amazing transformation of the communist regime from one that was infatuated with class struggle to one obsessed by growth rates. This "dot communism," characterized by the marriage of a Leninist party to bureaucratic capitalism with a globalist gloss, has merely disguised, rather than eliminated, these contradictions. But they are growing ever harder to ignore. The previously hidden costs of transition have begun to surface: Further change implies not simply a deepening of market liberalization but also the implementation of political reforms that could endanger the CCP's monopoly on power.

These emerging contradictions are embedded in the very nature of the Chinese regime. For example, the government's market-oriented economic policies, pursued in a context of autocratic and predatory politics, make the CCP look like a self-serving, capitalistic ruling elite, and not a "proletarian party" championing the interests of working people. The party's professed determination to maintain political supremacy also runs counter to its declared goals of developing a "socialist market economy" and "ruling the country according to law," because the minimum requirements of a market economy and the rule of law are institutionalized curbs on political power. The CCP's ambition to modernize Chinese society leaves unanswered the question of how increasing social autonomy will be protected from government caprice. And the party's perennial fear of independently organized interest groups does not prepare it for the inevitable emergence of such groups in an industrialized economy. These unresolved contradictions, inherent in the country's transition away from communism, are the source of rising tensions in China's polity, economy, and society.

During the go-go 1990s, the irreconcilable nature of these contradictions was obscured by rising prosperity and relative political tranquility. Economically, accelerating liberalization and deepening integration with the world marketplace produced unprecedented prosperity, even though some tough reforms (especially those affecting the financial sector and state-owned enterprises, or SOEs) lagged behind. Politically, the ruling elite drew its own lesson from the collapse of Soviet communism ("It's the economy, stupid") and closed ranks behind a strategy that prioritized economic growth and left the political system untouched.

This strategy worked for a decade. Within the regime, conservatives who opposed market reforms were marginalized. China's pro-democracy movement, which peaked with the Tiananmen Square protest in 1989, also waned after its leadership was decapitated through exile

HU JINTAO

or imprisonment. The resulting tranquility ended the polarized debate between liberals and conservatives of the 1980s. But ironically, this shift also silenced those at both ends of the ideological spectrum who would have cried that the emperor had no clothes. Thus, the regime escaped pressure to adopt deeper political reforms to relieve the tensions produced by the contradictions of dot communism. With rising wealth and loose talk of a "China century," even some skeptics thought the CCP had managed to square the circle.

The incompatibilities between China's current political system, however, and the essential requirements of the rule of law, a market economy, and an open society have not been washed away by waves of foreign investment. Pragmatists might view these contradictions as inconsequential cognitive nuisances. Unfortunately, their effects are real: they foreclose reform options that otherwise could be adopted for the regime's own long-term good. To be sure, China's pragmatic leaders have made a series of tactical adjustments to weather many new socioeconomic challenges, such as the CCP's recent outreach to entrepreneurs. But these moves are no substitute for genuine institutional reforms that would reinvigorate and relegitimize the ruling party.

THE BUBBLE BURSTS

IN RETROSPECT, the 1990s ought to be viewed as a decade of missed opportunities. The CCP leadership could have taken advantage of a booming economy to renew itself through a program of gradual political reform built on the rudimentary steps of the 1980s. But it did not, and now the cumulative costs of a decade of foot-dragging are becoming more visible. In many crucial respects, China's hybrid neo-authoritarian order eerily exhibits the pathologies of both the political stagnation of Leonid Brezhnev's Soviet Union and the crony capitalism of Suharto's Indonesia.

These pathologies—such as pervasive corruption, a collusive local officialdom, elite cynicism, and mass disenchantment—are the classic symptoms of degenerating governing capacity. In most political systems, a regime's capacity to govern is measured by how it performs three key tasks: mobilizing political support, providing public goods, and managing internal tensions. These three functions of governance—legitimation, performance, and conflict resolution—are, in reality, intertwined. A regime capable of providing adequate public goods (education, public health, law and order) is more likely to gain popular support and keep internal tensions low. In a Leninist party-state however, effective governance critically hinges on the health of the ruling party. Strong organizational discipline, account-ability, and a set of core values with broad appeal are essential to gov-erning effectively. Deterioration of the ruling party's strength, on the other hand, sets in motion a downward cycle that can severely impair the party-state's capacity to govern.

Numerous signs within China indicate that precisely such a process is producing huge governance deficits. The resulting strains are making the political and economic choices of China's rulers increasingly untenable. They may soon be forced to undertake risky reforms to stop the rot. If they do not, dot communism could be no more durable than the dot coms.

THE PARTY'S OVER

THE DECLINE of the CCP began during the rule of Mao Zedong, as the late leader's political radicalism, culminating in the mad-ness of the Cultural Revolution (1966–76), deeply damaged the ruling party. The ascent of Deng Xiaoping and his progressive reforms slowed this process, as economic gains, the end of mass repression, and the expansion of personal freedoms partially repaired the CCP's tarnished image.

But Deng's pro-market reforms produced a different set of dynamics that began to corrode the CCP's support. As economic reform deepened, large segments of Chinese society became poorer (such as grain-producing farmers and workers in SOEs). The revenue-starved state was unable to compensate these losers from reform. Consequently, the CCP had little means to secure the political support of these disaffected groups beyond exhorting self-sacrifice and making empty promises of better times ahead.

Some members of the ruling elite also converted their political power into economic gains, building and profiting from patronage machines. In one survey, about two-thirds of the officials being trained at a municipal party school said their promotion depended solely on the favors of their superiors; only five percent thought their own efforts could advance their careers. A ruling party fractured from within by such personalized patronage systems is hardly capable of building broad-based support within society.

It is worth noting that mass political campaigns, a previous hallmark of the CCP's prowess, have virtually vanished from the Chinese political scene. An obvious explanation is that such campaigns tend to be disruptive and lead to political excesses, as they did during the Mao years. A more likely cause, however, is that the CCP no longer possesses the political appeal or the organizational capacity required to launch such campaigns even when it desires them (as was the case during Beijing's efforts to contain pro-democracy dissidents in the late 1980s and the Falun Gong spiritual movement in the late 1990s). Increasingly, when faced with direct challenges to its authority, the CCP can rely only on repression rather than public mobilization to counter its opponents.

IMMOBILIZED

THE EXTENT of the CCP's decline can be measured in three areas: the shrinkage of its organizational penetration, the erosion of its authority and appeal among the masses, and the breakdown of its internal discipline. The organizational decline of the CCP is, in retrospect, almost predetermined. Historically, Leninist parties have thrived only in economies dominated by the state. Such an economy provides the economic institutions (SOEs and collective farms) that form the organizational basis for the ruling party. By pursuing market reforms that have eliminated rural communes and most SOEs, the CCP has fallen victim to its own success. The new economic infrastructure, based on household farming, private business, and individual labor mobility, is inhospitable to a large party apparatus. For instance, an internal CCP report characterized half of the party's rural cells as "weak" or "paralyzed" in recent years. In urban areas, the CCP has been unable to penetrate the emerging private sector, while its old organizational base has collapsed along with the SOEs. In 2000, the CCP did not have a single member in 86 percent of the country's 1.5 million private firms and could establish cells in only one percent of private companies.

The CCP's organizational decay is paralleled by the decline of its authority and image among the public. A survey of 818 migrant laborers in Beijing in 1997–98 revealed that the prevailing image of the ruling party was that of a self-serving elite. Only 5 percent of the interviewees thought their local party cadres "work for the interests of the villagers," and 60 percent said their local officials "use their power only for private gains." Other surveys have revealed similar negative public perceptions of the CCP. A 1998 study of 12,000 urban and rural residents across 10 provinces conducted by the CCP's antigraft agency found that only 43 percent of respondents agreed that "the majority of party and government officials are clean," and that fully one-third said "only a minority of party and government officials are clean."

At the same time as public officials are losing respect, the party's ideological appeal has all but evaporated. Polls conducted by the official national trade union in 1996 showed that only 15 percent of the workers surveyed regarded communism as "their highest ideal," while 70 percent said that their top priority was to pursue individual happiness. Even members of the ruling elite are beginning, albeit reluctantly, to admit this reality. A poll conducted in 1998 among 673 CCP officials in the northeastern province of Jilin found that 35 percent thought the status and authority of government officials had declined.

At the heart of the CCP's organizational and reputational decline is the breakdown of its members' ideological beliefs and internal discipline. Cynicism and corruption abound. The sale of government offices by local CCP bosses was unheard of in the 1980s but became widespread in the 1990s. A 1998 survey of 2,000 provincial officials, conducted by the official antigraft agency, found that 45 percent of respondents thought such practices were continuing unabated.

Even more worrying, the CCP appears unable to enforce internal discipline despite the mortal threat posed by corruption, which has surpassed unemployment as the most serious cause of social instability. Recent official actions, especially the prosecution and execution of several senior officials, create the impression that the CCP leadership is committed to combating corruption. But a comprehensive look at the data tells a different story. Most corrupt officials caught in the government's dragnet seem to have gotten off with no more than a slap on the wrist. For example, of the 670,000 party members disciplined for wrongdoing from 1992 to 1997, only 37,500, or six percent, were punished by criminal prosecution. Indeed, self-policing may be impossible for a ruling party accountable to no one. According to a top CCP official, the party has in recent years expelled only about one percent of its members.

Perhaps the greatest contributing factor to the CCP's political decline is, ironically, the absence of competition. Competition would have forced the party to redefine its mission and recruit members with genuine public appeal. But like monopoly firms, the CCP has devoted its energies to preventing the emergence of competition. Without external pressures, monopolies such as the CCP inevitably develop a full range of pathologies such as patronage systems, organizational dystrophy, and unresponsiveness. Moreover, one-party regimes can rarely take on the new competitors that emerge when the political environment changes suddenly. The fall of the Soviet bloc regimes and the defeat of similar monopolistic parties in the developing world (such as Mexico's Institutional Revolutionary Party) show that an eroding capacity for political mobilization poses a long-term threat to the CCP.

FAILING STATE?

IN A PARTY-STATE, the ruling party's weakness unavoidably saps the state's power. Such "state incapacitation," which in its extreme form results in failed states, is exemplified by the government's increasing inability to provide essential services, such as public safety, education, basic health care, environmental protection, and law enforcement. In China, these indices have been slipping over the past two decades. This decline is especially alarming since it has occurred while the Chinese economy has been booming.

Most of the evidence of the government's deteriorating performance is mundane but telling. Take, for example, the number of traffic fatalities (a key measure of a state's capacity to regulate a routine, but vital, social activity: transportation). Chinese roads are almost twice as deadly today as they were in 1985; there were about 58 road fatalities per 10,000 vehicles in 2000, compared to 34 in 1985. An international comparison using 1995 data shows that traffic fatality risks were much higher in China than in India or Indonesia. Indeed, China fared better only than Tonga, Bangladesh, Myanmar, and Mongolia in the Asia-Pacific region.

Although China has made tremendous progress in improving education, its recent performance lags behind that of many developing countries. China's education spending in 1998 was a mere 2.6 percent of GDP, below the average of 3.4 percent for low-income countries. In fact, China spends almost a third less on education than does India. As a result, access to primary and intermediate education is as low as 40 percent among school-age children in the country's poor western regions.

China's public health-care system has decayed considerably in recent years and compares poorly with those of its neighbors. According to the World Health Organization, China's health system ranked 144th worldwide, placing it among the bottom quartile of WHO members, behind India, Indonesia, and Bangladesh. China's agricultural population has been hit especially hard, as government neglect has led to a near-total collapse of the rural public-health infrastructure. According to the 1998 survey conducted by the Ministry of Health, 37 percent of ill farmers did not seek medical treatment because they could not afford it, and 65 percent of sick peasants needing hospitalization were not admitted because they could not pay. Both figures were higher than in 1993, when a similar survey was carried out. Poor health has become the chief cause of poverty in rural China; 40–50 percent of those who fell below the poverty line in 2000 in some provinces did so only after becoming seriously ill. Even more troubling, the crumbling public-health infrastructure is a principal cause of the rapid spread of HIV and AIDS in China. The UN warned in a recent study that "China is on the verge of a catastrophe that could result in unimaginable human suffering, economic loss, and social devastation."

State incapacitation also manifests itself in worsening environmental degradation. This problem poses perhaps the deadliest threat to China's continued economic development. About a third of the country suffers from severe soil erosion, 80 percent of wastewater is discharged untreated, 75 percent of the country's lakes and about half its rivers have been polluted, and nine of the ten cities with the worst air pollution in the world in 1999 were located in China.

China suffers huge direct economic losses from this environmental damage. The World Bank estimated in the mid-1990s that major forms of pollution cost the country 7.7 percent of its GDP. Beyond this measurable cost, environmental degradation, together with the collapse of much of the agricultural infrastructure built before the 1980s, may have exacerbated the effects of natural disasters. Grain losses resulting from natural disasters have more than doubled in the last 50 years, with most of the increase recorded in the 1990s.

BUSTING THE BUDGET

THE CENTRAL CAUSE of the declining effectiveness of the Chinese state is a dysfunctional fiscal system that has severely undercut the government's ability to fund public services while creating ample opportunities for corruption. Government data misleadingly suggest that the state experienced a massive loss of revenue over the last two decades, as its tax receipts fell from 31 percent of GDP in 1978 to 14 percent in 1999. The truth, however, is quite different. Aggregate government revenue over the past 20 years has held steady at about 30 percent of GDP. What has changed is the massive diversion of revenue from the government budget; increasingly, income collected by the government is not listed in the official budget. At their peak in the mid-1990s, such off-budget earnings exceeded budgeted tax revenue by two to one.

Provincial and municipal governments are the primary beneficiaries of this system because it allows them to raise revenue outside the normal tax streams. Because local officials are more likely to get promoted for delivering short-term growth or other such tangible results, off-budget revenue tends to be spent on building local industries and other projects that do little to improve education, health, or the environment. Moreover, since normal budget rules do not apply to such revenue, officials enjoy near-total discretion over its spending. Consequently, corruption is widespread. Large portions of this off-budget money have been found stashed away in secret slush funds controlled by government officials. In 1999, the National Auditing Agency claimed to have uncovered slush funds and illegal expenditures that amounted to 10 percent of 1998's tax revenue.

An important consequence of this dysfunctional fiscal system is the near collapse of local public finance in many counties and townships, particularly in the populous rural interior provinces (such as Henan, Anhui, and Hunan). Although counties and townships provide most government services, they rely on a slim tax base, collecting only 20 percent of total government revenue. In 1999, counties generated revenue barely equal to two-thirds of their spending, and about 40 percent of counties can pay for only half their expenditures.

The fiscal conditions for township governments are even more precarious because townships have practically no tax base and must extract their revenue from farmers, mostly through inefficient and coercive collection. The responsibilities of providing public services while supporting a bloated bureaucracy have forced many township governments deeply into debt. For instance, a survey in Hunan in 2000 found that township debts equaled half the province's total revenue.

In most countries, the state's declining fiscal health portends more serious maladies. The problems of the rural provinces should serve as an urgent warning to Beijing because these are historically the most unstable regions in the country, having previously generated large-scale peasant rebellions. Indeed, it is no coincidence that these agrarian provinces (where per capita income in 2000 was about half the national average) have in recent years seen the largest increase in peasant riots and tax revolts. Left to their own devices, local governments will not be able to provide effective remedies. A workable solution will require reforming the flawed fiscal system at the top and restructuring local governments at the bottom to make them more efficient and responsive.

ANGER MANAGEMENT

THE INSTITUTIONAL DECLINE of the ruling party and the weakness of the state have caused rising tensions between the state and society. The number of protests, riots, and other forms of resistance against state authorities has risen sharply. For instance, the number of collective protests grew fourfold in the 1990s, increasing from 8,700 in 1993 to a frightening 32,000 in 1999. The size and violence of such incidents have grown as well. There were 125 incidents involving more than 1,000 protesters in 1999, and the government itself admits that protests with more than 10,000 participants have become quite common. For example, in March 2002, more than 20,000 laid-off workers participated in a week-long protest in the northern city of Liaoyang. In rural areas, many towns have reported mob attacks by peasants on government buildings and even on officials themselves.

To be sure, rising social frustration results partly from the hardships produced by China's economic transition. In recent years, falling income in rural areas and growing unemployment in the cities have contributed to the rising discontent among tens of millions of peasants and workers. But the increasing frequency, scale, and intensity of collective defiance and individual resistance also reveal deep flaws in Chinese political institutions that have exacerbated the strains of transition. Social frustration is translated into political protest not merely because of economic deprivation, but because of a growing sense of political injustice. Government officials who abuse their power and perpetrate acts of petty despotism create resentment among ordinary citizens every day. These private grievances are more likely to find violent expression when the institutional mechanisms for resolving them (such as the courts, the press, and government bureaucracies) are inaccessible, unresponsive, and inadequate.

In rural China, where institutional rot is much more advanced, the tensions between the state and the peasantry have reached dangerous levels. In a startling internal report, the Ministry of Public Security admitted that "in some [rural] areas, enforcement of family-planning policy and collection of taxes would be impossible without the use of police force." In some villages, peasant resistance has grown so fierce that local officials dare not show their faces; these areas have effectively became lawless.

The most important source of this anger is the onerous tax burden levied on China's most impoverished citizens. The effective tax rate in 1996 for the agrarian sector (excluding village enterprises) was estimated at 50 percent. In fact, collecting taxes and fees has become practically the only task performed by public officials in rural areas, consuming 60–70 percent of their time. In some areas, local officials have even recruited thugs in their collection efforts; such practices have resulted in the illegal imprisonment, torture, and even deaths of peasants who are unable to pay. What has irked the peasantry even more is that their high taxes appear to have brought few government services in return. The combination of high payment, heavy-handed collection, and inadequate services has thus turned a large portion of the rural population against the state. Recent polls conducted in rural areas found that peasants consistently identify excessive taxes and fees as the most important cause of instability.

Significantly, relations between the state and society are growing more tense at a time of rising income inequality. To be sure, the reasons behind this process are extremely complex. Although the most important causes of overall inequality are the growing rural-urban income gap and regional disparities, the level of income inequality within regions and cities has been rising at an alarming pace as well. Recent surveys have found that inequality has become one of the top three concerns for the public. In the context of rampant official corruption, this rising inequality is likely to fuel public ire against the government because most people believe that only the corrupt and privileged can accumulate wealth. Such a perception is not off the mark: one academic study estimated that illegal income contributed to a 30 percent increase in inequality during the 1980s.

The absence of pressure valves within the Chinese political system will hamper the regime's ability to reduce and manage state-society tensions. Recent reforms, such as instituting village elections and improving the legal system, have proved inadequate. The CCP's failure to open up the political system and expand institutional channels for conflict resolution creates an environment in which aggrieved groups turn to collective protest to express frustrations and seek redress.

The accumulation of state-society tensions will eventually destabilize China, especially because the dynamics that generate such tensions trap the CCP in a hopeless dilemma. Rising tensions increase the risks that any reforms, even implemented as remedies, could trigger a revolution. Alexis de Tocqueville first observed this paradox: repressive regimes are most likely to be overthrown when they try to reform themselves. This sobering prospect could deter even the most progressive elements within the CCP from pursuing change.

THINK AGAIN

REMEDYING CHINA's mounting governance deficits should be the top priority of the country's new leaders. At present, these problems, brought on by the contradictions of dot communism, are serious but not life-threatening. If the new leadership addresses the institutional sources of poor governance, the CCP may be able to manage its problems without risking a political upheaval. The unfolding succession drama, however, will get in the way of meaningful change in the short term. Proposing even a moderate reform program could jeopardize a leader's political prospects. Moreover, undertaking risky reforms would require a high level of party unity—unlikely from a leadership jockeying for power.

Thus, China's governance deficits are likely to continue to grow and threaten the sustainability of its economic development. The slow-brewing crisis of governance may not cause an imminent collapse of the regime, but the accumulation of severe strains on the political system will eventually weigh down China's economic modernization as poor governance makes trade and investment more costly and more risky. The current economic dynamism may soon fade as long-term stagnation sets in.

Such a prospect raises questions about some prevailing assumptions about China. Many in the Bush administration view China's rise as both inevitable and threatening, and such thinking has motivated policy changes designed to counter this potential "strategic competitor." On the other hand, the international business community, in its enthusiasm for the Chinese market, has greatly discounted the risks embedded in the country's political system. Few appear to have seriously considered whether their basic premises about China's rise could be wrong. These assumptions should be revisited through a more realistic assessment of whether China, without restructuring its political system, can ever gain the institutional competence required to generate power and prosperity on a sustainable basis. As Beijing changes its leadership, the world needs to reexamine its long-cherished views about China, for they may be rooted in little more than wishful thinking.☯

When Should the
United States Intervene?

A Perfect Failure

NATO's War Against Yugoslavia

Michael Mandelbaum

ON THE NIGHT OF MAY 7, 1999—the 45th day of NATO's air campaign against Yugoslavia—bombs struck the Chinese embassy in downtown Belgrade, crushing the building and killing three Chinese who were said to be journalists. An investigation revealed that American intelligence had misidentified the structure as the headquarters of the Yugoslav Bureau of Federal Supply and Procurement. On that basis, NATO planners had put it on the list of approved targets and, guided by satellite, an American B-2 bomber destroyed it.

The attack on the embassy was therefore a mistake. It was not, however, an aberration. It symbolized NATO's Yugoslav war, a conflict marked by military success and political failure. The alliance's air forces carried out their missions with dispatch; the assault forced the Serb military's withdrawal from the southern Yugoslav province of Kosovo. The wider political consequences of the war, however, were the opposite of what NATO's political leaders intended.

Every war has unanticipated consequences, but in this case virtually all the major political effects were unplanned, unanticipated, and unwelcome. The war itself was the unintended consequence of a

MICHAEL MANDELBAUM is Director of the American Foreign Policy Program at the Johns Hopkins School of Advanced International Studies and Senior Fellow at the Council on Foreign Relations. This article originally appeared in the September/October 1999 issue of *Foreign Affairs*.

gross error in political judgment. Having begun it, Western political leaders declared that they were fighting for the sake of the people of the Balkans, who nevertheless emerged from the war considerably worse off than they had been before. The alliance also fought to establish a new principle governing the use of force in the post–Cold War world. But the war set precedents that it would be neither feasible nor desirable to follow. Finally, like all wars, this one affected the national interests of the countries that waged it. The effects were negative: relations with two large, important, and troublesome formerly communist countries, Russia and China, were set back by the military operations in the Balkans.

PAVED WITH GOOD INTENTIONS

AT THE OUTSET of the bombing campaign, the Clinton administration said that it was acting to save lives. Before NATO intervened on March 24, approximately 2,500 people had died in Kosovo's civil war between the Serb authorities and the ethnic Albanian insurgents of the Kosovo Liberation Army (KLA). During the 11 weeks of bombardment, an estimated 10,000 people died violently in the province, most of them Albanian civilians murdered by Serbs.

An equally important NATO goal was to prevent the forced displacement of the Kosovar Albanians. At the outset of the bombing, 230,000 were estimated to have left their homes. By its end, 1.4 million were displaced. Of these, 860,000 were outside Kosovo, with the vast majority in hastily constructed camps in Albania and Macedonia.

The alliance also went to war, by its own account, to protect the precarious political stability of the countries of the Balkans. The result, however, was precisely the opposite: the war made all of them less stable. Albania was flooded with refugees with whom it had no means of coping. In Macedonia, the fragile political balance between Slavs and indigenous Albanians was threatened by the influx of ethnic Albanians from Kosovo. The combination of the Serb rampage on the ground and NATO attacks from the air reduced large parts of Kosovo to rubble. In Serbia proper the NATO air campaign destroyed much of the infrastructure on which economic life depended.

Had this been a war fought for national interests, and had the eviction of Serb forces from Kosovo been an important interest of NATO's member countries, the war could be deemed a success, although a regrettably costly one. But NATO waged the war not for its interests but on behalf of its values. The supreme goal was the well-being of the Albanian Kosovars. By this standard, although the worst outcome—the permanent exile of the Albanians from Kosovo—was avoided, the war was not successful.

THE FATAL MISCALCULATION

ACCORDING TO THE CLINTON ADMINISTRATION, the harm to the people of the Balkans was inevitable and entirely the fault of Serbia. Yugoslav President Slobodan Milošević, the administration said, had long planned to evict all Albanians from Kosovo—where they had come to outnumber Serbs by almost ten to one—in order to ensure perpetual Serb control of the province. NATO could not honorably stand by while Milošević carried out his scheme of "ethnic cleansing" and thus had no choice but to respond as it did— with a 78-day bombing campaign.

Precisely when Belgrade decided on the tactics it employed in Kosovo after the bombing began, and indeed just what it decided— whether the displacement of almost 1.5 million Albanians was its original aim, simply a byproduct of a sweeping assault on the KLA, or a response to NATO's air campaign—are questions that cannot be seriously addressed without access to such records as the Milošević regime may have kept. To be sure, the practice of ethnic cleansing was scarcely unknown to the regime; indeed, it has been an all-too-familiar feature of twentieth-century Balkan history. And whatever their motives, those who killed and put to flight Albanians, and those with authority over the killers and ethnic cleansers bear personal responsibility for the epidemic of crimes in Kosovo.

But there are reasons for skepticism about the Clinton administration's assertion that Milošević's spring offensive against the Kosovar Albanians, like Hitler's war against the Jews, was long intended and carefully planned. Milošević had, after all, controlled the province for ten years without attempting anything approaching what happened in 1999. In October 1998, Serb forces launched an offensive against the KLA that drove 400,000 people from their homes. A cease-fire was arranged, and a great many returned. A team of unarmed monitors from the Organization for Security and Cooperation in Europe (OSCE) was dispatched to the province to give the Albanians a measure of protection. At the outset of 1999, the cease-fire broke down, violated by both sides. Although a concerted effort to reinforce the cease-fire and strengthen the international observers could not have ended the violence altogether, it might have limited the assaults on noncombatants and averted the disaster that Kosovo suffered. Containing the fighting could have bought time for what was necessary for a peaceful resolution of the conflict: a change of leadership in Belgrade. Removing Milošević from office was by no means an impossible proposition. He was not popular with Serbs (the subsequent NATO assault temporarily *increased* his popularity), he did not exercise anything resembling totalitarian control over Serbia, and prolonged demonstrations in 1996–97 had almost toppled him.

But NATO chose a different course. Led by Secretary of State Madeleine K. Albright, it summoned the Serbs and the KLA to the French chateau of Rambouillet, presented them with a detailed plan for political autonomy in Kosovo under NATO auspices, demanded that both agree to it, and threatened military reprisals if either refused. Both did refuse. The Americans thereupon negotiated with the KLA, acquired its assent to the Rambouillet plan, and, when the Serbs persisted in their refusal, waited for the withdrawal of the OSCE monitors and then began to bomb.

Albright later said that "before resorting to force, NATO went the extra mile to find a peaceful resolution," but the terms on which the bombing ended cast doubt on her assertion: they included important departures from Rambouillet that amount to concessions to the Serbs. The United Nations received ultimate authority for Kosovo, giving Russia, a country friendly to the Serbs, the power of veto. The Rambouillet document had called for a referendum after three years to decide Kosovo's ultimate status, which would certainly have produced a large majority for independence; the terms on which the war ended made no mention of a referendum. And whereas Rambouillet gave

NATO forces unimpeded access to all of Yugoslavia, including Serbia, the June settlement allowed the alliance free rein only in Kosovo.

Whether such modifications, if offered before the bombing began and combined with a more robust OSCE presence in Kosovo, could have avoided what followed can never be known. What is clear is that NATO's leaders believed that concessions were unnecessary because a few exemplary salvos would quickly bring the Serbs to heel. "I think this is . . . achievable within a short period of time," Albright said when the bombing began. She and her colleagues were said to consider Milošević a Balkan version of a "schoolyard bully" who would back down when challenged. Apparently the customs in Serbian schoolyards differ from those in the institutions where the senior officials of the Clinton administration were educated, for he did not back down. NATO thus began its war on the basis of a miscalculation. It was a miscalculation that exacted a high price. The people of the Balkans paid it.

Yet when the war ended, the political question at its heart remained unsettled. That question concerned the proper principle for determining sovereignty. The Albanians had fought for independence based on the right to national self-determination. The Serbs had fought to keep Kosovo part of Yugoslavia in the name of the inviolability of existing borders. While insisting that Kosovo be granted autonomy, NATO asserted that it must remain part of Yugoslavia. The alliance had therefore intervened in a civil war and defeated one side, but embraced the position of the party it had defeated on the issue over which the war had been fought.

This made the war, as a deliberate act of policy, a perfect failure. The humanitarian goal NATO sought—the prevention of suffering—was not achieved by the bombing; the political goal the air campaign made possible and the Albanian Kosovars favored—independence—NATO not only did not seek but actively opposed.

Moreover, the Albanian Kosovars were unlikely to accept any continuing connection to Belgrade, in which case NATO would face an awkward choice. An effort to grant independence to Kosovo would encounter opposition from Russia and China, which, as permanent members of the U.N. Security Council, would be able to block it. Denying independence, however, would risk putting the NATO troops in

Kosovo at odds with the KLA and repeating the unhappy experiences of the British army in Northern Ireland since the early 1970s and the American troops in Lebanon in 1982–83, both of which arrived as peacekeepers but eventually found themselves the targets of local forces.

THE CLINTON DOCTRINE

BESIDES PROTECTING THE ALBANIAN KOSOVARS, NATO aspired to establish, with its Yugoslav war, a new doctrine governing military operations in the post–Cold War era. This putative doctrine of "humanitarian intervention" had two parts: the use of force on behalf of universal values instead of the narrower national interests for which sovereign states have traditionally fought; and, in defense of these values, military intervention in the internal affairs of sovereign states rather than mere opposition to cross-border aggression, as in the Gulf War of 1991.

The first of these precepts contained a contradiction. Because no national interest was at stake, the degree of public support the war could command in NATO's member countries was severely limited. Recognizing this, the alliance's political leaders decreed that the war be conducted without risk to their military personnel. Its military operations were thus confined to bombardment from high altitudes. But this meant that NATO never even attempted what was announced to be the purpose of going to war in the first place: the protection of the Kosovar Albanians.

As for the second tenet of "humanitarian intervention," it is, by the established standards of proper international conduct, illegal. The basic precept of international law is the prohibition against interference in the internal affairs of other sovereign states. Without this rule there would be no basis for international order of any kind. But if the rule is inviolable, rulers can mistreat people in any way they like as long as the mistreatment takes place within legally recognized borders. Thus, in recent years international practice has begun to permit exceptions, but only under two conditions, neither of which was present in NATO's war against Yugoslavia.

One condition is a gross violation of human rights. The Serb treatment of Albanians in Kosovo before the NATO bombing was hardly exemplary, but measured by the worst of all human rights violations—murder—neither was it exceptionally bad. Far fewer people had died as a result of fighting in Kosovo before the bombing started than had been killed in civil strife in Sierra Leone, Sudan, or Rwanda—African countries in which NATO showed no interest in intervening. Thus NATO's war did nothing to establish a viable standard for deciding when humanitarian intervention may be undertaken. Instead, it left the unfortunate impression that, in the eyes of the West, an assault terrible enough to justify military intervention is the kind of thing that happens in Europe but not in Africa.

A second condition for violating the normal proscription against intervening in the internal affairs of a sovereign state is authorization by a legitimate authority. This means the United Nations, which, for all its shortcomings, is the closest thing the world has to a global parliament. But NATO acted without U.N. authorization, implying either that the Atlantic alliance can disregard international law when it chooses—a precept unacceptable to nonmembers of the alliance—or that any regional grouping may do so (giving, for example, the Russian-dominated Commonwealth of Independent States the right to intervene in Ukraine if it believes ethnic Russians there are being mistreated)—which is unacceptable to NATO.

Nor did the way the war was fought set a useful precedent. The basic procedure for the conduct of a "just war" is to spare noncombatants. NATO was scrupulous about trying to avoid direct attacks on civilians. But by striking infrastructure in Serbia, including electrical grids and water facilities, the alliance did considerable indirect damage to the civilian population there. Besides harming those whom NATO's political leaders had proclaimed innocent of the crimes committed in Kosovo—for which they blamed Milošević, not the Serb people—these strikes violated Article 14 of the 1977 Protocol to the 1949 Geneva Convention, which bars attacks on "objects indispensable to the survival of the civilian population."

The bombing of Serbia, moreover, continued an ugly pattern that the Clinton administration had followed in Haiti and Iraq, a pattern born of a combination of objection to particular leaders and reluctance to risk American casualties. As with Milošević, the administration had opposed the policies of the military junta that had seized power in Haiti and of Saddam Hussein in Iraq. As in the case of Yugoslavia, invading those two countries to remove the offending leadership was militarily feasible but politically unattractive for the Clinton administration. In all three countries, the administration therefore took steps short of invasion that inflicted suffering on the civilian population—the crushing embargoes of Haiti and Iraq were the equivalents of the bombing of the Serb infrastructure—without (until October 1994 in Haiti, and to the present in Iraq) removing the leaders from power. If there is a Clinton Doctrine—an innovation by the present administration in the conduct of foreign policy—it is this: punishing the innocent in order to express indignation at the guilty.

STRATEGIC DAMAGE

ALTHOUGH ostensibly waged on behalf of NATO's values, the war also affected two of its most important interests: relations with China and Russia. Its effect was to worsen relations with the only two countries in the world that aim nuclear weapons at the United States.

The Chinese leaders professed to be unconvinced by the American explanation for the accidental attack on their embassy. Whatever they thought, the attack was a political windfall for their regime. It deflected attention from the tenth anniversary of the bloody crackdown on the student rallies in Beijing and other cities and channeled against the United States popular sentiment that might otherwise have been directed toward the perpetrators of oppression. It was thus a double setback for American China policy: it strengthened the elements in the Chinese government least favored by Washington, and it stirred anti-American sentiment in some sectors of the Chinese population.

As for Russia, the war accelerated the deterioration in its relations with the West that the ill-advised decision to extend NATO membership to Poland, Hungary, and the Czech Republic had set in motion. In return for permitting a reunited Germany within NATO, Mikhail Gorbachev was promised that the Western military alliance would not expand further eastward. The Clinton administration broke that promise but offered three compensating assurances: that NATO was transforming itself into a largely political organization for the promotion of democracy and free markets; that insofar as NATO retained a military mission, it was strictly a defensive one; and that Russia, although not a NATO member, would be a full participant in European security affairs. The war in Yugoslavia gave the lie to all three: NATO initiated a war against a sovereign state that had attacked none of its members, a war to which Russia objected but that Moscow could not prevent.

Whereas NATO expansion had angered the Russian political class, the bombing of Serbia by all accounts triggered widespread outrage in the Russian public. Thus the sudden postwar occupation of the airport at Priština, the capital of Kosovo, by 200 Russian troops evoked enthusiastic approval in Russia and signaled a shift in the politics of Russian foreign policy in a nationalist direction.

Moscow sought to secure a separate Russian zone of occupation in postwar Kosovo; NATO refused. Russia could not reinforce its position at the airport (and in any case depended on the NATO governments for economic assistance), so it accepted something less: a presence within the American, French, and German zones. The war therefore had the same consequence for Kosovo that NATO expansion had for Europe as a whole: the stability of the military arrangements in both places came to depend less on Russian consent than on Russian weakness.

THE ALBRIGHT LEGACY

THE UNITED STATES dominated the prewar diplomacy and the air campaign, and the war was thus a monument to the efforts of the two officials with the greatest influence on American policy toward the Balkans.

The lesser of the two was President Clinton. He assumed the role of commander in chief with reluctance. Asked at an April 23 press conference with NATO Secretary-General Javier Solana during NATO's 50th anniversary celebration whether the alliance would consider inserting ground troops into Kosovo, Clinton deferred to Solana, as if it were the Spanish official and not he who had the power and responsibility to make that decision.

The official most closely identified with the war was Albright. When it ended, she spoke to troops in Macedonia preparing to enter Kosovo as peacekeepers. "This is what America is good at," she said, "helping people." The help the Albanian Kosovars needed was with rebuilding their homes and their lives. Here, the Clinton administration's track record was not encouraging: it had promised order in Somalia and left chaos. It had gone to Haiti to restore democracy and had left anarchy. It had bombed in Bosnia for the sake of national unity but presided over a de facto partition. But since Clinton had made clear that little money for recovery would come from the United States, the Kosovars' prospects depended on whether, at the end of the twentieth century, "helping people" was what *Europe* had come to be good at.

Albright was on firmer ground with another assertion. Kosovo, she said, was "simply the most important thing we have done in the world." This proved accurate, in no small part due to her efforts. And unlike the other political consequences of NATO's Yugoslav war, it was, for her, entirely intentional. In an administration increasingly preoccupied with its legacy, she had thereby produced one for herself. Focusing the vast strength of American foreign policy on a tiny former Ottoman possession of no strategic importance or economic value, with which the United States had no ties of history, geography, or sentiment, is something that not even the most powerful and visionary of her predecessors—not Thomas Jefferson or John Quincy Adams, not Charles Evans Hughes or Dean Acheson—could ever have imagined, let alone achieved. But as American bombs fell on Yugoslavia, Madeleine Albright had done both.🌀

Response

A Perfect Polemic

Blind to Reality on Kosovo

James B. Steinberg

DURING THE WAR OVER KOSOVO, most criticism of NATO's efforts
fell into two categories. Principled critics understood that important U.S. interests were at stake and that the cause was just but questioned the way NATO conducted the war. Rejectionist critics simply
saw no reason to be concerned about the expulsion or murder of a
whole people on NATO's doorstep. Since the war ended, the principled critics have largely shifted the focus of their skepticism to postwar challenges, urging the allies, appropriately, to make good on
their pledge to seek a more tolerant Kosovo, a democratic Serbia,
and a stable, integrated southeastern Europe. Most accept that
President Clinton's strategy ultimately succeeded: ethnic cleansing
was not only reversed but reversed in a way that kept NATO together,
prevented the destabilization of neighboring countries, and kept
Russia engaged without sacrificing NATO's stated goals.

But to the rejectionist critics, NATO's success remains an inconvenient
fact that cannot be allowed to get in the way of preconceived notions.
Michael Mandelbaum's article places him squarely in this category ("A
Perfect Failure," September/ October 1999). His broadside refuses to
see the slightest redeeming feature in ending Yugoslav President Slobodan Milošević's brutal and destabilizing campaign of atrocities. It is

JAMES B. STEINBERG is Vice-President and Director of Foreign
Policy Studies at the Brookings Institution. This article originally
appeared in the November/December 1999 issue of *Foreign Affairs*.

built on sweeping assertions that crumble on examination, unsupported assumptions about U.S. Kosovo policy, and predictable digressions on everything from NATO enlargement to Haiti to Iraq—all leading to a bitter and overly personalized trashing of Secretary of State Madeleine K. Albright. The only unifying principle I can discern in this attack is, "If the Clinton administration is for it, it must be wrong."

BETTER OFF AS WE ARE

START WITH MANDELBAUM'S MOST FUNDAMENTAL assertion: that NATO failed because the people of Kosovo and the Balkans "emerged from the war considerably worse off than they had been before." This is a breakdown of logic so elemental that it boggles the mind. Imagine if Mandelbaum had been around to apply the same standard to the end of World War II: "Sure, the Nazis have been defeated," he might have written, "but millions are dead, half of Europe is under Soviet control, and most Europeans are a lot worse off than in 1939. What a perfect failure."

NATO's victory is not an occasion for joyful celebration; too many people have lost their lives and homes in Kosovo over the last year for that. And there is much hard work ahead to build a peaceful society that respects the rights of all its people. But the real question in judging success is not whether people are better off than they were before, but whether people are better off than they would have been had the West not acted. The answer to that question is clearly yes. Had NATO not acted, the Serbs would have continued their offensive; more than a million and a half Kosovars would today be sitting in camps or starving in the hills with no hope of return; Milošević would be strengthened; and in a region with many unresolved ethnic tensions, potential dictators would have learned the lesson that massive violence will draw no response from the international community.

Mandelbaum writes that we will never know if Milošević actually intended to expel the Kosovars until we have "access to such records as the Milošević regime may have kept." But there is already a historical record of Milošević's aims and methods: the record of his brutal campaigns against Croatia and Bosnia, both launched long before a single NATO bomb fell on his forces. The same paramilitary warlords who did the dirty work in those campaigns led the charge again in Kosovo, including the notorious Arkan and his "Tigers" and the "White Lions" of Serbian Deputy Prime Minister Vojislav Šešelj. What does Mandelbaum think these people were sent to Kosovo to do—negotiate with Kosovar intellectuals over coffee and baklava? Does he really think they somehow needed to be incited by NATO to commit again the crimes they had committed so often before? Mandelbaum also conveniently forgets about the killings Serb troops committed in Kosovo well before NATO acted, including the January massacre in Racak, which took place despite the presence of monitors from the Organization for Security and Cooperation in Europe (OSCE). He forgets about the 40,000 troops and 300 tanks Milošević massed around Kosovo as he pretended to negotiate for peace and about the tens of thousands of people they pushed from their homes in the five-day period between the end of the Rambouillet peace talks and the start of the bombing. Milošević's goal may have been "simply" to crush the Kosovo Liberation Army (KLA) rebellion. But his method of crushing rebellions has long been well established: it is ethnic cleansing.

If Mandelbaum doubts all this, he can ask the very people for whom he affects such sympathy in his article: the returning Kosovar refugees, who would tell him that NATO rescued them from permanent exile. He can also ask the leaders of Romania, Bulgaria, Macedonia, Albania, Bosnia, and Hungary. He would find that none of them blames NATO for Milošević's decision to throw their region into turmoil, that all of them are grateful that NATO took a stand, and that all of them backed the alliance from beginning to end. He would find that real people get in the way of his hypothetical analysis.

Mandelbaum suggests that NATO might have avoided the horrors that befell the region's people had it made a "concerted effort to reinforce the cease-fire [in Kosovo] and strengthen the international observers." But that is precisely what America and our allies tried to do starting in October 1998, when Milošević agreed to cease his repression of the Kosovars and the OSCE launched an unprecedented effort, including the deployment of more than 1,000 monitors, to hold him to his word by peaceful means. Throughout this period,

Serbian forces repeatedly violated the ceasefire, exceeded the troop levels to which their leader had agreed in October, and steadily increased their harassment of the international observers until it was impossible for them to do their jobs.

The February talks in Rambouillet marked the end of this diplomatic process, not the beginning, as Mandelbaum implies. The administration's central position at the talks—that a greater tragedy could be avoided only if Serbian forces withdrew from Kosovo while an international force was deployed—was absolutely right. It was the conclusion drawn from a year of hard diplomacy, going back to March 1998, when, with America's European partners and Russia, the United States first asked Milošević to pull his police out of Kosovo. If anything, Secretary Albright's assertion that "NATO went the extra mile to find a peaceful resolution," which Mandelbaum disparages, was an understatement.

Mandelbaum also mischaracterizes what happened at the Rambouillet talks. The plan the allies presented there did not call for a "referendum after three years to decide Kosovo's ultimate status." Instead, it offered an international meeting that would determine a mechanism for defining Kosovo's future, which would take into account the will of the people concerned, the opinions of relevant authorities, the degree of compliance by the parties, and the Helsinki Final Act. Moreover, the KLA delegates did not "refuse" to agree to the allies' plan for Kosovar autonomy. They accepted it in principle, went home, and then returned to accept it formally. Milošević's delegates never seriously engaged at the talks—because he was simultaneously preparing the offensive that he believed would destroy the KLA once and for all. That was clearly his fundamental aim from the beginning, and the "concessions" Mandelbaum suggests offering would have been highly unlikely to divert him from trying to achieve it.

Once Rambouillet broke down, NATO had little alternative but to act. Milošević would not accept any solution that required him to pull his troops from Kosovo. Those troops were starting their offensive, violating every previous commitment Milošević had made to the international community, and the situation was deteriorating rapidly. America and our allies hoped that military action would prevent further suffering. But we knew that it was equally possible that it would not and that a sustained campaign might be necessary to stop the killing and reverse the expulsions. And we were prepared to do what it took to win.

A DOG IN THIS FIGHT

MANDELBAUM'S HEART does not really seem to be in the policy alternatives he suggests. Perhaps that is because he sees little reason to care about what happens in faraway Kosovo, a place he dismisses as a "tiny former Ottoman possession of no strategic importance or economic value, with which the United States had no ties of history, geography, or sentiment." Overlook the sweeping insensitivity and historical myopia of that statement—hardly surprising from someone who also opposed NATO's effort to end the bloodshed in Bosnia in 1995—and simply focus on Mandelbaum's claim that "no national interest was at stake" in this conflict.

In fact, 19 NATO allies, with all the diversity of their political cultures and historical relationships with the Balkans, felt they had a compelling interest in ending the violence in Kosovo. A prolonged conflict there would have had no natural boundaries. The allies had an interest in not seeing Kosovars driven from their land, across national borders into fragile new democracies that would be overwhelmed and destabilized by their presence. If NATO had not acted, Kosovo's neighbors might have felt compelled to respond to this threat themselves, and a wider war might have begun. The allies clearly had an interest in preserving the stability of southeastern Europe—and protecting the strides it has made away from a violent past toward a more democratic future. And the allies had an interest in maintaining the unity and credibility of NATO, which would have been impossible had the alliance done nothing in the face of unspeakable atrocities committed at its doorstep—a lesson learned in Bosnia. One can dispute whether these interests justified NATO's decision to use force. But one cannot dispute that these interests exist.

Mandelbaum also argues that the conflict undermined far more important American interests—namely, U.S. relations with Russia and China. True, Russia strongly opposed NATO's action in Kosovo.

But Mandelbaum neglects to consider what would have happened to that relationship had America let the slaughter of innocents continue in Kosovo simply because Russia objected to the use of force. It would have been far harder to sustain a domestic consensus for U.S.-Russian relations under those circumstances. It is far better to try to resolve the source of the tension itself: a decade of war and instability in the Balkans.

As it is, the Kosovo conflict is over. Russia played a key role in ending it. Just as in Bosnia, Russia and NATO now are serving side by side to keep the peace. And Washington and Moscow have already begun to refocus on their common interests: beginning discussions on a START III treaty, working together to get START II ratified and to preserve the ABM treaty, safeguarding Russia's nuclear technology and expertise, strengthening Russia's political and economic institutions, and more.

As for the bombing of the Chinese embassy in Belgrade, that was an error—tragic, but of the sort possible in any conflict. Surely Mandelbaum does not believe that Washington should avoid the use of force under all circumstances simply because a wrong target may be hit. And President Clinton's recent meeting with Chinese President Jiang Zemin in Auckland was a reminder that the bombing has not derailed the common commitment to strengthening this strategically important bilateral relationship.

DOCTRINAIRE

ANOTHER BASIC MISTAKE Mandelbaum makes is ascribing motives to NATO that were never shared by its leaders. For example, he writes that the political question at the heart of the campaign was "the proper principle for determining sovereignty." Since NATO fought on behalf of the Kosovar Albanians while embracing the Serb-backed view that Kosovo should remain part of Serbia, he claims that NATO's effort was an incoherent failure.

But NATO did not go to war in Kosovo over any principle of sovereignty. NATO fought to end Serb repression in Kosovo and to protect southeastern Europe from its consequences. The allies have long argued that the status of Kosovo should be settled peacefully—and thanks to NATO's actions, that can now start to happen. Kosovo's status could be settled far more easily if Serbia was a democracy and the Balkans were more closely integrated with Europe, goals to which the allies have made a long-term commitment.

Mandelbaum also asserts that NATO fought to establish "a new doctrine governing military operations in the post–Cold War era"— a doctrine of humanitarian intervention. But in initiating the conflict, President Clinton made it plain that NATO had a clear and limited rationale. The administration's goal was to stop a vicious campaign of ethnic cleansing in a place where important American interests were at stake and where America and its allies had the ability to act effectively.

Since the conflict ended, the president has said that when governments single out an entire people for destruction or displacement because of their heritage or faith and America can do something about it, America should act—in a way that takes into account both its interests and its values. Americans would rather not live in a world where whole peoples can be hauled off to the slaughter or driven into exile just because of who they are. And such tragedies can launch cycles of violence that throw whole regions into chronic turmoil, overwhelm the world's ability to help the innocent, and inevitably lead to future wars.

At the same time, President Clinton has never suggested that America can or should respond to every humanitarian tragedy the way it responded to Kosovo, or that military force is the only way to respond. In fact, East Timor shows that in some situations, U.S. goals can be better achieved through concerted economic and political pressure. How the United States responds to each case will depend on its capacity to act, on the willingness of others to act with it, and on the national interests at stake. The most important thing America can do is work with other nations and institutions, from regional organizations to the United Nations, to strengthen the collective capacity to prevent—and, if necessary, defeat—outbreaks of mass killing. That is the way to avoid both the heartlessness of doing nothing in the face of human suffering and the callousness of making promises we cannot keep.

A PROUD LEGACY

MANDELBAUM CLOSES with an attack on the Clinton administration's overall policy in the Balkans and central Europe, which he calls the Albright "legacy." In fact, the American people can be proud of what Madeleine Albright, Warren Christopher, William Perry, William Cohen, Anthony Lake, Sandy Berger, and countless others have tried to help President Clinton achieve in Europe over the last six and a half years.

Americans can be proud that NATO has put to rest predictions of its demise—that it is united, adapting to meet 21st-century challenges, and strengthened by the addition of new members. (Today Mandelbaum denounces the policies that brought NATO to this point; ironically, when the alliance was still debating whether to pursue them, he was one of their strongest proponents. He wrote in 1993 that the admission to NATO of Poland, Hungary, and the Czech Republic would be "good for them, good for the West, and good for Russia." He argued that it would help begin the "necessary process of transforming NATO from a defensive alliance against a threat that no longer exists into a broader security community capable of contributing to the establishment of democracy and the maintenance of peace from the English Channel to the Pacific Coast of Russia," and that this process might well involve "undertaking out of area missions, such as policing a negotiated settlement in the former Yugoslavia.")

Americans can be proud as well that four years ago, the new NATO stopped the slaughter in Bosnia and helped put that country on the road to normality. Americans can be proud that in 79 days over Kosovo, America and its allies stopped the most terrible crimes against humanity Europe has seen since World War II. Americans can be proud that at the Balkan summit in Sarajevo this July, the leaders of every democratic nation in that long-troubled region joined with their fellow European and North American democracies to embrace a common plan for shared security and prosperity—not least because the promise of NATO and European Union enlargement have made them feel part of a new Europe. Americans can be proud that our country has been able to work through its disagreements with Russia, supporting its efforts to build an open and prosperous society within the European mainstream while defending American interests and staying true to American principles.

One shudders to think of what might have happened had America and its allies followed a different path. The Balkans would have been wracked by continuous conflict, crowned by the ultimate triumph of ethnic cleansing and genocide. Southeastern Europe would be overrun by refugees and would become a fertile ground for turmoil and instability. Ten years after the fall of the Berlin Wall, NATO would still be maintaining the Iron Curtain as its eastern frontier— that is, if NATO still existed as a functioning, relevant alliance. The new democracies of central and southeastern Europe would feel abandoned by the West, left to fend for themselves in their search for security. America's relationship with Europe would be frayed at best, and its relationship with Russia would suffer under the weight of these mounting tensions.

It is better by far to have worked to build a Europe undivided, democratic, and at peace. When the history of this decade is written, it will be said that the Clinton administration brought that goal within reach—and that in Kosovo, President Clinton and his fellow leaders did the right thing in the right way.🌀

Rwanda in Retrospect

Alan J. Kuperman

A HARD LOOK AT INTERVENTION

SEVERAL YEARS after mass killings in Bosnia, Somalia, and Rwanda, the United States is still searching for a comprehensive policy to address deadly communal conflicts. Among Washington policymakers and pundits, only two basic principles have achieved some consensus. First, U.S. ground troops generally should not be used in humanitarian interventions during ongoing civil wars. Second, an exception should be made for cases of genocide, especially where intervention can succeed at low cost. Support for intervention to stop genocide is voiced across most of the political spectrum.

Despite this amorphous consensus that the United States can and should do more when the next genocide occurs, there has been little hard thinking about just what that would entail or accomplish. A close examination of what a realistic U.S. military intervention could have achieved in the last clear case of genocide this decade, Rwanda, finds insupportable the oft-repeated claim that 5,000 troops deployed at the outset of the killing in April 1994 could have prevented the genocide. This claim was originally made by the U.N.'s commanding general in Rwanda during the genocide and has since been endorsed by members of Congress, human rights groups, and a distinguished panel of the Carnegie Commission on Preventing Deadly Conflict. Although some lives could have been saved by intervention of any size at any point dur-

ALAN J. KUPERMAN is Resident Assistant Professor of International Relations the Bologna Center of John Hopkins University School of Advanced International Studies. This article originally appeared in the January/February 2000 issue of *Foreign Affairs*.

ing the genocide, the hard truth is that even a large force deployed immediately upon reports of attempted genocide would not have been able to save even half the ultimate victims.

PRELUDE TO GENOCIDE

RWANDAN POLITICS were traditionally dominated by the Tutsi, a group that once made up 17 percent of the population. Virtually all the rest of the population was Hutu, and less than one percent were aboriginal Twa. All three groups lived intermingled throughout the country. During the transition to independence starting in 1959, however, the Hutu seized control in a violent struggle that spurred the exodus of about half the Tutsi population to neighboring states.

The Hutu themselves were divided into two regional groups. The majority lived in the central and southern part of the country and supported the PARMEHUTU (Parti du mouvement et de l'émancipation des Bahutu), which assumed power upon independence, while a minority lived in the northwest, historically a separate region. During the first decade of independence, Tutsi refugees invaded Rwanda repeatedly, seeking a return to power. The ruling Hutu responded by massacring domestic Tutsi. In 1973, a northwestern Hutu officer, Juvénal Habyarimana, led a coup that shifted political power to his region. Northwestern Hutu came to dominate Rwanda's political, military, and economic life, engendering resentment from other Hutu as well as from the Tutsi. But large-scale violence against domestic Tutsi largely disappeared for 15 years in the absence of any further attempted invasions by refugees.

Stability began to unravel in October 1990, when an expatriate rebel force composed mainly of Uganda-based Tutsi refugees, the Rwandan Patriotic Army (RPA), invaded northern Rwanda. The RPA and its political arm, the Rwandan Patriotic Front (RPF), were led by battle-tested soldiers who had fought with the Ugandan guerrilla Yoweri Museveni to overthrow Uganda's government in 1986 before turning their efforts toward home. By early 1993, the rebels had made substantial inroads against the Hutu-dominated Rwandan Armed Forces (or FAR, in the French acronym). This military advance, combined with diplomatic pressure from the international community, compelled Habyarimana to agree to share power in the Arusha accords of August 1993.

The peacekeepers of the U.N. Assistance Mission for Rwanda (UNAMIR) then arrived, but for eight months the Rwandan leader obstructed and tried to modify the power-sharing provisions. The extremist wing of his northwestern Hutu clique viewed the accords as abject surrender to the Tutsi, who they feared would seize the spoils of rule and seek retribution. Habyarimana attempted to retain power by co-opting the opposition Hutu through bribery and appeals to solidarity against the Tutsi, and he succeeded in splitting off radical factions from the main opposition parties. But he and the extremists also developed a forceful option—training militias, broadcasting anti-Tutsi hate radio, and plotting to kill moderate Hutu leaders and Tutsi civilians. On April 6, 1994, as Habyarimana appeared to be acquiescing to international pressure to implement the accords, his plane was mysteriously shot down. The genocide plan was put in motion.

In most areas of Rwanda, violence began on the following day. The government radio station and the extremists' counterpart—Radio-Télévision Libre des Mille Collines—urged the Hutu to take vengeance against the Tutsi for their alleged murder of the president. Led by militias, Hutu began to attack the homes of neighboring Tutsi, attempting to rob, rape, and murder them, and often setting fire to their homes. This initial step did not eliminate a high proportion of Tutsi, however, because their attackers were generally poorly armed. The vast majority of Tutsi fled their homes and sought refuge in central gathering places—churches, schools, hospitals, athletic fields, stadiums, and other accessible spaces. Tutsi often passed through more than one such site to gather in larger concentrations, either voluntarily or at government direction. Within a few days, most of Rwanda's Tutsi had congregated at such centralized sites throughout the country, in groups ranging from a few hundred to tens of thousands.

At first, the assembled Tutsi gained a defensive advantage. The surrounding crowds of militia-led Hutu were generally armed only with swords, spears, and machetes—or with the traditional *masu*, a large club studded with nails. By using walls and buildings for defense, Tutsi groups could often fend off attacks merely by throwing rocks. By contrast, individual Tutsi who attempted to flee were often killed immediately by the surrounding Hutu masses or caught and killed at roadblocks. For several days, this produced a standoff. Tutsi living conditions were deteriorating and supplies were dwindling, but most Hutu were unwilling to risk casualties by attacking.

This situation changed in most of Rwanda within a week, by about April 13, when better-armed Hutu reinforcements—composed of members of the regular army, the reserves, the Presidential Guard (PG), or the national police—began arriving at the Tutsi gathering sites. Although these forces were few in number at each site, they were armed with rifles, grenades, or machine guns, which tilted the balance of force. They would typically toss a few grenades on the Tutsi and follow with light-arms fire. Survivors who attempted to flee were usually mowed down by gunfire or caught and killed by the surrounding mob. Militia-led Hutu would then enter the site, hacking to death those still alive. Some Tutsi escaped in the initial mayhem or avoided death by hiding beneath their dead compatriots, but many were later caught at roadblocks and killed on the spot or taken to other central sites to face a similar ordeal. A few lucky Tutsi survived by hiding in places such as pit latrines or the homes of sympathetic Hutu, living to tell their harrowing tales.

Perhaps the most remarkable aspect of the genocide was its speed. According to survivor testimonies gathered by African Rights and Human Rights Watch, the majority of Tutsi gathering sites were attacked and destroyed before April 21, only 14 days into the genocide. Given that half or more of the ultimate Tutsi victims died at these sites, the unavoidable conclusion is that a large portion of Rwanda's Tutsi had been killed by April 21—perhaps 250,000 in just over two weeks. That would be the fastest genocide rate in recorded history.

Despite this generally rapid pace, two factors constrained the speed and extent of the killing in Rwanda. First, Hutu extremists generally avoided large-scale massacres when international observers were present—as part of a comprehensive strategy to hide the genocide from both the outside world and Rwanda's

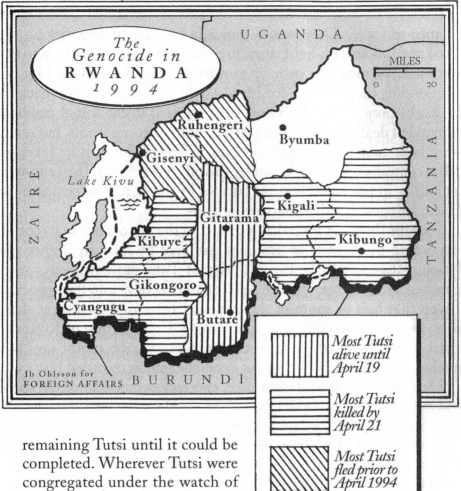

The
Genocide in
RWANDA
1994

UGANDA

MILES

0   20

ZAIRE

Ruhengeri

Byumba

Gisenyi

Lake Kivu

Kigali

Gitarama

Kibuye

Kibungo

TANZANIA

Gikongoro

Cyangugu

Butare

Ib Ohlsson for
FOREIGN AFFAIRS   BURUNDI

Most Tutsi
alive until
April 19

Most Tutsi
killed by
April 21

Most Tutsi
fled prior to
April 1994

Many Tutsi
saved by RPF
occupation

remaining Tutsi until it could be
completed. Wherever Tutsi were
congregated under the watch of
outside observers, the extremists
favored an alternate strategy of
slow, stealthy annihilation: Hutu
leaders would arrive each day at
such sites with a list of up to sev-
eral dozen names, usually starting with the Tutsi political elite.
These Tutsi would be removed under a false pretense such as inter-
rogation before being taken to a remote location and executed. This
occurred at several places across Rwanda: Kamarampaka Stadium and
the Nyarushishi camp in Cyangugu prefecture, where Red Cross aid
workers were present; the Kabgayi Archbishopric in Gitarama, under

the watchful eyes of the pope's subordinates; Amahoro stadium in Kigali, where U.N. troops stood guard; and smaller sites in Kigali such as the St. Famille and St. Paul's churches. At such sites, the slower pace of killing meant that the vast majority of Tutsi there were still alive at the end of April, and a good number survived the entire ordeal.

Second, the killing varied among Rwanda's ten original prefectures. Byumba prefecture in the north was the base of the Tutsi-led rebels, who generally prevented large-scale massacres of Tutsi there. The two prefectures most dominated by Hutu extremists, Gisenyi and Ruhengeri in the northwest, also suffered relatively little killing because much of their Tutsi populations had fled prior to the genocide in response to earlier threats and harassment.

Two prefectures with high Tutsi populations and strong Hutu opposition movements also initially managed to avoid the genocide. Butare prefecture in the south was governed by a Tutsi prefect who managed to keep matters relatively calm until he was removed from office on April 18. Widespread killing then began with a vengeance, and tens of thousands of Tutsi perished in the next few days. Similarly, Gitarama prefecture, the heart of central Rwandan Hutu opposition to the northwestern Hutu regime, generally resisted implementing the genocide until government forces arrived to spur them on. Large-scale killing commenced there about April 21. Finally, the nature of killing in the capital, Kigali, also differed significantly from that in the rest of the country. During the first two days, a highly organized and thorough assassination campaign was carried out there against opposition politicians and prominent liberals such as human rights advocates. Unlike elsewhere, many of Kigali's initial victims of Hutu extremism were fellow Hutu.

Civil war also erupted in Kigali almost immediately. On April 7, an RPA battalion that had been stationed in the capital since December 1993 under the Arusha accords demanded a halt to atrocities against civilians—and then clashed with government forces when its demand was ignored. With the president and the moderate opposition dead, war breaking out in Kigali, and radio broadcasts urging Hutu to kill their neighbors, the capital descended into chaos. Corpses began to pile up, totaling as many as 20,000 during the first week. Unlike in the countryside, however, Tutsi had a decent chance of gaining some

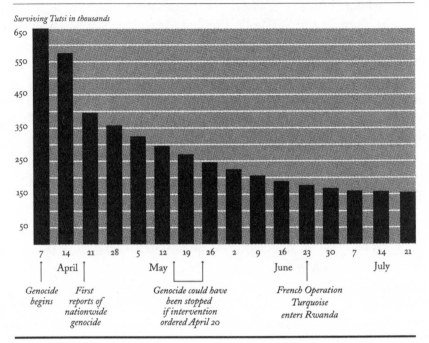

ESTIMATED PACE OF GENOCIDE IN RWANDA
APRIL – JULY 1994

Surviving Tutsi in thousands

7 14 21 28	5 12 19 26	2 9 16 23 30	7 14 21
April	May	June	July

Genocide begins

First reports of nationwide genocide

Genocide could have been stopped if intervention ordered April 20

French Operation Turquoise enters Rwanda

refuge by reaching a central gathering site where foreigners stood guard. Although the extremists could not hide the chaos and violence in the capital, they generally avoided wholesale massacres before such witnesses in hopes of averting foreign military intervention.

By late April, only three weeks after the president's plane crash, almost all the large massacres were finished. The rebels themselves acknowledged on April 29 that "the genocide is almost completed." Human Rights Watch concurs that "in general, the worst massacres had finished by the end of April." By that time, it notes, "perhaps half of the Tutsi population of Rwanda"—some two-thirds of the ultimate Tutsi victims—already had been exterminated. Killing of the remaining Tutsi continued at a slower pace for another two and a half months until halted by the rebels' military victory and a belated French-led intervention.

Precise Tutsi death totals are difficult to determine because of several factors, including the inability to distinguish Tutsi from Hutu corpses. But estimates can be made by subtracting the number of Tutsi survivors from the number living in Rwanda immediately prior to the genocide. Estimated 1994 population figures, which are extrapolated from the 1991 census and account for annual population growth of three percent, indicate that Rwanda's pre-genocide population included approximately 650,000 Tutsi. There is no evidence for other, higher claims.[1] After the genocide and civil war, some 150,000 Tutsi survivors were identified by aid organizations. Thus an estimated 500,000 Rwandan Tutsi were killed, more than three-quarters of their population. The number of Hutu killed during the genocide and civil war is even less certain, with estimates ranging from 10,000 to well over 100,000.

THE KNOWLEDGE GAP

ALTHOUGH U.S. intelligence reports from the period of the genocide remain classified, they probably mirrored those of the international news media, human rights organizations, and the U.N.—because U.S. intelligence agencies committed virtually no in-country resources to what was considered a tiny state in a region of little strategic value. During the genocide's early phases, the U.S. government actually received most of its information from nongovernmental organizations. A comprehensive review of such international reporting—by American, British, French, Belgian, and Rwandan media, leading human rights groups, and U.N. officials—strongly suggests that President Clinton could not have known that a nationwide genocide was under way in Rwanda until about April 20.

This conclusion is based on five aspects of the reporting during the first two weeks. First, violence was initially depicted in the context of a two-sided civil war—one that the Tutsi were winning—

---

[1] Some accounts claim that one million Tutsi lived in Rwanda before the genocide, making up 12 percent of the population, which would correspond with the estimate of 850,000 killed. But historical demographic data suggest otherwise. In 1956, a Belgian census counted almost 17 percent of the population as Tutsi, but half of those fled or died in the violence that accompanied independence. The remaining 9 percent subsequently had a lower fertility rate than the Hutu, reducing the Tutsi population to the 8 percent reported in the 1991 census.

rather than a one-sided genocide against the Tutsi. On April 13, the Western press accurately reported that Rwanda's Hutu interim government had fled the capital for refuge in Gitarama and that "the fall of Kigali seems imminent" (Paris Radio France International). When Western troops arrived to evacuate foreign nationals, the Tutsi rebels did not seek assistance but rather demanded that the troops depart immediately so as not to interfere with their imminent victory. The Canadian commander of the U.N. peacekeepers in Rwanda, General Romeo Dallaire, also identified the problem as mutual violence, stating on April 15 that "if we see another three weeks of being cooped up and seeing them pound each other" (*The Guardian*), the U.N. presence would be reassessed. In addition, until April 18 both the government and the rebels stated publicly that the FAR was not participating in massacres. (The government was engaged in a cover-up, and the rebels initially avoided implicating the FAR in the vain hope of winning its allegiance against the extremist Hutu.)

Second, the violence was reported to be waning when it actually was accelerating. Just four days in, on April 11, *The New York Times* reported that fighting had "diminished in intensity" and *Le Monde* wrote three days later that "a strange calm reigns in downtown" Kigali. The commander of Belgian peacekeepers stated that "the fighting has died down somewhat, one could say that it has all but stopped" (Paris Radio France International). On April 17, Dallaire told the BBC that except for an isolated pocket in the north, "the rest of the line is essentially quite quiet." Only on April 18 did a Belgian radio station question this consensus, explaining that the decline in reports of violence was because "most foreigners have left, including journalists."

Third, most early death counts were gross underestimates and never suggested genocidal proportions. Three days into the killing, on April 10, *The New York Times* quoted varying estimates of 8,000 or "tens of thousands" dead. But during the second week, media estimates did not rise at all. On April 18, the *Times* still reported only 20,000 deaths, underestimating the actual carnage at that point by about tenfold. The true scope of the killing emerged only on April 20, when Human Rights Watch estimated that "as many as 100,000 people may have died to date," followed the next day by a Red Cross estimate of perhaps "hundreds of thousands."

Fourth, the initial focus of international reporting was almost exclusively on Kigali, a relatively small city, and thus failed to indicate the broader scope of violence—a consequence both of Hutu concealment efforts and of the Western evacuation of expatriates and reporters from the countryside. Although a few early reports of rural violence did trickle out to the West, these indicated military combat, mutual ethnic violence, or criminal looting rather than an extermination campaign. An RPF official told the BBC on April 12 only that "we want to stop the senseless killing that is going on in Kigali." The first international report of a large-scale massacre outside the capital did not emerge until April 16. As late as April 20, U.N. Secretary-General Boutros Boutros-Ghali still described the killings as "mainly in Kigali." This initial obsession with the capital, which contained only four percent of Rwanda's population, obscured the national scope of violence and thus its genocidal intent.

The rebels' own radio station did not report the nationwide scope of the violence until April 19. American newspapers failed to give any such indication until April 22, when they belatedly reported that fighting bands had reduced "much of the country to chaos" (*The New York Times*). Many foreign observers still could not conceive that a genocide was under way. On April 23, *The Washington Post* pondered why only 20,000 refugees had crossed the border—even though half a million Tutsi had fled their homes—and reported that aid workers had concluded that "most of the borders have been sealed by the Rwandan Army." Only on April 25 did *The New York Times* solve the riddle, reporting that violence had "widened into what appears to be a methodical killing of Tutsi across the countryside." The missing refugees "either have been killed or are trying to hide."

Fifth, no credible and knowledgeable observers, including human rights groups, raised the prospect that genocide was occurring until the end of the second week. In opinion articles published on April 14 and 17, Human Rights Watch gave no hint of an attempted nationwide genocide. The rebels did not use the term until April 17. Human Rights Watch finally raised the prospect in an April 19 letter to the U.N. Security Council. Other international observers remained considerably more cautious. The pope first used the word "genocide" on April 27. The U.S. Committee for Refugees waited until May 2 to urge the Clinton administration to make such a determination. Only on May 4 did Boutros-Ghali finally declare a "real genocide." Thus the earliest President Clinton credibly could have made a determination of attempted genocide was about April 20, 1994—two weeks into the violence.

THE MILITARY SCENE

AT THE TIME of Habyarimana's death, Rwanda hosted three military forces—those of the government, the rebels, and the United Nations. Government forces totaled about 40,000, including the army, the national police, and 1,500 PG troops. But except for the PG and a few other elite battalions, this force was largely hollow, having expanded sixfold in three years responding to the rebel threat. Another 15,000 to 30,000 Hutu were scattered around the country in militias, but many apparently did not possess firearms or ammunition. Rebel arms were more primitive than the FAR's and included few motorized vehicles and no aircraft.

UNAMIR had about 2,500 peacekeepers, most either in Kigali or in the north near the demilitarized zone. Their presence was subject to the consent of the Rwandan government. Rules of engagement were somewhat ambiguous but were generally interpreted to bar the use of force except in self-defense or in joint operations with Rwandan national police.

On the first day of violence, the PG executed ten Belgian peacekeepers who were attempting to protect Rwanda's opposition prime minister. These deaths and the emerging chaos in Kigali prompted Western governments to evacuate their nationals. European troops began arriving on April 9 and evacuated several thousand Westerners before departing on April 13. On April 10, Dallaire also requested 5,000 more U.N. troops to halt what he perceived to be mutual killing confined to the capital. Instead, Belgium announced on April 14 that it would be withdrawing its UNAMIR battalion, which triggered unease among the other troop-contributors and led the U.N. Security Council a week later to cut authorized troop levels to a skeleton crew of 270.

Rebel forces, estimated at 20,000, had been constrained by the Arusha accords to a small area of northern Rwanda; the exception was one authorized Kigali battalion, which the RPF had reinforced clandestinely to about 1,000 troops. When the civil war was renewed on April 7, the northern-based rebels set out to help the stranded battalion in the capital and engage FAR troops elsewhere, making quick progress down Rwanda's entire eastern flank by late April. Thereafter, the war had two stationary fronts, in Kigali and Ruhengeri, until the end of June, as well as a broad mobile front moving westward through southern Rwanda. In just three months, the rebels captured most of the country—Gitarama on June 9, Kigali on July 4, Butare on July 5, Ruhengeri on July 14, and Gisenyi on July 17—before finally declaring a cease-fire on July 18.

As reports of genocide reached the outside world starting in late April, public outcry spurred the United Nations to reauthorize a beefed-up "UNAMIR II" on May 17. During the following month, however, the U.N. was unable to obtain any substantial contributions of troops and equipment. As a result, on June 22 the Security Council authorized France to lead its own intervention, Operation Turquoise, by which time most Tutsi were already long dead.

POTENTIAL U.S. INTERVENTIONS

IN RETROSPECT, three levels of potential U.S. military intervention warrant analysis: maximum, moderate, and minimal. None would have entailed full-blown nationwide policing or long-term nation-building by American troops. Based on historical experience, full-blown policing would have required some 80,000 to 160,000 personnel—that is, ten to twenty troops per thousand of population—an amount far more than logistically or politically feasible. Nation-building would have been left to a follow-on multinational force, presumably under U.N. authorization.

Maximum intervention would have used all feasible force to halt large-scale killing and military conflict throughout Rwanda. Moderate intervention would have sought to halt some large-scale killing without deploying troops to areas of ongoing civil war, in order to reduce U.S. casualties. Minimal intervention would have relied on air power alone.

A maximum intervention would have required deployment of a force roughly the size of one U.S. division—three brigades and supporting units, comprising about 15,000 troops and their equipment—with rules of engagement permitting the use of deadly force to protect endangered Rwandans. After establishing a base of operations at Kigali airport, the force would have focused on three primary goals: halting armed combat and interposing itself between FAR and RPF forces on the two stationary fronts of the civil war; establishing order in the capital; and finally fanning out to halt large-scale genocidal killing in the countryside. None of these tasks would have been especially difficult or dangerous for properly configured and supported American troops once they were in Rwanda. But transporting such a force 10,000 miles to a landlocked country with limited airfields would have been considerably slower than some retrospective appraisals have suggested.

The first brigade to arrive would have been responsible for Kigali: coercing the FAR and RPF to halt hostilities, interposing itself between them, and policing the capital. The second brigade would have deployed one battalion in the north to halt the civil war in Ruhengeri and another as a rapid-reaction force in case American troops drew fire. The third brigade, supplemented by a battalion of the second brigade, would have been devoted to halting the killing in the countryside. Such an effort would have required roughly 2,000 troops to halt the war in Kigali, 3,000 to police Kigali, 1,000 to stop the fighting in the north, 1,500 for a rapid-reaction force, and 6,000 to stop the genocide outside Kigali—a total of about 13,500 troops, in addition to support personnel.

The time required to deploy such a force would have depended mainly on its weight. A division-size task force built around one brigade each from the 101st Air Assault, 82nd Airborne, and a light army division can be approximated as the average of those divisions—26,550 tons, including 200 helicopters and 13,500 personnel. (The Marines could also have substituted for the one of the brigades.) Because Rwanda is a landlocked country in Central Africa, and because speed is critical in stopping a genocide, the entire force would have been airlifted. The rate of airlift would have been constrained by factors such as the delay in loading planes at U.S. bases, excessive demand for air refueling, fuel shortages in Central Africa, and the limited airfield capacity in Kigali and at the potential staging base at Entebbe in neighboring Uganda. At an optimistic rate of 800 tons

	Force size	Airlift in days	Tutsi saved	Percentage of death toll
Maximum	Division 13,500 troops; 27,000 tons	40	125,000	25
Moderate	Reinforced Brigade 6,000 troops; 10,000 tons	21	100,000	20
Minimum	Air Assault Brigade 2,500 troops (outside Rwanda); 4,500 tons	14	75,000	15

daily, the task force would have required 33 days to airlift. Personnel, which are much quicker to transport than their cargo, could have been sent first—but it would have been imprudent to deploy them into the field without sufficient equipment and logistics. Several additional days would also have been required for the delay between the deployment order and start of airlift, for the gradual increase in the capacity of theater airfields unaccustomed to such traffic, and for travel to and unloading at the theater. In addition, the rate of force deployment might have been slowed by the need to use limited airlift capacity for food, medicine, and spare parts to sustain the first troops to arrive. Thus the entire force could not have closed in the theater until about 40 days after the president's order.

Advance units, however, could have begun operations much sooner. Approximately four days after the order, a battalion or two of Army Rangers could have parachuted in and seized Kigali airport at night. Follow-on troops could have expanded outward from the airfield to establish a secure operating base. Within about two weeks, sufficient troops and equipment could have arrived to halt the fighting, form a buffer between the FAR and the RPF in Kigali and northwest Rwanda, and fully police the capital. Only later, however, could the intervention force have turned in earnest to stopping the genocide in the countryside as helicopters, vehicles, and troops arrived.

Some observers have suggested that the genocide would have ceased spontaneously throughout Rwanda upon the arrival of Western enforcement troops in Kigali—or possibly even earlier, upon the mere announcement of a deployment. They claim that the extremists would have halted killing in hopes of avoiding punishment. But these Hutu were already guilty of genocide and could not have imagined that stopping midway would gain them absolution. More likely, the announcement of Western intervention would have accelerated the killing as extremists tried to finish the job and eliminate witnesses while they had a chance. Such was the trend ahead of the RPA advance, as Hutu militias attempted to wipe out remaining Tutsi before the rebels arrived. During the genocide, the ringleaders even trumpeted false reports of an impending Western intervention to help motivate Hutu to complete the killings. Although the Hutu generally held back from mass killing at sites guarded by foreigners to avoid provoking Western intervention, they would have lost this incentive for restraint had such an intervention been announced.

The 6,000 U.S. troops deployed to the countryside would have been insufficient to establish a full police presence, but they could have found and protected significant concentrations of threatened Rwandans. Ideally, helicopter reconnaissance could have identified vulnerable or hostile groups from the air and then directed rapid response forces to disperse hostile factions and secure the sites. Alternately, ground troops could have radiated out from Kigali in a methodical occupation of the countryside. Displaced Rwandans could have been gathered gradually into perhaps 20 large camps for their protection.

Depending on the search method, large-scale genocide could have been stopped during the fourth or fifth week after the deployment order, by May 15 to May 25. Interestingly enough, this would have been before the task force's airlift had been completed. Based on the genocide's progression, such an intervention would have saved about 275,000 Tutsi, instead of the 150,000 who actually survived. Maximum credible intervention thus could not have prevented the genocide, as is sometimes claimed, but it could have spared about 125,000 Tutsi from death, some 25 percent of the ultimate toll.

A more modest intervention would have refrained from deploying U.S. troops to any area in Rwanda in which FAR and RPA troops were actively fighting. In late April, this would have limited U.S. troops to a zone consisting of six prefectures in the south and west of Rwanda. A single reinforced brigade would have sufficed given the reduced territory, population, and threat of potential adversaries. Ideally, the ready brigade of the 101st Air Assault Division would have been designated and supplemented by two additional light-infantry battalions, supporting units for peace operations, and additional helicopters and motorized vehicles: a force of 6,000 personnel, weighing about 10,000 tons.

For such an action, three main objectives would have been set: first, to deter and prevent entry of organized military forces into the above-mentioned zone; second, to halt large-scale genocide there; and third, to prepare for a handoff to a U.N. force. Strategic airlift would not have relied on Kigali airport, which was still a battleground in the civil war, but rather on neighboring Bujumbura in Burundi and Entebbe in Uganda—which would have further constrained the deployment rates. Still, facing little military threat in the zone, these troops probably could have stopped large-scale genocide there within three weeks after the deployment order, by May 11, 1994. About 200,000 Tutsi from the zone could have survived, as opposed to about 100,000 from this part of Rwanda who actually did. Elsewhere in Rwanda, genocide would have continued until stopped by the RPA, as occurred, leaving only 50,000 survivors outside the zone of intervention. Moderate intervention thus could have spared about 100,000 Tutsi from death, or 20 percent of the ultimate toll. Surprisingly, moderate intervention in this case would have saved almost as many lives as the maximum alternative, because by avoiding combat areas the interveners could have turned sooner to counter genocide in the zone where most Tutsi lived.

The third alternative, a minimal intervention, would have attempted to mitigate the genocide without introducing U.S. ground troops into Rwanda, relying on airpower alone from bases in neighboring countries. For example, the United States could have threatened to bomb the extremist ringleaders and the FAR's military assets unless the killing was halted—and then followed through if necessary. But if the threat alone failed to coerce, U.S. pilots would have had difficulty locating the ringleaders or hitting FAR positions without killing rebels as well. Even if air coercion had succeeded in Rwanda, a follow-on ground force would have been needed to keep the peace.

Alternatively, the United States could have pursued airborne policing, which would have attempted to interdict physically and intimidate psychologically the perpetrators of the genocide throughout Rwanda. Significant numbers of U.S. attack helicopters and fixed-wing aircraft could have patrolled Rwanda daily from bases in neighboring countries. If armed factions threatening large groups of civilians were spotted, air-to-ground fire could have dispersed the assailants, at least temporarily. Such air patrols would have continued until deployment of non-American ground troops or until the RPF won the civil war. But airborne policing could not have prevented smaller acts of violence in the meantime.

Another minimal approach would have been to help the Rwandan Tutsi escape to refugee camps in bordering states—Burundi, Tanzania, Uganda, or Zaire—by using helicopter patrols to ensure safe passage. Rwanda has only about 600 miles of paved roads. Assuming a team of 20 helicopters with standard maintenance needs, five helicopters could have been kept aloft at a time, with each responsible for 120 miles of roadway. If these helicopters flew at a ground speed of 120 miles per hour, each section of roadway could have been patrolled approximately every hour. Airborne broadcasts and leaflets would have directed the Tutsi to the exit routes. Air-to-ground fire would have broken up roadblocks and dispersed armed gangs to ensure the free flow of refugees. But this strategy could not have saved those Tutsi unable to reach major roads and would have caused a major refugee crisis.

Each of the airpower options would have had drawbacks, including the risk of losing airborne personnel to anti-aircraft fire, but each also had the potential to save tens of thousands of Tutsi. Coercion might have stopped the genocide quickly, potentially facilitating a cease-fire in the civil war. Airborne policing could have allowed more Tutsi to be saved by France's Operation Turquoise or a similar follow-up deployment. Free passage also would have kept more Tutsi alive, albeit as refugees, and they might have returned home quickly after the RPF's victory. About 300,000 Tutsi still were alive in late April 1994, of whom about 150,000 subsequently perished. If minimum intervention had been able to avert half these later killings, it could have spared about 75,000 Tutsi from death, or 15 percent of the genocide's ultimate toll.

Rwanda in Retrospect

A WESTERN FAILURE OF WILL?

MANY OBSERVERS have claimed that timely intervention would have prevented the genocide. Some even asserted at first that UNAMIR itself could have done so, although most now acknowledge that the peacekeepers lacked sufficient arms, equipment, and supplies. Conventional wisdom still holds that 5,000 well-armed reinforcements could have prevented the genocide had they been deployed promptly when the killing began—and that the West's failure to stop the slaughter resulted exclusively from a lack of will. Rigorous scrutiny of six prominent variations of this assertion, however, finds all but one dubious.

Human Rights Watch makes the boldest claim: Diplomatic intervention could have averted the genocide without additional military deployment. These advocates contend that a threat from the international community to halt aid to any Rwandan government that committed genocide would have emboldened Hutu moderates to face down the extremists and extinguish violence. As proof, they note that moderate FAR officers appealed for support from Western embassies during the first days of violence, and that the intensity of massacres waned after the West intensified its condemnations in late April.

However, this argument ignores the fact that virtually all of Rwanda's elite military units were controlled by extremist Hutu, led by Colonel Theoneste Bagosora. These forces demonstrated their power and ruthlessness by killing Rwanda's top political moderates during the first two days of violence. By contrast, moderate Hutu officers had virtually no troops at their disposal. The moderates avoided challenging the extremists not because of a lack of Western rhetorical support but because of mortal fear for themselves and their families. This fear was justified given that the extremists stamped out any nascent opposition throughout the genocide—coercing and bribing moderate politicians, removing them from office or killing them if they did not yield, shipping moderate soldiers to the battlefront, and executing civilian opponents of genocide as "accomplices" of the rebels. The decline in massacres in late April is explained simply by the dwindling number of Tutsi still alive. International condemnation did little except compel extremists to try harder to hide the killing and disguise their rhetoric. Even these superficial gestures were directed mainly at persuading France to renew its military support for the anti-Tutsi war—hardly an indication of moderation.

The only way that the army's Hutu moderates could have reduced the killing of Tutsi civilians would have been to join forces with the Tutsi rebels to defeat the Hutu extremists. This was militarily feasible, given that the Tutsi rebels alone defeated both the FAR and the Hutu militias in just three months—but it was politically implausible. By April, Rwanda had already been severely polarized along ethnic lines by four years of civil war, the calculated efforts of propagandists, and the October 1993 massacre of Hutu by Tutsi in neighboring Burundi. Even moderate Hutu politicians once allied with the rebels had come to fear Tutsi hegemony. Although the moderate Hutu officers sincerely favored a cease-fire and a halt to the genocide, they could not realistically have defected to the Tutsi rebels—at least until the FAR's defeat became imminent.

The second claim is that 5,000 U.N. troops deployed immediately upon the outbreak of violence could have prevented the genocide. But this assertion is problematic on three grounds. It assumes such troops could have been deployed virtually overnight. In reality, even a U.S. light-infantry ready brigade would have required about a week after receiving orders to begin significant operations in the theater and several more days for all its equipment to arrive. Further delays would have resulted from reinforcing the brigade with heavy armor or helicopters, or from assembling a multinational force. Even if ordered on April 10, as requested at the time by Dallaire, reinforcements probably could not have begun major operations to stop genocide much before April 20. Moreover, it is unrealistic to argue that urgent intervention should have been launched on April 10—given that the international community did not realize genocide was under way until at least ten days later.

Intervention advocates, such as the Carnegie Commission, also erroneously characterize the progression of the genocide. The commission claims that there was a "window of opportunity ... from about April 7 to April 21" when intervention "could have stemmed the violence in and around the capital [and] prevented its spread to the countryside." In reality, killing started almost immediately in most of Rwanda, and by April 21, the last day of this purported "window," half the ultimate Tutsi victims already were dead. Even if reinforcements had arrived overnight in Kigali, Dallaire was unaware of genocide outside the capital and thus would not have deployed troops to the countryside in time to prevent the massacres.

Furthermore, 5,000 troops would have been insufficient to stop genocide without running risks of failure or high casualties. Only 1,000 troops would have been available for policing Kigali—some three troops per thousand residents, which is grossly inadequate for a city in the throes of genocide. In the countryside, U.S. commanders would have faced a stark choice: either concentrate forces for effective action, leaving most of the country engulfed in killing; or spread forces thin, leaving troops vulnerable to attack. To avoid such painful choices in the past, U.S. military planners have insisted on deploying more than 20,000 troops for interventions in the Dominican Republic, Panama, and Haiti—all countries with populations smaller than Rwanda's.

A third claim is that U.N. headquarters had three months' advance notice of genocide and could have averted the killing simply by authorizing raids on weapons caches. Critics cite the so-called genocide fax—a January 11, 1994, cable from Dallaire to U.N. headquarters in New York that conveyed a Hutu informant's warning that extremists were planning to provoke civil war, kill Belgian peacekeepers to spur their withdrawal, and slaughter the Tutsi with an *Interahamwe* militia of 1,700 troops that the informant was training. The cable also reported an arms cache containing at least 135 weapons, which Dallaire wanted to seize within 36 hours.

Dallaire, however, raised doubts about the informant's credibility in this cable, stating that he had "certain reservations on the suddenness of the change of heart of the informant.... Possibility of a trap not fully excluded, as this may be a set-up." Raising further doubt, the cable was the first and last from Dallaire containing such accusations, according to U.N. officials. Erroneous warnings of coups and assassinations are not uncommon during civil wars. U.N. officials were prudent to direct Dallaire to confirm the allegations with Habyarimana himself, based on the informant's belief that "the president does not have full control over all elements of his old party/faction." Dallaire never reported any confirmation of the plot.

Even if the U.N. had acquiesced to Dallaire in January 1994, it is unlikely the weapons cache could have been seized or that doing so would have prevented the genocide. The U.N. actually did reverse itself barely three weeks later, on February 4, 1994, granting Dallaire authorization to raid weapons depots. But his forces failed in every attempt, even after an informant identified three new caches on February 7. By mid-March, six weeks after receiving authorization, the peacekeepers had captured only a paltry total of 16 weapons and 100 grenades; their rules required cooperating with Rwandan police, who tipped off the extremists. If the U.N. had permitted Dallaire to act without consulting local authorities, Kigali could have responded under Chapter VI of the U.N. Charter (which governs consensual peacekeeping operations) by simply expelling the force. The peacekeepers also were vulnerable to violent retaliation, as they were dispersed and still lacked armored personnel carriers at the time. In addition, Dallaire's cable identified a cache of only 135 weapons—a tiny fraction of the 20,000 rifles and 500,000 machetes imported by the government over the preceding two years. Even had Dallaire managed to seize this cache without prompting expulsion or retaliation, he could not have derailed the wider genocide plot without significant reinforcements.

A fourth claim holds that quickly jamming or destroying Hutu radio transmitters when the violence broke out could have prevented the genocide. A Belgian peacekeeper who monitored broadcasts testified, "I am convinced that, if we had managed to liquidate [Radio Mille Collines], we could perhaps have avoided, or in any case limited, the genocide." A human rights advocate characterized the jamming as "the one action that, in retrospect, might have done the most to save Rwandan lives." But radio broadcasts were not essential to perpetuating or directing the killing. By April, Rwandans had been sharply polarized along ethnic lines by civil war, propaganda, and recent massacres in Burundi. Habyarimana's assassination was a sufficient trigger for many extremist Hutu to begin killing. Moderate Hutu were usually swayed not by radio broadcasts but by threats and physical intimidation from extremist authorities. Furthermore, orchestration of the genocide relied not merely on radio broadcasts but on the government's separate military communications network. Silencing the radio might have had most impact prior to the genocide, when broadcasts were fostering polarization, but such action would have been rejected at the time as a violation of sovereignty. Even if hate radio had been preventively extinguished, the extremists possessed and used other means to foster hatred.

The fifth variant of the intervention argument is that the Western forces sent to evacuate foreign nationals during the first week could have restored order in Kigali—and thereby prevented the genocide had they merely been given the orders to do so. Just four days after Habyarimana's assassination, some 1,000 lightly armed Western evacuation troops, mainly French and Belgian soldiers, had arrived in Kigali, where Belgium's 400-troop UNAMIR contingent was already stationed. Another 1,100 reserves were less than two hours away by air. But it is doubtful that this small force, lacking the right equipment or logistical support, could have quickly quashed violence in the capital—or that doing so would have stopped the genocide elsewhere. The Western evacuators had to commit half their force to guarding the airport at the town's outskirts and a few key assembly points, leaving few available for combat. In addition, coordinated action would have been inhibited by the widespread perception that France and Belgium sympathized with opposite sides in the civil war. Moreover, Kigali was defended by 2,000 elite Rwandan army troops and several thousand regulars equipped with heavy weapons, another 2,000 armed fighters of the Hutu militia, and 1,000 national police. Also located there were more than 1,000 Tutsi rebels who had access to surface-to-air missiles and had explicitly threatened to attack the evacuators if they extended their mission. Even if the small Western force had somehow halted the violence in Kigali, it lacked the equipment and logistics to deploy troops quickly to the countryside. Rural killing probably would have continued unless the ringleaders were captured and coerced to call off the slaughter. Such a search would not have been a quick or simple matter for any force, as demonstrated by the failed search for the Somali warlord Mohamed Farah Aidid by U.S. troops in 1993. Ill-equipped evacuation troops could have wasted weeks looking for the ringleaders while genocide continued at a torrid pace in the countryside, where 95 percent of Rwandans lived.

The sixth claim is most realistic: Had UNAMIR been reinforced several months prior to the outbreak of violence, as Belgium urged at the time, genocide might have been averted. More troops with the proper equipment, a broad mandate, and robust rules of engagement could have deterred the outbreak of killing or at least snuffed it out early. Such reinforcement would have required about 3,500 additional high-quality troops in Kigali, armored personnel carriers, helicopters, adequate logistics, and the authorization to use force to seize weapons and ensure security without consulting Rwandan police. This would have been the 5,000-troop force that Dallaire envisioned—but one deployed prior to the genocide.

Under the U.N.'s peacekeeping rules, Rwanda's government would have had to consent to such a change—and probably would have. Prior to the genocide, its cabinet still was dominated by the Hutu opposition moderates who had negotiated the Arusha accords, which called for a neutral international force to "guarantee [the] overall security of the country." The U.N. Security Council had watered down implementation of this provision, authorizing UNAMIR only to "contribute to the security of the city of Kigali." As tensions mounted in early 1994, the Rwandan government again asked the U.N. to dismantle armed groups, but the peacekeepers were too weak. Belgium pleaded for reinforcements and a new mandate from the Security Council in January and February 1994 on the grounds that UNAMIR could not maintain order. But the United States and Britain blocked this initiative before it could even reach a vote, citing the costs of more troops and the danger that expanding the mission could endanger peacekeepers—as had occurred in Somalia the previous October.

The Rwandan government, however, almost certainly would have welcomed a reinforcement of UNAMIR prior to the genocide. Five thousand troops in the capital would have meant 16 troops for every thousand Rwandans, a ratio historically sufficient to quell severe civil disorders. Such a force might well have deterred the genocide plot. Failing that, well-equipped peacekeepers could have protected moderate Hutu leaders and Tutsi in the capital and captured some of the extremists during the first days of violence, thereby diminishing the chance of large-scale massacres in the countryside. Indeed, such early reinforcement of UNAMIR is the only proposed action that would have had a good chance of averting the genocide.

LESSONS

THE MOST OBVIOUS LESSON of Rwanda's tragedy is that intervention is no substitute for prevention. Although the 1994 genocide represents a particularly tough case for intervention in some respects—such as its rapid killing and inaccessible location—it would have been a relatively easy mission in other respects, including the limited strength of potential opponents. Yet even an ideal intervention in Rwanda would have left hundreds of thousands of Tutsi dead. To avert such violence over the long term, there is no alternative to the time-consuming business of diplomacy and negotiation. Tragically, international diplomatic efforts in Rwanda prior to the genocide were ill conceived and counterproductive.

Whether pursuing prevention or intervention, policymakers must use their imagination to better anticipate the behavior of foreign actors. In Rwanda, Western officials failed to foresee the genocide, despite numerous warning signs, in part because the act was so immoral that it was difficult to picture. Increased awareness of such risks demands that any peacekeeping force deployed preventively to a fragile area be adequately sized and equipped to stop incipient violence—rather than be sent as a lightly armed tripwire that serves mainly to foster a false sense of security. If the West is unwilling to deploy such robust forces in advance, it must refrain from coercive diplomacy aimed at compelling rulers to surrender power overnight. Otherwise, such rulers may feel so threatened by the prospect of losing power that they opt for genocide or ethnic cleansing instead. Western diplomacy that relies mainly on the threat of economic sanctions or bombing has provoked a tragic backlash not just in Rwanda, but also in Kosovo and East Timor over the last few years as local rulers opted to inflict massive violence rather than hand over power or territory to lifelong enemies. In each case, Western military intervention arrived too late to prevent the widespread atrocities.

Obviously, time is of the essence once large-scale attacks against civilians begin. Most such violence can be perpetrated in a matter of weeks, as was demonstrated in Rwanda, Kosovo, and East Timor. Despite this reality, domestic politics often prevents an American president from quickly launching a major intervention. Thus U.S. defense planners should be more creative in developing limited alternatives. The case of Rwanda underscores that lighter intervention options that avoid combat areas and focus mainly on stopping violence against civilians could save almost as many lives if pursued seriously and expeditiously. Rapid responses would be facilitated by the development of pre-prepared plans for known trouble spots and by better coordinating intelligence from available sources, including nongovernmental organizations.

That said, tradeoffs are inevitable if the United States hopes to increase its effectiveness in humanitarian military intervention. To deploy troops faster, additional "ultra-light" units (like the Tenth Mountain Division) would have to be created, either by converting existing heavier units intended for major contingencies or by increasing defense spending. The Pentagon's recent proposal to trim some heavy mechanized forces down to medium-weight units would not solve the problem, because they would still be too heavy for a quick airlift. Lighter units probably could save more lives abroad but would also be subject to more casualties and potential failure. Such tradeoffs should be made only after rigorous debate, which to date has been virtually absent in the United States.

Finally, no policy of humanitarian military intervention should be implemented without a sober consideration of its unintended consequences. Recent interventions, whether in Bosnia, Kosovo, or East Timor, have been motivated by the impulse to provide humanitarian aid to a party visibly suffering in an internal conflict. But intervention in those cases also resulted in the weaker sides being bolstered militarily. This pattern creates perverse incentives for weaker parties in such conflicts to reject compromise and escalate fighting because they expect foreign intervention or hope to attract it. The result is often tragedy, as intervention arrives too little or too late to protect civilians. Thus a policy of intervening to relieve humanitarian emergencies that stem from internal conflicts may actually increase the number and extent of such emergencies—a classic instance of moral hazard.

Inevitably, decisions on whether and how to intervene in specific cases will be caught up in politics. But this challenge should not deter hard thinking on when and how such intervention can be most beneficial—or detrimental. If Rwanda demonstrates nothing else, it is that thousands of lives are at stake in such decisions.🌐

Response

Shame

Rationalizing Western Apathy on Rwanda

Alison L. Des Forges

ALAN J. KUPERMAN plays word games when he asserts that President Clinton could not have known of the "attempted genocide" of Tutsi in Rwanda until April 20, 1994—two weeks into the slaughter—because the press, nongovernmental organizations (NGOs), and the U.N. did not call it a genocide ("Rwanda in Retrospect," January/February 2000).

Two days, not two weeks, after the slaughter began on April 6, U.S. officials knew that extremists with an avowedly genocidal agenda had murdered legitimate Rwandan authorities and were claiming control of the government. U.S. officials knew that these extremists had used the radio to spew anti-Tutsi propaganda for months and that they had recruited, trained, and armed militias. U.S. officials knew that Rwandans had previously used the highly centralized administrative system to organize massacres of Tutsi. And at least some of these officials knew that an eerily prescient CIA study three months before had foreseen a death toll of half a million if violence began again.

ALISON L. DES FORGES is Senior Advisor for Human Rights Watch/Africa. ALAN J. KUPERMAN is Resident Assistant Professor of International Relations the Bologna Center of John Hopkins University School of Advanced International Studies. This article originally appeared in the May/June 2000 issue of *Foreign Affairs*.

As an April 8 State Department briefing made clear, U.S. officials also knew that Hutu soldiers had been killing Tutsi for two days and that the violence was not limited to the capital. They learned this from U.S. embassy personnel and from the French and the Belgians, who had extensive contacts in Rwanda and with whom Washington was planning a joint evacuation of their citizens. U.S. officials had similar reports from the commander of the U.N. peace-keeping force in Rwanda, as well as from Human Rights Watch and other NGOs, which had been calling the State Department since the preceding day.

During the crucial first weeks, the U.N., at the behest of the United States, ordered the more than 2,000 peacekeepers in Rwanda to do nothing to halt the killing and then withdrew all but a rump force of 400 soldiers. Some 1,000 elite French and Belgian troops (backed by 250 U.S. Marines just across the border) swooped in to rescue foreign nationals (most of them not at risk) and then left, ignoring the slaughter of Rwandan civilians. Clinton and other international leaders said nothing of substance. Seeing the international indifference, Rwandans became convinced that the genocidal government would succeed. Those who hesitated at first now yielded to fear or opportunism and carried the slaughter throughout Rwanda.

U.N. peacekeepers and the evacuation force could have deterred the killings had they acted promptly. Belgian military records show cases in which they did just that when permitted to use their weapons. Firm and coherent international censure could have influenced the organizers of the genocide. On the two occasions when they received outraged telephone calls from foreign governments, the organizers halted attacks on hundreds of Tutsi at the Hotel des Mille Collines in Kigali. Jamming the genocidal radio broadcasts would have kept the organizers from passing orders directly to the population. The military radio, the only other channel accessible to the genocide's organizers, did not broadcast to civilians.

Kuperman scoffs at such measures. He takes seriously only the possibility of dispatching U.S. troops, who, he states, could easily have ended the genocide. Yet he goes on to argue that even a major American force could have saved no more than a quarter of the intended victims. He presents figures, computations, a chart, and a graph that lend apparent solidity to this conclusion.

But this solidity vanishes when his underlying premises are examined. Kuperman's assertion that troops could not have been deployed until several days after April 20 rests on the incorrect assumption that Clinton learned of the genocide only on that date. Kuperman also assumes that the genocide swept through "most" of Rwanda "immediately" after its start and killed half the victims by April 21. This assumption exaggerates the early extent and the speed of the slaughter.

In 1994, the Clinton administration confounded genocide and internal war, and now Kuperman does it again. He slides without explanation from discussing the genocide to speculating about intervention in an "internal war," arguing that helping the "weaker" side may spur it to reject compromise and escalate fighting.

Let us be clear: There was a war in Rwanda, but the weaker party was the genocidal government fighting the militarily stronger Rwandan Patriotic Front. Tutsi civilians were not a party to the conflict. They were a people targeted for extermination. Helping them would not have escalated fighting but would have saved their lives.

Americans must face the truth, as all the other major international actors in Rwanda—the Belgians, the French, the U.N., and the Organization of African Unity—have already done by investigating their roles in the genocide. Congress should have the courage to follow this lead and investigate what the U.S. government did do and, even more important, what it could have done during a genocide that slaughtered half a million people.

KUPERMAN REPLIES
Alan J. Kuperman

ALISON L. DES FORGES' response and William F. Schulz's letter to the editor (March/April 2000) call into question my recent article on Rwandan genocide.

My article relies on three main findings. First, the Rwandan genocide of 1994 was perpetrated extremely quickly; about half the ultimate Tutsi victims were dead before the end of the third week.

Second, because of the intentional deception by the perpetrators of the genocide and incomplete reporting by Western sources, President Clinton could not have known that a nationwide genocide against Rwanda's Tutsi was occurring until two weeks into the killing. Third, owing to constraints of strategic airlift and military doctrine, several weeks would have been required for a U.S. intervention to stop the genocide. Thus, my article concludes that even if President Clinton had ordered a maximum intervention as soon as he knew genocide was occurring in Rwanda, at most one-fourth of the ultimate Tutsi victims could have been saved, but the majority would not have survived.

Des Forges takes issue with each of these findings. First, she asserts that my article "exaggerates the early extent and the speed of the slaughter." This is puzzling, given her own recent writing on the subject. My article states that "perhaps 250,000 [Tutsi were killed] in just over two weeks." But her 1999 book for Human Rights Watch, *Leave None to Tell the Story*, states, "By two weeks into the campaign, they had slain hundreds of thousands of Tutsi." If anything, my estimate is more conservative than her own.

Second, Des Forges claims that President Clinton knew almost immediately that a genocide was under way because of past ethnic violence in Rwanda, an earlier CIA analysis, and news reports during the first two days that extremists had taken control. Each of these arguments falls apart under closer analysis. Des Forges' book estimates that during the approximately three years of civil war prior to the genocide, about 2,000 Tutsi civilians had been killed—a rate of about 50 per month. Although such killing was extremely troubling, it did not suggest that the death rate would suddenly jump to 250,000 in the following month.

Furthermore, the CIA study was a "desk-level" analysis that contained three possible scenarios, only one of which predicted such mass killings. Intelligence analysts routinely include such a worst-case scenario to cover themselves in case events go awry. Moreover, low-level studies of this sort rarely reach the president. U.S. officials did know, by the second day, about the bloody coup, the large-scale violence in the capital, and the renewed civil war. But they also expected the Tutsi rebels to win quickly. There is no reason to believe that

President Clinton or any other U.S. observer knew immediately of the nationwide genocide. Indeed, Des Forges herself, in a *Washington Post* op-ed published on April 17, 1994 (11 days after the outbreak of violence), failed to raise even the prospect of "genocide." Des Forges' hindsight may be 20-20, but the picture was more muddled at the time.

Third, Des Forges claims that deploying intervention forces throughout Rwanda would not have been necessary to stop the genocide. Either "international censure" or quick military action in the capital by the few European evacuation troops present would have been sufficient, she claims. Although anything is possible, this smacks of wishful thinking. The lightly armed Western evacuators were outnumbered five to one by Hutu forces in the capital, so quick victory would have been unlikely. Meanwhile, large-scale massacres ignited throughout most of the country within the first week and continued for three months—in the face of repeated international condemnation and sanctions—until Tutsi rebels and late-arriving French troops ventured out to the countryside to stop them. This strongly suggests that once nationwide genocide began, only large-scale military intervention could have assured its rapid end.

Schulz, by contrast, criticizes three purported claims that are nowhere to be found in my article. First, he claims that I am "at pains to deny ... [that] the U.N.'s inaction ... was caused by an utter failure of will." To the contrary, my article discusses how a lack of will led the United States and the United Kingdom to quash efforts to bolster the peacekeeping force prior to the genocide. Moreover, my article underscores that if the West had possessed sufficient will to launch an intervention immediately upon learning of the attempted genocide, it could have saved up to 125,000 Tutsi.

Second, Schulz claims that my "thesis is that we are under a moral imperative to stop genocide only when we can stop it completely." Although my article debunks previous claims that military intervention in Rwanda after the outbreak of violence could have averted the genocide completely, it never suggests that this "exempts us from making the effort." Rather, it offers detailed recommendations for improving the effectiveness of military intervention. In addition, my article suggests devoting more attention to diplomacy, which offers the best hope of actually averting genocide.

Alison L. Des Forges, Alan J. Kuperman

Third, Schulz writes that I "cannot seriously contend" that the innocent victims in ethnic conflict "calculatedly invited their fates." What my article actually states is that the leaders of such groups sometimes provoke retaliation against their own civilians in order to galvanize domestic and, especially, international support. This was a repeated tactic of the Bosnian government in its 1992–95 war, as documented by at least two U.N. commanders on the ground. More recently, this cynical tactic was copied with even greater success by the Kosovo Liberation Army. As long as the West comes to the military assistance of groups being victimized because of their own violent provocations, we risk fostering an escalation of ethnic conflict.

Ultimately, Des Forges, Schulz, and I share the same goal—to reduce genocide and other massive abuses of human rights. Where we differ is in tactics. Their organizations, Human Rights Watch and Amnesty International USA, respectively, call for coercive pressure to force oppressive rulers to hand over their powers overnight. But when such rulers face the prospect of losing power and suffering retribution, they may opt instead for a final solution of murdering or expelling their opponents—as in Rwanda, the Balkans, and East Timor. Western military intervention has not and cannot arrive quickly enough to save many innocents. Thus, I offer an alternative prescription: Give less support for violent insurgencies, more incentives for gradual reform, and golden parachutes for departing authoritarian leaders in cases in which forgiving past crimes is the price of preventing future ones.

The best way to stop genocide is not military intervention after the fact but wise diplomacy that prevents genocide from starting in the first place.✪

Do Sanctions Work?

Sanctioning Madness

Richard N. Haass

A ROTTEN CORE

ECONOMIC SANCTIONS are fast becoming the United States' policy tool of choice. A 1997 study by the National Association of Manufacturers listed 35 countries targeted by new American sanctions from 1993 to 1996 alone. What is noteworthy, however, is not just the frequency with which sanctions are used but their centrality; economic sanctions are increasingly at the core of U.S. foreign policy.

Sanctions—predominantly economic but also political and military penalties aimed at states or other entities so as to alter unacceptable political or military behavior—are employed for a wide range of purposes. The United States, far more than any other country, uses them to discourage the proliferation of weapons of mass destruction and ballistic missiles, promote human rights, end support for terrorism, thwart drug trafficking, discourage armed aggression, protect the environment, and oust governments.[1] To accomplish these ends, sanctions may take the form of arms embargoes, foreign assistance reductions and cutoffs, export and import limitations, asset freezes, tariff increases, import quota decreases, revocation of most favored nation (MFN) trade status, votes in international organizations, withdrawal of diplomatic relations, visa denials, cancellation of air links, and credit, financing, and investment prohibitions. Even U.S. state and local governments are introducing economic sanctions. Dozens have adopted "selective purchasing laws" that prohibit

RICHARD N. HAASS is President of the Council on Foreign Relations. This article originally appeared in the November/December 1997 issue of *Foreign Affairs*.

public agencies from purchasing goods and services from companies doing business with such countries as Burma and Indonesia.

With a few exceptions, the growing use of economic sanctions to promote foreign policy objectives is deplorable. This is not simply because sanctions are expensive, although they are. Nor is it strictly a matter of whether sanctions "work"; the answer to that question invariably depends on how demanding a task is set for a particular sanction. Rather, the problem with economic sanctions is that they frequently contribute little to American foreign policy goals while being costly and even counterproductive. A recent study by the Institute for International Economics concluded that in 1995 alone, sanctions cost U.S. companies between $15 billion and $19 billion and affected some 200,000 workers. Secondary sanctions, levelled against third-party states that do not support a particular sanctions regime, add to this cost by jeopardizing the United States' trade relations. Thus, policymakers need to give more serious consideration to the impact of a sanction and weigh alternative policies more carefully.

THE SANCTIONS BOOM

ECONOMIC SANCTIONS are popular because they offer what appears to be a proportional response to challenges in which the interests at stake are less than vital. They are also a form of expression, a way to signal official displeasure with a behavior or action. They thus satisfy a domestic political need to do something and reinforce a commitment to a norm, such as respect for human rights or opposition to weapons proliferation. Reluctance to use military force is another motivation. As the National Conference of Catholic Bishops points out, "Sanctions can offer a nonmilitary alternative to the terrible options of war or indifference when confronted with aggression or injustice."

---

[1]Excluded here are sanctions introduced to ensure market access or compliance with trade pacts. Economic sanctions for economic purposes tend to be used pursuant to the rules that guide trade. By contrast, economic sanctions for political purposes work in the absence of any agreed-on political or legal framework.

The frequency with which the United States uses sanctions is also a result of the increased influence, especially on Congress, of single-issue constituencies, notably those promoting human rights, environmentalism, or ethnic, religious, or racially oriented causes. The media, too, plays a part. The so-called CNN effect can increase the visibility of problems in another country and stimulate Americans' desire to respond. Sanctions offer a popular and seemingly cost-free way of acting. The end of the Cold War and the demise of the Soviet Union have also contributed to the sanctions boom. Sanctions can now usually be introduced without opposition from Moscow, which in the past meant a veto in the U.N. Security Council or a Soviet subsidy for a target of U.S. sanctions.

Some evidence supports the efficacy of economic sanctions. One influential study concludes from analysis of more than 100 cases that economic sanctions have worked to some extent about a third of the time.[2] Other advocates are more selective in their views of history. For groups on the left, it is an article of faith that sanctions helped dismantle apartheid, just as the right argues that sanctions played a major role in the demise of the "evil empire."

Under the right circumstances, sanctions can achieve, or help achieve, various foreign policy goals ranging from the modest to the fairly significant. Sanctions introduced against Iraq after the Persian Gulf War have increased Iraqi compliance with U.N. resolutions calling for the elimination of its weapons of mass destruction. They have also diminished Baghdad's ability to import weapons and related technology. Iraq today is considerably weaker militarily and economically than it would have been without these sanctions.

Sanctions were one reason for the Serbs' decision to accept the Dayton agreement in August 1995 ending the fighting in Bosnia.

---

[2] Gary Clyde Hufbauer, Jeffrey J. Schott, and Kimberly Ann Elliott, *Economic Sanctions Reconsidered: History and Current Policy*, 2nd ed., Washington: Institute for International Economics, 1990. This relatively positive assessment is hotly disputed on the grounds that the authors were overly generous in judging what constitutes "success" and in not properly disaggregating the effects of sanctions from the impact of the threat or use of military force. See Robert A. Pape, "Why Economic Sanctions Still Do Not Work," *International Security*, Fall 1997, pp. 90-136.

The threat of sanctions may have also deterred several European firms from investing in Iran's oil and gas industry. Sanctions have burdened the economies of Iran, Cuba, and Libya, and may eventually contribute to change in those societies or in their behavior. U.S. sanctions against Pakistan, while having little discernible effect on that country's nuclear weapons program, have hurt Islamabad both economically and militarily, possibly influencing Pakistan's future actions as well as those of other would-be proliferators.

MORE HARM THAN GOOD

THE LIMITATIONS of sanctions are more pronounced than their accomplishments. Sanctions alone are unlikely to achieve results if the aims are large or time is short. Even though they were comprehensive and enjoyed almost universal international backing for nearly six months, sanctions failed to compel Saddam Hussein to withdraw from Kuwait in 1990. In the end, it took nothing less than Operation Desert Storm.

Other sanctions have also fallen short of their stated purposes. Despite sanctions against Iran, Tehran remains defiant in its support of terrorism, its subversion of its neighbors, its opposition to the Middle East peace process, and its pursuit of nuclear weapons. Fidel Castro still commands an authoritarian political system and a statist economy. Pakistan's nuclear program is well advanced; it now has enough material for at least a dozen bombs. Libya has refused to hand over the two individuals accused of destroying Pan Am Flight 103 over Lockerbie, Scotland. Sanctions did not persuade Haiti's junta to honor the results of the 1990 election that brought Jean Bertrand Aristide to power, nor did they convince Serbia and the Bosnian Serbs for several years to call off their military aggression. Unilateral sanctions are particularly ineffective. In a global economy, unilateral sanctions impose higher costs on American firms than on the target country, which can usually find substitute sources of supply and financing. Unilateral sanctions did, however, prove more costly for Haiti and Cuba, which were heavily dependent on trade with the United States. They also hurt Pakistan, which had been receiving substantial U.S. military and economic aid. Such cases are the exception, though; most unilateral sanctions will be little more than costly expressions of opposition except in those instances in which the ties between the United States and the target are so extensive that the latter cannot adjust to an American cutoff.

Generating international support for sanctions is often extremely difficult. In most instances, other governments prefer minimal sanctions, or none at all. They tend to value commercial interaction more than the United States does and are less willing to forfeit it. In addition, the argument that economic interaction is desirable because it promotes more open political and economic systems normally has more resonance in other capitals, although it has been used successfully by both the Bush and Clinton administrations to defeat Congress' attempts to revoke China's MFN status. Such thinking makes achieving multilateral support for sanctions more difficult for the United States. It usually takes something truly egregious, like Saddam Hussein's occupation of Kuwait, to overcome this anti-sanctions bias. Even with Iraq, generous compensation for third-party states affected by the sanctions, including Egypt and Turkey, was a prerequisite for their support.

Trying to compel others to join a sanctions regime by threatening secondary sanctions can seriously harm U.S. foreign policy interests. Congress is increasingly turning to secondary sanctions to bolster ineffective unilateral sanctions regimes, as with Cuba, Iran, and Libya; in all three instances, sanctions now apply to overseas firms that violate the terms of U.S. legislation like the Iran-Libya Sanctions Act and Helms-Burton Act. This threat appears to have deterred some individuals and firms from entering into proscribed business activities, but it has increased anti-American sentiment, threatened the future of the World Trade Organization (WTO), distracted attention from the provocative behavior of the target governments, and made Europeans less likely to work with the United States in shaping policies to contend with post–Cold War challenges.

MISSING THE TARGET

SANCTIONS OFTEN produce unintended and undesirable consequences. Haiti is a prime example. Sanctions exacerbated the island's economic distress, causing a massive exodus of Haitians to the United States that proved life-threatening for them and expensive and disruptive for Florida. In Bosnia, the arms embargo weakened the Muslims, since Bosnia's Serbs and Croats had larger stores of military supplies and greater access to outside sources. This military imbalance contributed to the fighting and to the disproportionate Muslim suffering. Military sanctions against Pakistan may actually have increased Islamabad's reliance on a nuclear option because they cut off its access to U.S. weaponry and dramatically weakened Pakistan's confidence in Washington.

All this demonstrates that sanctions can be a blunt instrument. Most sanctions do not discriminate within the target country. There is a rationale for this: funds and goods can easily be moved around, and governments can often command what is in the hands of others. The problem with such a broad-brush approach is that sanctions tend to affect the general population, while those in the government and the military are able to skirt the sanctions.

Thus, the tendency to see economic sanctions as "below" the use of military force on some imagined ladder of foreign policy escalation must be revised. Sanctions can be a powerful and deadly form of intervention. The danger inherent in broad sanctions—beyond missing the true target—is both moral, in that innocents are affected, and practical, in that sanctions that harm the general population can bring about undesired effects, including strengthening the regime, triggering large-scale emigration, and retarding the emergence of a middle class and a civil society. Mass hardship can also weaken domestic and international support for sanctions, as with Iraq, despite the fact that those sanctions have included from the outset a provision allowing Iraq to import humanitarian goods and services.

"NOT-SO-SMART" SANCTIONS

"SMART" OR "designer" sanctions, which penalize leaders while sparing the general public, are only a partial solution. It is possible that Haiti's military leaders were bothered by the fact their families could no longer shop in Florida. And executives who risk being denied access to the United States under the 1996 Helms-Burton act may think twice before entering into proscribed business deals. But opportunities to employ effective sanctions with precision are rare. Gathering the necessary information about assets, and then moving quickly enough to freeze them, can often prove impossible. Leaders and governments have many ways to insulate themselves, and designing "smart" sanctions to target only them is extraordinarily difficult, especially with a totalitarian or authoritarian state run by a few people.

In addition, authoritarian, statist societies are often able to hunker down and withstand the effects of sanctions. There are several possible reasons: sanctions sometimes trigger a "rally around the flag" nationalist reaction; by creating scarcity, they enable governments to better control the distribution of goods; and they create a general sense of siege that governments can exploit to maintain political control. This conclusion is consistent with literature suggesting that market economic reform reinforces the development of civil society; by reducing the scope for independent action, sanctions can work against forces promoting political pluralism.

Last, but far from least, sanctions can be expensive for American business. There is a tendency to overlook or underestimate the direct costs of sanctions, perhaps because, unlike the costs of military intervention, they do not show up in U.S. government budget tables. Sanctions do, however, affect the economy by reducing revenues of U.S. companies and individuals. Moreover, this cost is difficult to measure because it includes not only lost sales but also forfeited opportunities: governments and overseas companies can elect not to do business with the United States for fear that sanctions might one day be introduced, wreaking havoc with normal commercial relations.

TAKING SANCTIONS SERIOUSLY

A FUNDAMENTAL change in thinking and attitude is required. Economic sanctions are a serious instrument of foreign policy and should be employed only after consideration no less rigorous than for other forms of intervention, including the use of military force. The likely benefits of a particular sanction to U.S. foreign policy should be greater than the anticipated costs to the U.S. government and the American economy. Moreover, the sanction's likely effect on U.S. interests should compare favorably to the projected consequences of all other options, including military intervention, covert action, public and private diplomacy, or simply doing nothing. Broad sanctions should not be used as a means of expression. Foreign policy is not therapy; its purpose is not to make us feel good but to do good. The same holds for sanctions.

For pragmatic more than normative reasons, multilateral support for economic sanctions should typically be a prerequisite for the United States' imposition of them. Such support need not be simultaneous, but it should be all but certain to follow. Except when the United States is in a unique position to exert leverage based on its economic relationship with the target, unilateral sanctions should be avoided. Building international support will require intense, often high-level diplomatic efforts and even then may not succeed. Policymakers must then consider whether some alternative would not be better than weaker or unilateral sanctions.

International compliance with sanctions regimes can be increased by providing assistance to third parties to offset the economic cost of implementing sanctions. Greater use should be made of Article 50 of the U.N. Charter, which allows such states to approach the Security Council for redress. In addition, a fund for this purpose should be established within the U.S. foreign assistance budget. The cost would be more than offset by the benefits of multilateral cooperation.

By contrast, secondary sanctions are not a desirable means of securing multilateral support. They are not only an admission of diplomatic failure but they are also expensive. The costs to U.S. foreign policy, including the damage to relations with major partners and U.S. efforts to build an effective WTO, almost always outweigh the potential benefits of coercing unwilling friends to join sanctions regimes.

Sanctions should focus, as far as possible, on those responsible for the offending behavior and on limiting penalties to the particular area of dispute. Such limited sanctions would avoid jeopardizing other interests or an entire bilateral relationship. They would cause less collateral damage to innocents, and make it easier to garner multinational support. Sanctions designed to stem the proliferation of weapons of mass destruction are a prime example. Where there are transgressions, the United States should direct any sanctions toward nuclear or weapons-related activity, for example by cutting off associated technological cooperation or trade. Similarly, political responses such as event boycotts and visa denials might be the best way to signal opposition to objectionable behavior when no appropriate economic or military sanction is available or as a complement to something as specific as freezing an individual's assets. Political sanctions should not, however, extend to breaking diplomatic relations or canceling high-level meetings. Such interactions help the United States as much as the targeted party.

Sanctions should not hold major or complex bilateral relationships hostage to one or two issues. This is especially true with a country like China, where the United States has to balance interests that include maintaining stability on the Korean peninsula, discouraging any support for "rogue" states' weapons of mass destruction or ballistic missile programs, managing the Taiwan-China situation, and promoting trade, market reform, and human rights. Similarly, the United States has a range of interests with Pakistan that go well beyond nuclear matters, including promoting democracy, economic development, and regional stability. The principal alternative to broad sanctions in such instances is sanctions that are narrow and germane to the issue at hand. With Pakistan, for example, sanctions could focus on specific defense articles and technologies but exempt all economic assistance and military education and training.

Humanitarian exceptions should be part of any comprehensive sanctions regime. In part this is a moral judgment, that innocents should not be made to suffer any more than is absolutely necessary. But it is also pragmatic, since it is easier to generate and sustain domestic and international support for sanctions that allow the importation of food and medicine. Sanctions, however, should not necessarily be suspended if the humanitarian harm is the direct result of cynical government policy, such as Iraq's, that creates shortages among the general population in order to garner international sympathy.

Any imposition of sanctions should be swift. As with other forms of intervention, including military action, gradual escalation allows the target to adapt and adjust. Such an approach forfeits shock value and allows asset shifting, hoarding, and other arrangements to circumvent sanctions—as Libya and Iran found. This recommendation is easier said than done, since gaining international support for sanctions will in many cases require that the United States move slowly and gradually, further limiting the potential effectiveness of economic sanctions in today's world.

GETTING IT RIGHT

RESTRAINT WILL not materialize by itself. Policymakers should be required to prepare and send to Congress a policy statement similar to the reports prepared and forwarded under the 1973 War Powers Act before or soon after a sanction is put in place. Such statements should clearly explain the sanction's purpose, the legal or political authority supporting its use, the expected impact on the target, retaliatory steps the target or third parties may take, the probable humanitarian consequences and what is being done to minimize them, the expected costs to the United States, prospects for enforcement, the expected degree of international support or opposition, and an exit strategy, including the criteria for lifting the sanction. In addition, policymakers should be able to explain why a particular sanction was selected over other sanctions or policies. If necessary, portions of this report could be classified to avoid providing information that would be useful to the target. Any sanction Congress initiates should be approved only after the relevant committees have carefully considered the matter; members being asked to vote on the proposal would then be able to refer to a report that addresses their questions.

All sanctions embedded in legislation should allow the president to suspend or terminate them in the interest of national security. Beyond being consistent with the Constitution's bias in favor of executive primacy in foreign affairs, such latitude is needed if relationships are not to fall hostage to one interest and if the executive is to have the flexibility to explore whether limited incentives could bring about a desired policy result. The benefits of this latitude outweigh any diminution of automatic sanctions' deterrent power. Current legislation that mandates sanctions in specific circumstances should be repealed or modified.

The federal government, together with affected firms, should challenge in court states' and municipalities' right to institute economic sanctions against companies and individuals operating in their jurisdiction. This practice is eliciting protests not just from the targeted countries but from the European Union, which argues convincingly that such sanctions violate commitments made by the U.S. government to the World Trade Organization. The Constitution may not settle the struggle between the executive and legislative branches in foreign affairs, but it limits it to the federal branch of government.[3] State and local sanctions undermine the flexibility necessary for the executive branch to effectively carry out foreign policy. To paraphrase Justice Louis Brandeis, states may be laboratories of democracy, but not of diplomacy. Unfortunately, the Clinton administration—like the Reagan administration, which never challenged the more than 100 state and local sanctions targeting firms involved with South Africa—has chosen not to confront this issue. Beyond using the legal system, companies might consider deploying their economic power and avoid investing in states that have a history of supporting sanctions. Firms would also be wise to build broader coalitions (including labor unions) that would have a stake in opposing certain state and local sanctions.

Any sanction should be the subject of an annual impact statement, prepared by the executive branch and submitted in unclassified form to Congress, which would provide far more information and analysis than the pro forma documents written to justify many current sanctions. Like the report that would accompany a new sanction, the annual statement would introduce much-needed rigor into the sanctions decision-making process. A more careful calculation of eco-

---

[3]David Schmahmann and James Finch, "The Unconstitutionality of State and Local Enactments in the United States Restricting Business Ties with Burma (Myanmar)," *Vanderbilt Journal of Transnational Law*, March 1997, pp. 175-207.

nomic costs would also provide a basis for determining payments to workers and companies being asked to bear a disproportionate share of the sanctions burden. Such seriousness has not been the hallmark of the American embrace of sanctions, which are often imposed and maintained with only cursory analysis of likely or actual effects.

The consequences of what is recommended here—less frequent and more modest use of economic sanctions—would risk creating something of a policy vacuum. In Washington it is difficult to beat something with nothing. So how does one beat economic sanctions?

Sometimes military force will be required. This was the lesson of Desert Storm and Bosnia. In Cuba, for example, instead of tightening sanctions—which increased the misery of the Cuban people—and going along with Congress' introduction of secondary sanctions against U.S. allies, the Clinton administration might have been wiser to launch a cruise missile salvo or use stealth aircraft to take out the MiGs that in 1996 shot down the unarmed plane flown by Cuban exiles from the group Brothers to the Rescue.

In other instances, focused sanctions could be useful. A more appropriate response to Pakistan's nuclear program would have been export controls designed to slow missile and nuclear bomb development. With Haiti, narrow sanctions aimed at the illegitimate leadership would not have triggered the human exodus that pressured the administration into an armed intervention that could well have proved far more costly than it did. China was stung by the U.S. decision to oppose Beijing's bid to host the Olympic games in the year 2000 and is bothered by being singled out in various international bodies for its treatment of its citizens.

The principal alternative to economic sanctions is best described as constructive or conditional engagement. Such an approach, involving a mix of narrow sanctions and limited political and economic interactions that are conditioned on specified behavioral changes, might be preferable, especially if the goal is to weaken the near-monopoly of an authoritarian leadership over a country like Cuba, Iran, or China. Such an approach is not as simple as imposing economic sanctions; nor does it yield as dramatic a sound bite. Its principal advantage is that it might have a more desirable impact at less cost to Americans and American foreign policy.✪

What Sanctions Epidemic?

U.S. Business' Curious Crusade

Jesse Helms

IN THE PAST YEAR, a handful of Washington business lobbyists have waged a blistering campaign to persuade the world that Congress has been engaged in a spasm of sanctions proliferation.

Reliance on unilateral sanctions, these lobbyists warn us, is a disturbing new epidemic. Their campaign has sparked dozens of news articles and editorials decrying the "sanctions frenzy" and castigating Congress' "voracious appetite" for sanctions. Normally responsible journalists parrot statistics—conveniently furnished by these business lobbyists—alleging that in the last few years the United States has placed anywhere from one-half to two-thirds of the world's population under the yoke of unilateral economic sanctions. *The New York Times* clamors that "more than 60 laws or executive orders authorizing sanctions . . . have been enacted in the last five years." Even President Clinton jumped on the antisanctions bandwagon, announcing in 1998 that the United States has gone "sanctions happy."

This is sheer nonsense. The statistics peddled by these lobbyists are grossly inflated and intentionally misleading. Half of the world is not living under American sanctions—nowhere near it. There is no epidemic. Congress has been cautious and circumspect, passing just a handful of carefully targeted sanctions laws. And unilateral economic sanctions are by no means new: they have been vital weapons in America's foreign policy arsenal for more than 200 years. I have been

---

SENATOR JESSE HELMS was Chairman of the Senate Foreign Relations Committee. This article originally appeared in the January/February 1999 issue of *Foreign Affairs*.

and continue to be a friend of American business. But the distortions spread by this small cabal of lobbyists in the name of American business are inexcusable. The time has come for a reality check.

LIES, DAMNED LIES, AND STATISTICS

THE STATISTIC HAS BECOME CONVENTIONAL wisdom: in just four years the United States has imposed sanctions 61 times, burdening 2.3 billion people (42 percent of the world). That would be pretty awful, save for one thing—it is not true. These figures have been circulated by the antisanctions business group USA Engage, based on a study by the National Association of Manufacturers (NAM). They are a fabrication. At my request, the Congressional Research Service (CRS) evaluated the NAM claim that from 1993 through 1996, "61 U.S. laws and executive actions were enacted authorizing unilateral sanctions for foreign policy purposes." CRS reported that it "could not defensibly" justify the number. "We find the calculation used in . . . the NAM study to be flawed, even if the specific [sanctions] were fairly characterized, which is not always the case," CRS concluded.

How did NAM come up with 61 sanctions? The study alleges that 20 laws were passed by Congress and 41 were imposed by presidential action. This is a gross distortion. Nearly three-quarters of the congressional measures were not sanctions at all but conditions, limitations, or restrictions on U.S. foreign aid. One measure placed conditions on assistance to the Palestine Liberation Organization. Another barred aid for military or police training to Haitians involved in drug trafficking or human rights abuses. One "sanction" blocked assistance to countries knowingly harboring fugitives wanted by the international war crimes tribunals for Rwanda and the former Yugoslavia. Still another prohibited Defense Department aid to countries supporting terrorists. Are these the measures that NAM and USA Engage want Congress to curtail? Let's hope not.

But what about those 41 "sanctions" imposed by the executive branch? Five are not unilateral, as NAM charges, but rather represent U.S. compliance with U.N. Security Council sanctions—multilateral, by definition. In seven cases, the NAM study counts the same sanction repeatedly, identifying it each time as a separate sanction. For example, the measure declaring Sudan a terrorist state is counted five different times. NAM lists two cases when no sanction was ever imposed, including a November 1994 executive order that even NAM concedes in fine print "did not impose any specific new sanctions on any countries." Eight cases represent mere restrictions on U.S. foreign aid. Five are limited bans affecting only military exports to Zaire, Nigeria, Sudan, Haiti, and Angola. Thirteen affect only a specific foreign company or person—not an entire country, not an entire industry, but one specific entity—for example, banning imports from the Chinese Qinghai Hide and Garment Factory for its use of prison slave labor or seizing the assets of individual Colombian drug traffickers.

These actions are obviously not what most people think of as "sanctions." They think instead of broad trade bans affecting whole countries, entire industries, vast populations, or access to large markets—not conditioning U.S. foreign aid, blocking imports from a single prison factory in China, seizing the assets of drug barons, or halting the sale of lethal weapons to terrorist states.

The claim that 42 percent of the world's population has been affected is also bogus. The study lists the entire population of the former Zaire (now the Congo) as being under U.S. sanction because the United States barred sales of defense items to the government. The same goes for China, Nigeria, Mauritania, and Pakistan, where CRS notes that such highly targeted actions "put the entire populations of these countries into NAM's calculation, even though most people . . . are not likely to experience significant impact from or awareness of [the] imposition." U.S. access to those countries' commercial goods-and-services markets remains unaffected.

What is the reality? Between 1993 and 1996, Congress passed and the president signed a grand total of five new sanctions laws: the Nuclear Proliferation Prevention Act of 1994, the Cuban Liberty and Democratic Solidarity Act of 1996, the Antiterrorism and Effective Death Penalty Act of 1996, the Iran-Libya Sanctions Act of 1996, and the Free Burma Act of 1996. During the same period, the president imposed just four new sanctions: declaring Sudan a terrorist state; banning imports of munitions and ammunition from China; tightening travel-related restrictions, cash remittance levels, and the sending of gift parcels to Cuba (restrictions that have since been lifted); and imposing a ban on new contractual agreements or investment in Iran. Nine new sanctions. That is it. The allegation of a sanctions epidemic is demonstrably false—a myth spread with the intention of misleading Congress, the American public, and the American business community.

UNMENTIONABLES

EVEN MORE TELLING is what the business lobbyists leave out of their inflated inventory of sanctions. As they rail against "unilateral economic sanctions for foreign policy purposes" (NAM's phrase), they conveniently omit discussing unilateral economic sanctions for *trade* purposes. Retaliatory trade sanctions are not mentioned by NAM and are not covered by the proposed Sanctions Reform Act— a stunning admission of the efficacy of sanctions. After all, if uni- lateral sanctions did not work, why on earth would business want to protect the U.S. ability to impose them in trade disputes? The ability to threaten and impose unilateral economic sanctions is a vital tool of U.S. trade policy, just as it is in U.S. foreign policy.

What these lobbyists really dislike is not the idea of sanctions themselves but the reason some sanctions are imposed. They tacitly admit that sanctions work but insist that sanctions are good only if they defend business interests, not national interests. According to the lobbyists, the United States should be hamstrung when a govern- ment proliferates weapons of mass destruction, commits genocide, tortures its people, or supports terrorists. But if that same government floods the American market with cheap television sets, America should throw the book at it. But, of course, the business lobbyists can- not say that, so they attempt to confuse the issue with cooked-up data and claims of an epidemic. They establish groups with clever monikers like "USA Engage," whose very name implies that those who disagree with them are isolationists. But what they really stand for is not engagement but mercantilism—an amoral foreign policy.

GOOD ENOUGH FOR THE FOUNDERS

Sanctions have always been an American foreign policy weapon. Economic sanctions were imposed by the American colonies against

Britain in response to the Stamp and Townsend Acts, in both cases forcing their repeal. Jefferson and Madison both passionately advocated economic sanctions, believing not only that they were legitimate but that they should be America's primary diplomatic tools. In an 1805 letter to Jefferson, Madison argued, "The efficacy of an embargo . . . cannot be denied. Indeed, if a commercial weapon can be properly crafted for the Executive hand, it is more and more apparent to me that it can force nations . . . to respect our rights." Jefferson, for his part, contended that in foreign affairs "three alternatives alone are to be chosen from. 1. Embargo. 2. War. 3. Submission and tribute."

Jefferson is right. There are, indeed, three tools in foreign policy: diplomacy, sanctions, and war. Take away sanctions and how can the United States deal with terrorists, proliferators, and genocidal dictators? Our options would be empty talk or sending in the marines. Without sanctions, the United States would be virtually powerless to influence events absent war. Sanctions may not be perfect and they are not always the answer, but they are often the only weapon.

Unilateral sanctions, in fact, are the linchpin of our nonproliferation policy. According to a recently declassified analysis by the Arms Control and Disarmament Agency, "the history of U.S.-China relations shows that China has made specific nonproliferation commitments only under the threat or imposition of sanctions." Short of war, sanctions are the main leverage the United States has over China.

They have also played a crucial role in trade disputes. The threat of unilateral sanctions on China over intellectual property rights and unfair trade barriers has forced China several times to yield. In November 1991, the U.S. trade representative threatened $1.5 billion in trade sanctions if an intellectual property rights agreement was not reached by January 1992. Not surprisingly, such an agreement was struck on January 16, 1992. No wonder business lobbyists are so keen to retain unilateral sanctions in the trade arsenal—even as they campaign to remove them from our nation's foreign policy.

U.S. sanctions helped bring down the Soviet Union. They played a pivotal role in forcing communist Poland to release political prisoners and legalize Solidarity—sparking the collapse of communism. Our targeted Nigerian sanctions are beginning to bear fruit as the military government wearies of its pariah status. In Guatemala, the decision to freeze $47 million in U.S. aid (one of the "sanctions" that business is lobbying to curtail) and the mere threat of lost trade convinced business, labor, and military leaders to roll back President Jorge Serrano Elías' May 1993 coup. Swiss banks' recent decision to pay $1.25 billion in reparations to Holocaust survivors was a direct result of threatened sanctions, as admitted by the Union Bank of Switzerland.

Critics respond that sanctions have failed to bring down regimes in Iraq, Iran, Syria, Sudan, Libya, and Cuba. Perhaps—but they have effectively contained the Saddam Husseins, Mu'ammar al-Qadhafis, and Hafiz al-Asads of the world. Without sanctions, Saddam would now be threatening the world with vx missiles, Qadhafi would be blowing up U.S. passenger planes, and Asad would be planning terrorist operations against U.S. citizens. If this policy represents failure, it beats capitulation any day. As for Cuba, until 1991 the U.S. embargo was offset by $5 billion to $7 billion in Soviet subsidies. Only without them has the embargo begun to take a toll on Castro's regime. The moment the embargo kicked in, Castro's efforts to finance Marxist insurgencies stopped, allowing the nearly complete democratic transformation of the western hemisphere. Castro's regime is teetering; unless America gives up its leverage by unconditionally lifting the embargo, his successors will be anxious to exchange normalized relations with the United States for a democratic transition in Cuba.

STAYING THE COURSE

WHEN SANCTIONS DO NOT WORK, it is often because the target government doubts our resolve to keep them imposed. And with good reason: the Clinton administration views sanctions as domestic public relations tools rather than as foreign policy weapons. For example, President Clinton signed the Iran-Libya Sanctions Act live on CNN. But once the camera lights dimmed and the time came to implement it, he lost his nerve. This sent the message to Iran and other rogue states that the administration talks tough but caves in under pressure. It is the same with Cuba. After the Castro regime murdered four innocent people, including three Americans, by shooting down two civilian planes flying over international waters,

Clinton made a bold speech for the cameras and signed the Helms-Burton law. Since then, he has done everything in his power to avoid enforcing it. Clinton has also gone to extraordinary lengths to avoid imposing sanctions on China for its missile proliferation, despite incontrovertible evidence from American intelligence that sanctionable activities have taken place.

Congress has given the president great flexibility in most U.S. sanctions laws. National-interest waivers let the White House temporarily or permanently suspend prescribed sanctions. Even so, when the administration feels Congress has set the bar too high for these waivers, it can get around it by, as President Clinton recently said, "fudg[ing] an evaluation of the facts." If anything, Congress has already given the president too much flexibility.

HANDCUFFING AMERICA

IRONICALLY, those who criticize sanctions as a one-size-fits-all foreign policy propose a worse solution—the Sanctions Reform Act. This cookie-cutter legislation is no solution at all. Instead of providing greater flexibility on sanctions policy—the clarion call of the reform crowd—this law does the exact opposite by tying the hands of both Congress and the president.

The bill prohibits the president from implementing any sanctions for a mandatory 45-day "cooling-off" period. That may sound reasonable, but in practice placing a six-week shackle on all U.S. sanctions in every situation and circumstance is dangerous folly. Ponder one example: after Libyan terrorists blew up Pan Am flight 103, the United Nations spent months debating appropriate sanctions. Meanwhile, Libya divested itself of all its reachable assets, thereby avoiding the sanctions' impact. The Sanctions Reform Act would essentially afford other terrorist states the same courtesy. While the United States "cools off" for six weeks, terrorists, proliferators, and dictators will take evasive measures—quietly divesting assets, concealing evidence, and finding safe haven for fugitives.

The Sanctions Reform Act would also impose a mandatory two-year "sunset" on all new U.S. sanctions. Another bad idea. A two-year sunset writes "sanctions fatigue" into law, sending the target state a clear message: hunker down and wait out the storm since U.S. resolve will collapse on a fixed date. The bill also mandates the "sanctity of contracts." Again, this sounds reasonable, but it is not. What happens if a U.S. company contracts to sell militarily sensitive technology to a country that suddenly tests a nuclear bomb (India, Pakistan), invades a neighbor (Iraq), engages in genocide (Serbia), or commits an act of terrorism (Iran, Libya)? The Sanctions Reform Act would prevent the United States from breaching the contract by stopping those militarily sensitive sales.

None of this means that the United States should never protect existing business contracts with sanctioned states. In most cases, it does just that. The Clinton administration's recent executive order imposing new sanctions on Iran bars only "new investments and contracts." The Helms-Burton law affects only those investments made in stolen U.S. properties in Cuba after the date of its enactment. But Congress and the White House should decide these matters case by case and not be tied down by a mandatory provision that could have unintended consequences.

Congress already has a system for considering U.S. economic sanctions. It is called congressional debate. Each sanctions law is considered carefully, every provision is debated openly, and varying levels of flexibility are written into the law. Business gets a chance to weigh in, as do other constituencies. In the end, the president can veto any law. And Congress can always go back and amend sanctions if necessary—as it just did with India and Pakistan. The system the Founders established to decide such matters works just fine. It does not need "reform" inspired by a "sanctions epidemic" fabricated in some Washington lobbying firm's offices.

SELLING THUMBSCREWS TO TYRANTS

WHY have some American companies invested so much in fighting sanctions? In Europe, business and government opposition to sanctions is understandable. Slumping welfare-state economies and double-digit unemployment drive Europeans to employ increasingly trade-obsessed foreign policies. But American business has no such excuse. Thanks to the vigilance of congressional Republicans, they have not been saddled with high taxes and regulations. The U.S. economy is booming, and unemployment is at an all-time low.

The lobbyists' cry that sanctions cost the United States vital access to large markets is a sham. The cost of U.S. sanctions is minuscule. According to Jan Paul Acton of the Congressional Budget Office, "to date, the cost of existing sanctions to the overall economy has been quite modest. CBO's review of research indicates that the net cost may be less than $1 billion annually. That compares with $6.6 trillion of total national income in 1997." The United States *gave away* roughly $13 billion in foreign aid during 1997. Besides, cutting foreign aid to punish misbehavior actually saves taxpayers' money. Even if we use the business lobbyists' standard tactic of applying costs to entire populations, the price tag for U.S. economic sanctions comes to a whopping $3.77 per American—about the cost of a Big Mac and fries.

That is a small price to pay for a moral foreign policy—and a price most Americans are willing to bear. A 1998 *Wall Street Journal*/NBC News poll taken on the eve of the president's visit to China showed that less than one-third of Americans agreed that "We should maintain good trade relations with China, despite disagreements we might have with its human rights policies." Fully two-thirds of Americans agreed that "we should demand that China improve its human rights policies if China wants to continue to enjoy its current trade status with the United States."

This may shock the business lobbyists. It should not. Americans do not need to sell their souls or their national security to create jobs and economic prosperity. The lobbyists behind this antisanctions crusade are saying, "If you can't beat 'em, join 'em." America cannot stop rogue states from acquiring weapons of mass destruction, they say, so why cede markets for sensitive technology to our European competitors? The United States cannot stop dictators from torturing people, so why not close our eyes and trade with them as if nothing is happening? That is not the American way. Americans do not need to create jobs by selling thumbscrews to the world's tyrants.

U.S. policies should isolate terrorist regimes like Iran, Iraq, Libya, Syria, and Cuba. U.S. aid should not go to countries that commit genocide, harbor war criminals, support terrorism, or export illegal drugs that poison American children. Lethal weapons should not be sold to violent regimes in Nigeria and Sudan; assets of drug traffickers should be seized; imports from Chinese companies that use prison slave labor should be banned; and government procurement contracts should not be given to foreign companies that sell dangerous technologies to terrorist states. There should be sanctions on companies and governments that proliferate nuclear, chemical, and biological weapons and countries that murder women and children and pile them into mass graves. America should not hesitate for one second to place a cost on these reprehensible acts and to restrain those few American companies who would actually conduct business with the perpetrators of such heinous crimes.

With their antisanctions crusade, these lobbyists are fighting for business as usual with thugs, tyrants, and terrorists. They do not represent the views of the American people or most American businesses. They should be ashamed.⊗

Is Trade Policy on Track?

A Renaissance
for U.S. Trade Policy?

C. Fred Bergsten

LIBERALIZATION IN RETREAT

U.S. TRADE POLICY has been facing widespread criticism around the world. Under threat of congressional action, the Bush administration initiated an investigation of steel imports, imposed tariffs of up to 30 percent on a sizable portion of foreign steel shipments to the United States, and launched an effort to organize global steel production—all within the past year. The administration and Congress have agreed to roll back some apparel imports from the Caribbean and Central America. Sharp new tariffs have been slapped on lumber imports from Canada, a nation with which the United States supposedly has free trade. Both Congress and the president have backed a new farm bill that perpetuates substantial subsidies for U.S. agriculture, even though the United States has railed for years against such practices abroad. All these steps have reinforced the concern that America is pursuing a unilateralist rather than a globally cooperative foreign policy.

Moreover, these protectionist initiatives have surfaced at a time when the global trading system is already under severe strain. U.S. trade retaliation against Europe is still in place from a previous dispute over beef. Europe is considering up to $4 billion of counteraction against U.S. tax subsidies for exports—a practice found illegal under the rules of the World Trade Organization (wTO)—and

C. FRED BERGSTEN is Director of the Institute for International Economics. This article originally appeared in the November/December 2002 issue of *Foreign Affairs*.

is fighting Washington's new steel measures. Last year, Japan and China engaged in a cycle of retaliation and counterretaliation. There has been continuing concern about trade wars among the largest economies, and the recent U.S. actions are widely viewed as throwing fuel on the fire. U.S. backtracking on liberalization gives other countries an excuse to do likewise and reduces the prospects for future reduction of barriers.

At a more subtle level, some of the most crucial components of the global system are coming under considerable stress. The WTO's new dispute-settlement mechanism, a crowning achievement of the 50-year drive to forge an effective rules-based trade regime, could crack under the intense pressure of a rapidly growing case load; politically sensitive cases that should be negotiated rather than litigated are proliferating. The advent of scores of additional members has turned the WTO into an extremely unwieldy organization, pushing more and more countries to turn to regional and bilateral deals instead. Repeated financial crises and disappointing growth, as seen currently in Latin America, reinforce hostility toward globalization. The United States, which championed the global system from its outset after World War II through the completion of the latest negotiations in the Uruguay Round a decade ago, has been viewed as taking steps that add to these pressures rather than resolve them.

The administration should see this drumbeat of criticism as a highly desirable reminder of the costs of protectionist trade measures and the breadth of support for continued liberalization. But the legitimate questions about U.S. trade policy can be understood only by putting current developments into broader historical perspective, along three dimensions. One is the most recent context, deriving from the evolution of the globalization debate in the United States in the 1990s and its deep impact on U.S. trade policy. The second looks back over the past 40 years and the frequently tawdry tactics that politicians have had to use to exercise the justly renowned "U.S. leadership of the system." The third is more optimistic, drawing from the postwar negotiating record the hope that renewed progress in the global trade regime is more possible than most observers believe.

A Renaissance for U.S. Trade Policy?

THE STALEMATE OVER GLOBALIZATION

THE CLINTON ADMINISTRATION enjoyed a spectacular start on trade. It completed the Uruguay Round in 1993, subsequently concluded its three follow-on sectoral compacts, and won congressional approval for both the round and the North American Free Trade Agreement (NAFTA). It launched the Free Trade Area of the Americas (FTAA) and the Asia-Pacific Economic Cooperation initiative (APEC) aiming to achieve "free and open trade and investment" in that huge and dynamic region by 2010 or 2020. President Bill Clinton's first two years in office in fact represented the zenith of postwar U.S. trade policy while reaffirming the traditional bipartisanship of that policy by concluding major deals that had been launched by the first Bush and Reagan administrations.

But the situation deteriorated rapidly thereafter. The president received no negotiating authority from Congress after the expiration in June 1994 of "fast track," which greatly strengthens the president's hand by forcing Congress to approve or reject trade agreements without amendments, within a set time period. Very little progress was made in pursuing the FTAA, and APEC did nothing to approach its ambitious goals. The effort to launch new global negotiations in the WTO collapsed in the debacle at Seattle in 1999. Initiatives to conclude bilateral deals with several small countries (Jordan, Singapore, and Chile) were left incomplete. Even the legislative successes of Clinton's last year—the implementation of permanent normal trade relations with China and the substantial freeing of trade with Africa and the Caribbean— were replete with limitations and required enormous expenditures of presidential and private-sector effort despite carrying virtually no costs for the United States. Hence the forward momentum of liberalization stalled badly, opening the door for protectionist and mercantilist pressures to fill the vacuum quickly— as they have traditionally done.

Most important, nothing was done to overcome the domestic stalemate over globalization that plagued the United States throughout the 1990s and underlay the stagnation of trade policy. Clinton said repeatedly that one of his greatest frustrations in office was his inability to convince the country, and especially his own party, to support globalization despite its enormous contribution to the sharp improvement in U.S. economic performance in the 1990s.

The three congressional rejections of fast-track authority in the 1990s, as well as the paper-thin majorities that granted such authority to President George W. Bush in 2001–2, were influenced by a number of partisan as well as intraparty considerations. More broadly, however, the legislative stalemate reflects the basic political fact that the U.S. public is split almost evenly over the wisdom of further globalization. But studies at the Institute for International Economics point the way toward overcoming the stalemate—because the single key variable that determines public attitudes is education. Workers with college experience welcome globalization, regardless of where they are currently employed, because they feel they can take advantage of it. Workers with a high school diploma or less, who still constitute half the labor force, fear the required adjustment and thus oppose it even if they have good jobs now. The number of actual job losses due to globalization is relatively small, but some workers do take substantial lifetime earnings hits. As a result, many other workers think, "There but for the grace of God go I." But the split in opinion would shift to solid proliberalization majorities in the short run if the government were seen to be credibly helping those workers who lose from increased trade. The key steps would be improved social safety nets to cushion their transition and training programs to improve their skills.

Yet very little was done on these crucial domestic adjustment fronts in the 1990s, even by a Democratic administration that was ostensibly sympathetic to such measures. Indeed, its failure to effectively implement the modest domestic adjustment provisions of NAFTA badly hurt its effort to win fast-track authority in 1997. The legitimate debate over the costs of globalization shifted toward issues that hold very little promise for helping American workers (such as international labor standards) and wind up pitting the United States against the entire developing world. Hence the stalemate persisted, undermining U.S. trade policy and, through it, the global system.

LESSONS FROM THE PAST

THE BUSH ADMINISTRATION thus faced a Herculean task in regenerating U.S. trade policy when it took office in early 2001. Moreover, the overall climate for trade policy had soured badly. The U.S. economy slowed sharply from the middle of 2000 through the end of 2001, with unemployment jumping from four to six percent. The continued climb of the dollar through 2000–1 meant that it was at least 20 to 25 percent overvalued, and the strong dollar in turn lifted the annual current account deficit to almost $500 billion by 2002. Making matters even worse, the terrorist attacks of September 11 generated new pressures to "close the borders."

The new administration nevertheless placed high priority on getting trade policy back on track. To do so, it correctly decided to pursue the two-part strategy that had worked repeatedly throughout the postwar period: the launch of far-reaching new international negotiations and congressional passage of fast-track legislation (renamed trade promotion authority, or TPA) to authorize their pursuit. The new negotiations, which the administration planned to conduct simultaneously at the multilateral, regional, and bilateral levels, would restart the forward momentum of liberalization on the international front. They would further open world markets and write new trade rules while seizing the initiative from the antiglobalization forces. Passage of TPA would achieve the same outcome domestically. Neither part of the package was possible without the other: other countries would not negotiate seriously with the United States unless the president had congressional authority to make commitments, and Congress would not provide that authority without a clear indication that doing so would bring substantial benefits to the United States through extensive concessions by other countries.

That strategy had been successfully deployed in the three prior cycles of postwar U.S. trade policy. It produced the Kennedy Round under John Kennedy and Lyndon Johnson, the Tokyo Round under Richard Nixon, Gerald Ford, and Jimmy Carter, and both the Uruguay Round and NAFTA under Ronald Reagan, George H.W. Bush, and Clinton. Indeed, the approach has been deployed by administrations and Congresses controlled by both parties.

It is far too early to know whether George W. Bush's version of the strategy will work. But so far the first two steps have been navigated successfully. Working closely with the European Union (EU), the administration forged an agreement at Doha in November 2001 to launch a comprehensive new round in the WTO that could wind up tackling virtually all relevant trade issues, as well as completing the accession of China and Taiwan to the WTO. Combined with the existing prospects for an FTAA and bilateral negotiations both inherited from Clinton (Chile and Singapore) and newly envisaged (Australia and perhaps New Zealand, Central America, Morocco, southern Africa, and possibly Thailand), the Doha Round paves the way for a substantial package. Indeed, it should bring enough benefits both to the United States and to other countries to persuade all of them to complete the deals. This strategy also clearly reaffirms the global rather than unilateral approach of the United States in a policy area that is even more crucial to other countries than it is to Washington.

Congressional passage of TPA in the summer of 2002 was a major step forward. The new legislation authorizes the administration to participate in all these negotiations without facing crippling amendments from Congress that could have limited their scope. It even unilaterally lowers U.S. barriers to a significant volume of textile imports from a number of developing countries, an unprecedented element in a trade authorization bill. Both Doha and the TPA were very close calls, and the domestic legislative battle left partisan wounds that may bedevil U.S. trade policy into the future. But they put in place the building blocks for new advances in the global trading system and for U.S. trade policy.

Indeed, the new version of the presidential negotiating authority may carry the seeds of a fundamental transformation of U.S. policy toward globalization, especially toward trade and other international economic issues. The TPA legislation dramatically expands the Trade Adjustment Assistance program to sharply increase worker eligibility and financing for both safety-net provisions and retraining, and it starts providing partial coverage for losses of wages and health insurance by trade-dislocated workers. These reforms, championed by Senate Democrats, could begin to allay the fears of globalization. And if implemented effectively, they could begin shifting public attitudes within the United States in a more supportive direction.

This last outcome would be further strengthened if the new trade-related steps were coupled with continued improvements in the American educational system. Such progress would empower more workers to take advantage of globalization rather than feel victimized by it. Lifting the education level of the average American worker from high school to junior college would garner a solid majority for globalization; our studies show that, on average, each additional year of formal education increases support for globalization by 10 percent. These domestic policy approaches offer far more promise for helping globalization's victims in the United States than even the most ambitious reforms of international labor standards. The revealed preference in the new legislation for such a strategy may turn out to represent a lasting reorientation of the policy debate.

ONE STEP BACKWARD, TWO STEPS FORWARD

THE CONTEXT laid out above is necessary to assess the administration's recent protectionist steps. None of these steps is defensible on its merits. All of them, in fact, represent extremely bad policies. Most of them were directly related to electoral politics. But they were also essential components of restoring an effective U.S. trade policy. The entire strategy could not have even begun without congressional passage of TPA. The three key votes on that legislation in the House of Representatives carried by margins of three or fewer. Hence there was literally no room to spare. Unsavory political bargains simply had to be struck to get the basic approach off the ground.

The most obvious example was the blatant rollback of some of the previous textile liberalization for the Caribbean and Central America to win the final three votes in the initial House action of December 2001. (That said, the final legislation did include much more significant liberalizing steps for the same products from the same countries.) But it is also noteworthy that nine more steel-caucus members voted for TPA than for fast track in 1998. The administration's initiation of the safeguard case on steel imports in the summer of 2001 and its subsequent decision to impose relief in early 2002 were presumably critical to avoiding large losses of votes from this group. And in the case of the farm bill, the administration did not block the congressional initiatives to sustain the increased support levels of recent years and to undo earlier efforts to decouple farm policies from trade flows—again, all to avoid losing TPA support. The political economy of trade policy was obviously in play in motivating all these deviations from a liberal approach.

History reveals that such domestic maneuvering is a sad but true constant of U.S. trade policy. Every president who has wanted to obtain the domestic authority to conduct new international liberalizing negotiations has had to make concessions to the chief protectionist interests of the day. The entire history of U.S. postwar trade policy can be characterized as "one step backward, two steps forward." On all previous occasions, the gamble has succeeded, and the ultimate benefits have turned out to be well worth the costs.

In 1961, for example, Kennedy faced the prospect that the textile lobby would block congressional approval of the Trade Expansion Act. That bill would have enabled him to launch the Kennedy Round—a centerpiece of both his overall foreign policy, especially with the newly unifying Europe, and his economic policy. Kennedy thus directed his administration to negotiate the first comprehensive U.S. import quotas on cotton textiles, paving the way for more than 40 years of extensive protection for that sector. But he extracted in return a promise from the industry to support his legislation. He also applied new "escape clause" protection to carpets and glass, even though Europe retaliated and triggered a minor trade war. The strategy worked. The Kennedy Round achieved a major breakthrough in across-the-board reduction of tariffs and set a benchmark for all postwar trade talks.

Nixon encountered a similar dilemma a decade later. To combat the first widespread surge of postwar protectionism and pave the way for Congress to approve the launch of the Tokyo Round in 1974, including the initial fast-track authority, Nixon had to go even further than Kennedy did. He converted the cotton textile quotas into a more sweeping arrangement (the Multi-Fiber

Agreement), installed a temporary surcharge on most imports and a permanent tax subsidy for U.S. exports, and devalued the dollar twice before eventually floating it. Later on, the Carter administration extended new protection to the shoe, steel, and color television industries, thereby maintaining the necessary domestic consensus to support the negotiations and eventual congressional approval of the Tokyo Round.

These trade-offs became even more extensive in the mid-1980s, when protectionist pressures reached their postwar peak due to the dollar's massive overvaluation and the resulting record trade deficits. Reagan, in the words of his secretary of the Treasury, James Baker, "thus granted more import relief to U.S. industry than any of his predecessors in more than half a century." His administration installed "voluntary export restraint agreements" on automobiles, steel, and machine tools; substantially tightened the existing quotas on textiles and apparel; negotiated an agreement to expand U.S. exports of semiconductors; and accepted the infamous "Super 301" authority that permitted retaliation against "priority foreign countries" of whose trade policies the United States disapproved. But it was able to win renewal of fast-track authority in 1988, which the subsequent administrations used to achieve both NAFTA and the Uruguay Round.

Hence the same approach has played out in all three of the previous postwar trade-policy cycles in the United States. The president adopts the two-part strategy described above. He successfully seeks international agreement to launch new negotiations. But he is blocked from obtaining the necessary domestic authority by the protectionist interests of the day. He thus has no choice but to placate those interests sufficiently to neutralize their opposition to his proposed negotiations. With those interests assuaged, Congress provides the needed authority. The president then completes the international negotiations. He essentially trades protection that is modest and temporary (albeit long-lived for textiles and frequently renewed for steel) for liberalization and international rule-making that is sizable and permanent. In all three episodes, the net outcome has represented major progress for the U.S. economy, for U.S. trade-policy leadership and hence overall foreign policy, and for the world trading system and economy as a whole.

It is of course impossible to know whether this occasion will record similar success. But the administration has added several innovations to the traditional strategy that enhance the prospects. In particular, its simultaneous pursuit of regional and bilateral as well as multilateral negotiations generates substantial pressure on other countries to cooperate via a process of "competitive liberalization." For example, a bilateral trade accord with Central America will increase the incentives for Mercosur (South America's major trade bloc) to agree on an FTAA; in turn, the latter will encourage the EU to agree to reduce barriers globally. This dynamic should restore the forward momentum of liberalization. Along with periodic roundups of partial deals in the WTO, it should also generate early tangible results that will help sustain domestic support for the policy in the United States while it awaits the results of the Doha Round (which are likely to be delayed until 2007). In any event, the strategy would never have gotten off the ground without TPA. Hence the protectionist steps were necessary evils for achieving the greater goals.

For the price to be worth paying, however, the payoff from the negotiations that have now been authorized must be considerable in both economic and foreign-policy terms. The recent turmoil in South America is a reminder of just how great the gains could be, in both respects, from an FTAA that replicated even partially the enormous payoff to Mexico (and thus to the United States) from NAFTA. Thus it is essential that the Doha Round, in particular, be comprehensive in its coverage. Everything must be on the table so that each country's goals can be achieved and each will, in turn, be willing to satisfy the objectives of the other key players. A mini round would simply not be worth the effort.

For that reason, U.S. Trade Representative Robert Zoellick was correct and courageous in reversing the Clinton administration's refusal to place the most politically sensitive U.S. trade policies on the table (a position that had produced the failure at Seattle). These include high tariffs on textiles, apparel, and other industrial products; high agricultural tariffs, quotas, and subsidies, whose importance is now greatly heightened due to the farm bill; and antidumping and countervailing duties, the chosen U.S. instruments of "process protection" in recent years. Unless Washington is willing to put its most sensitive restraints on the table too, other countries will not be able to overcome their domestic political constraints and meet U.S. demands for reductions in their tariffs, liberalization of their farm supports and services sector, and strengthening of the global trading rules. The administration also deserves credit for its steadfast resistance to congressional efforts to hamstring its negotiating position by excluding such issues from the talks before they even start. Elimination of the Senate's Dayton-Craig amendment, which would essentially have taken antidumping (and countervailing duties) off the table, was particularly important in this regard.

SECRETS TO SUCCESS

CRITICS of current U.S. trade policy, even if they accept the analysis to this point, will still point to two huge obstacles: implacable congressional hostility to liberalization of present antidumping practices and the new farm bill. They believe that the whole approach is bound to founder on one or both. But again, history suggests a potentially brighter interpretation.

With respect to antidumping, it must be remembered that the United States has entered the last two multilateral trading rounds with at least one apparently non-negotiable demand from Congress each time. But in both cases, a skillful blend of international and domestic politics overcame this hurdle and permitted a comprehensive negotiating outcome to succeed. In the Tokyo Round, that issue was countervailing duties. At that time, the Treasury Department, which managed the issue in those days, could increase duties against any foreign practice that it deemed a subsidy as long as a domestic U.S. interest group offered a petition, whether or not the industry was suffering any injury. Needless to say, foreign outrage over this practice was intense.

The U.S. negotiators overcame that seemingly intractable problem with a twofold approach. First, they rolled that specific U.S. practice into negotiations over a much broader subsidies code that, for the first time, brought international discipline to bear on the export subsidies deployed by most countries. They then obtained commitments from more than 30 countries to eliminate or sharply reduce their existing subsidies and, in turn, embedded that agreement in the Tokyo Round agreement itself, which advanced a number of other important U.S. trade objectives. Congress was persuaded that the United States would now be better protected against foreign subsidy practices and that the overall package was in the national interest. Thus it endorsed the Tokyo Round by overwhelming majorities in both chambers.

Approaching the Uruguay Round in the late 1980s, the domestic political constraint for the United States was textile and apparel trade. Yet the three administrations involved in the negotiations agreed to a total phaseout of the long-standing import quotas and the entire Multi-Fiber Agreement. The strategy was again twofold. It sought to achieve specific benefits for the sector itself through reductions in foreign barriers to U.S. textile exports (and parallel agreements that actively promoted U.S. textile exports under NAFTA) and an overall outcome from the Uruguay Round that met many top U.S. goals.

In both these cases, the impossible was in fact achieved. As the Doha Round unfolds, creative U.S. negotiating should be able to craft and sell a similar strategy with respect to antidumping. As it did in the Tokyo Round, it could install new disciplines on other countries' practices (including their continued export subsidies and the lack of transparency in their antidumping procedures, which are of increasing concern to U.S. exporters). Such an approach would also enable Washington to achieve a comprehensive outcome that will advance major U.S. interests and improve the global trading regime.

The new farm bill created another firestorm over U.S. policy and complicated the prospects for the global system. But here, too, the problem can be converted into an opportunity. Fortunately, the administration has already begun to move in that direction with its aggressive proposals for using the Doha Round to dramatically reduce agricultural tariffs, phase out all export subsidies, and sharply cut domestic support levels—including its own. It won widespread support from the farm community for this approach and was able to launch it even before final passage of TPA.

The farm bill's increased supports for American agriculture, of course, will increase the incentive for other countries to negotiate on the topic to produce a reversal of the new U.S. actions. The United States can use that incentive to increase its leverage in the agriculture talks as long as it is willing to roll back its new subsidies as part of a multilateral deal—and in fact cut them even further, as it has clearly and forcefully said it will. Furthermore, the new farm payments are technically within the bounds that the United States accepted in the Uruguay Round. As a result, in negotiating terms the effect will be identical to many developing countries' insistence on negotiating tariff reductions on the basis of their much higher "bound" rates (the highest tariff allowed) rather than their much lower applied rates. Even the farm bill, if properly managed, can thus turn out to enhance the prospects for a successful Doha Round rather than sounding its death knell, as has been widely suggested.

THE ROAD AHEAD

THE BUSH administration has a very long road ahead over the next several years to convert these strategic purposes into a successful conclusion for Doha and the other negotiations it will be undertaking. The domestic politics of trade are now much more difficult than in the past. Trade has tripled its share of the economy over the past generation and therefore become enormously more important to the United States. The traditional bipartisanship of trade policy has been severely eroded as congressional partisanship has risen; only 20 to 25 Democrats supported TPA in the three key House votes. Global and even regional trade negotiations are far more complex now because of the much larger number of countries involved and the far broader (and more complicated) array of issues to be tackled. There is also the fact that an organized group of developing countries (as well as the EU) can now block any outcome. Finally, the end of the Cold War eliminated the security glue that compelled the largest trading countries to keep their disputes from disrupting their alliance systems.

But the first two major hurdles—the launch of the Doha Round and the passage of TPA—have now been cleared. History suggests that these initial steps may be the hardest parts of the entire enterprise; their payoffs are much less tangible than the ultimate outcomes, and Congress is quite properly reluctant to reject a "done deal" that other countries have already processed politically. There will be many more close calls, both internationally and domestically, down the road. But the alternative would have been a prolonged U.S. absence from serious international trade negotiations, which would mean increasingly heavy costs for the United States as the rest of the world negotiated additional deals on its own and expanded dis-crimination against American exports. The United States and the world would have suffered severely from the continued absence of effective participation from the largest trading nation and traditional champion of open markets.

The historical perspectives described here suggest that the prospects for an eventually favorable outcome are quite good. The administration will have to negotiate skillfully abroad to bring home a series of saleable packages, but its innovative additions to the traditional strategies offer excellent promise for doing so. It will have to use the intervening years to make Trade Adjustment Assistance and education reform work at home, chipping away at the opposition to globalization. But the new legislation provides an effective foundation for building the stronger domestic political base that is essential. The year 2002 may thus turn out to represent a renaissance for U.S. trade policy rather than the demise that has been so widely feared.⊛

A High-Risk Trade Policy

Bernard K. Gordon

A STEP IN THE WRONG DIRECTION

ROBERT ZOELLICK, the U.S. trade representative and the main force shaping U.S. foreign trade policy today, combines prodigious negotiating skills with an equally solid background in realpolitik. Nevertheless, the current American approach to trade, over which he has presided, promises to severely damage U.S. foreign policy and trade. At the heart of the problem is Washington's unwise return to economic "regionalism"—an approach evident in the many U.S. efforts now underway to build new bilateral or regional trade agreements with a number of small trading partners.

Washington's regionalism aims, in principle, to induce the world's major trade actors, especially Europe and Japan, to complete the broader, multilateral agenda of the World Trade Organization (WTO). This strategy is no secret; in fact, it has been publicly discussed several times. In a letter to the author in late 2001, for example, Zoellick wrote,

> I believe a strategy of trade liberalization on multiple fronts—globally, regionally, and bilaterally—enhances our leverage and best promotes open markets. As Europeans have pointed out to me, it took the completion of NAFTA [North American Free Trade Agreement] and the first APEC [Asia-Pacific Economic Cooperation] Summit in 1993–94 to persuade the EU to close out the Uruguay Round. I favor a "competition in liberalization" with the U.S. at the center of the network.

BERNARD K. GORDON is Professor of Political Science Emeritus at the University of New Hampshire. This article originally appeared in the July/August 2003 issue of *Foreign Affairs*.

Zoellick's description of events in the early 1990s is dead on. That was a time when the former main framework for world trade, the General Agreement on Tariffs and Trade (GATT), was notoriously in trouble—"GATT is dead," economist Lester Thurow declared at the time—and its weaknesses led to the establishment of the considerably more institutionalized WTO. American efforts were key to that change, and the WTO's present Doha Round of negotiations likewise owes much to Washington. Two recent and very bold American proposals—dealing with trade in agricultural goods and industrial products—could make the Doha Round the most successful round thus far.

Yet at the same time the United States has also accelerated its "free trade areas" policy, and these FTAS—precisely because they are not broadly multilateral—are bound to cause serious problems. Aside from the conceptual and practical challenge they pose to the WTO (a point its leaders recognize and often condemn), regional FTAS are also fundamentally incompatible with America's national interests. Nowhere is that incompatibility clearer than in East Asia, where local FTAS are proliferating, and where all are justified as a necessary response to American initiatives.

China, for example, since 2001 has embarked on a mission to achieve a free trade area with all of Southeast Asia and has begun work on a similar arrangement in Northeast Asia. In direct response to that Chinese initiative, Japan has announced that it is ending its 50-year commitment to multilateral trade. Recognizing how large is its policy shift, Japan frankly calls it a "departure." Yet both countries, to explain and justify their new emphasis on regionalism, regularly blame the United States for starting the trend.

The Japanese shift dates to 1999, when the director of the Japan External Trade Organization (JETRO), Japan's foreign trade body, wrote that in a world of regional trading blocs, "we cannot prevail alone. We have to face reality. ... 26 of the world's 30 main economies were or would be partners in such [regional] accords—the European Union, the North American Free Trade Agreement and the Association of Southeast Asian Nations' planned Free Trade Agreement (AFTA)."

Since then, and especially in light of China's economic successes and its announced FTA with the Association of Southeast Asian

Nations (ASEAN), Tokyo has hardened its rhetoric still further. Old rivalries between Japan and China, among Asia's longest-standing, have resurfaced. Today, however, the antagonism is marked by an ascendant China and a possibly declining Japan. A Tokyo official put the issue simply: "If Japan does nothing, its economic leadership in East Asia would be taken over by the Chinese."

This new and developing competition between Beijing and Tokyo is not something Washington could possibly want. Nor would American interests be served by the most likely alternative: formal collaboration between China and Japan on East Asia's trade. Yet that is precisely the pattern now forming. Since early last year, and culminating in November 2002—when the foreign ministers of China, Japan, and South Korea met on the fringes of the annual ASEAN meetings—evidence of such cooperation has proliferated, coming under the rubric of "ASEAN + 3" (or the reverse), which combines the ten ASEAN countries with Japan, China, and South Korea.

As many will remember, "ASEAN + 3" is exactly the model first proposed in the mid-1980s by Malaysian Prime Minister Mahathir bin Mohamad. He called at the time for an "East Asian Economic Caucus," a proposal that was quickly resisted and successfully put down by U.S. Secretary of State James Baker, who believed the Mahathir plan would in effect draw a line down the Pacific separating the United States from East Asia. Because the grouping would also have excluded Australia, New Zealand, and Canada, it was quickly labeled a "caucus without Caucasians," and those racist overtones have been perpetuated by the fact that ASEAN continues to rebuff Australia's membership.

LESS IS LESS

THE GROWTH in regionalism was thrown into new and urgent focus earlier this year, when preliminary 2002 trade data were released. Most attention centered on Japan because, for the first time since 1961, Japan imported more from China than from the United States. Similar dramatic changes were reported by the other East Asian economies. Taiwan and South Korea, along with the principal ASEAN nations, all recorded 50 percent increases in their exports to China in 2002, while their exports to the United States remained flat.

This was sobering news, but it should not have been surprising. Signs of change, particularly of a relatively reduced U.S. trade presence in East Asia, have been evident since at least the mid-1990s. Those signs were discounted or ignored by many observers because they ran counter to the widespread belief that large and growing exports from Asia to the United States were a reliable fixture of the environment. Indeed, the "Asian miracle" analysis identified exports to the United States as a key element in East Asia's growth, so much so that they were taken for granted.

Many American observers were so blinded that they ignored the evidence and dismissed as naive any suggestion that Asia's economies were intensifying their regional interactions and becoming less reliant on the U.S. market. Whenever that suggestion was made, the common rejoinder was that "the Japanese [or the Koreans, or the Chinese] would never do anything so foolish and so much opposed to their own interests." The response recalls a comment made by John Foster Dulles when he was supervising the end of America's occupation of Japan in the early 1950s. In a memorable remark on Japan's economic future, he urged that Tokyo concentrate on nearby Asian markets because Japanese products would never be attractive to Americans. Needless to say, the seeds had already been planted that would soon become known to Americans as Honda and Sony.

Incipient trends are once again present in U.S.–East Asian trade, but this time in the reverse direction. As the accompanying charts illustrate, the rise of China and the relative decline of the United States—the two events that raised eyebrows in 2002—have already been evident for a number of years. The chart on the facing page shows that Japan's imports from China rose from $36 billion to almost $60 billion between 1995 and 2001, while its imports from the United States fell, from $76 billion to $63 billion. It is hardly surprising, then, that in the year following, Japan's imports from China exceeded those from the United States.

Although Japan's shift is the most dramatic in absolute dollar terms among the several East Asian economies, there were similar striking trends across the board. South Korea's exports to China rose by 100 percent (from $9 billion to $18 billion), while its exports to the United States grew by just 30 percent. Likewise for

its imports: from China they nearly doubled, to $13 billion, while
from the United States they fell by
a quarter. Again, in absolute dollar
terms, South Korea's trade with
the United States still remains
larger than its trade with China,
but the very different growth rates
are not promising—and the same
applies to Thailand, Singapore,
and Malaysia. For each of these
four countries, trade with China
has been rising much faster than
trade with the United States. In
three out of four, imports from
China rose by more than 70 percent, while imports from the
United States fell. Singapore's
experience is particularly dramatic:
its imports from China rose by 120
percent, while those from the
United States fell by 6 percent.

These trends, to borrow a Wall
Street reminder, do not necessarily
predict the future, but they do
highlight several important realities.
One is the mammoth size of U.S.
exports to East Asia. In 2001, pre-

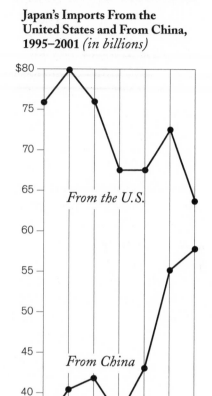

**Japan's Imports From the
United States and From China,
1995–2001** *(in billions)*

SOURCE: Calculated from data in the
International Monetary Fund's *Direction of
Trade Statistics Yearbook*, 2002.

cisely a quarter of the United States' total exports of goods went
to the Pacific Rim. Their value, at $182 billion, was identical to
the value of the United States' exports to Europe. In 2002, U.S.
exports to the Pacific Rim rose still further, to 26 percent of the
U.S. total, while Europe's share dropped slightly, to 24 percent.

The sharply different trade growth rates underline a second reality:
East Asia's tightening economic ties. That process was accelerated
by the region's financial crisis in 1997–98 and reinforced by
Washington's initially cool response. Tokyo, in contrast, stepped up

to the plate with several imaginative offers of help, including its sponsorship of the "Asian Monetary Fund," an idea quickly—and, some would say, brutally—crushed by then Treasury Secretary Lawrence Summers. The contrast in behavior strengthened the view, especially in Southeast Asia, that the United States was prepared to write off several of the Asian economies; some even believed that Americans were anxious to benefit from Asia's plight.

A good reflection of this sentiment were the statements of a senior official in Thailand's Foreign Ministry. In 1997, at the onset of the crisis, he complained that while the United States benefited from globalization, Thailand suffered. Three years later, when Bangkok was planning to host an economic conference, his bitterness had ripened to a conviction that the United States was simply unconcerned with Southeast Asia: "The leaders of eight ASEAN countries have confirmed participation. The Japanese prime minister will attend. ... EU leaders will ... attend [but] I am a bit disappointed with the U.S. participation. ... The U.S. domestic economy is large and sound, which is probably why it does not attach much importance to participation in international forums."

Much the same disappointment with the United States was reflected this past March, in a Washington speech given by Emil Salim, one of Indonesia's most prominent economists. Salim co-chairs the United States–Indonesia Society, and in remarks there, he spoke of a fundamental change in Indonesia's future economic orientation. Gone was the familiar talk of first-rung manufacturing progress, of the sort typified by Nike footwear and garments destined for the United States. Instead Salim spoke of how Indonesia must now fit in with "China's role in Asia's economies," of "ASEAN + 3," and of how Indonesia's future must depend not on manufactured exports but on exports of its traditional "tropical products." His statements, like those of many others in Southeast Asia today, reflect a shift away from the region's 30-year effort to integrate with America and the West. They signal instead a turn toward planning for prosperity as part of a resurgent and postcrisis Asia.

The third reality these illustrations point to is the global distribution of U.S. exports. As the chart on the facing page demonstrates, half of American exports are divided almost equally between Europe and Asia, and more than a third go to immediate neighbors, Canada and Mexico. Putting this another way, almost 90 percent of U.S. exports are directed, in roughly equal proportions, to the globe's three main economic regions: North America, East Asia, and the EU. None of the world's other major economic players, whose exports go mainly to nearby markets, has a distribution even approaching this U.S. record. The EU export pattern is the least diversified, with two-thirds of the exports staying within the EU, and Japan's exports are almost as concentrated.

Global Shares of U.S. Merchandise Exports in 2002; *Total $693.5 billion*

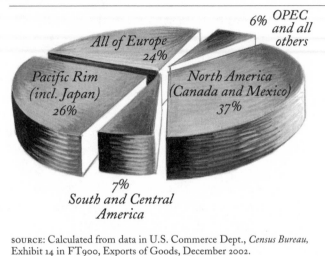

SOURCE: Calculated from data in U.S. Commerce Dept., *Census Bureau,* Exhibit 14 in FT900, Exports of Goods, December 2002.

NOTE: OPEC share excludes Venezuela and Indonesia.

ONE AFTA THE OTHER

THESE CONTRASTS are a reminder of the enormity of the United States' stake in all of the world's regions, and of the corollary U.S. need to strengthen and maintain its commitment to the global trade system symbolized by the WTO. Yet both recent presidents have undermined that goal by their insistence on new regional or bilateral free trade agreements. None of those agreements is remotely analogous to NAFTA, the creation of which was justified by the political and strategic advantages it brought to the United States. The items on today's FTA agenda represent no such political or economic gain to Washington.

The most recent, a proposed "Central American Free Trade Area," can hardly be taken seriously from a U.S. perspective, in part because Central America is a tiny market, but more important because U.S. exports there already account for at least 40 percent of Central America's imports. In contrast, the United States' supposed "competitors," the EU and Japan, have less than 10 and 5 percent of the Central American market, respectively. Yet so strong is today's FTA fetish that when President George W. Bush called for a Central American FTA, all perspective (and humor) went out the window. The White House solemnly announced that U.S. exports to Central America were "more than to Russia, Indonesia, and India combined"—conveniently forgetting that those three have long ranked at the bottom of America's markets.

How to explain this belief in the future of FTAS? Zoellick hopes that they will act as "building blocks" of global free trade, but that has always been a debatable proposition, and now there is clear evidence that trade blocs in one region simply beget trade blocs in other regions. This is the real lesson of the Asian experience and Asia's new FTA proposals. Whether under Chinese or Japanese sponsorship, these proposals are responses to burgeoning FTAS elsewhere—especially those in the western hemisphere, which are U.S.-sponsored—and they will likewise have two consequences for the United States. The first, as the above data demonstrate, will be to threaten the United States' major economic stake in East Asia. The second will be to help build a political and strategic counterweight to Washington's long-term security interests in the Pacific.

Critics will object that there is no tradeoff between the two: that East Asia and the western hemisphere are quite separate, and that U.S. policy can readily handle that separation. But events in the two regions are far from separate, as Henry Kissinger was forcefully reminded when he visited Tokyo in the early 1990s. Kissinger spoke with Ryutaro Hashimoto, who was then Japan's finance minister and would soon become its prime minister. In his book *Vision of Japan,* Hashimoto reported on their conversation and recalled that its background was two policy questions that directly connected the western hemisphere and East Asia.

The first issue was Malaysia's proposal for an "East Asia Economic Caucus" (EAEC). The second was the debate then current in the United States about NAFTA, specifically its possible expansion to Central and South America. Those developments, which of course later led to President Bill Clinton's call for a hemisphere-wide Free Trade Area of the Americas (FTAA), were closely monitored by Asian leaders, who worried that an enlarged NAFTA would give South Americans preferential treatment in the enormous U.S. market and that those preferences would come at Asia's expense. Some also feared that this FTAA talk in the western hemisphere would give added support and justification to those Asians who had long contemplated establishing their own regional trade bloc in the Pacific.

It was in that context that Hashimoto spoke with Kissinger about the link between the EAEC proposal, which Japan was being pressed to support, and the possibility of NAFTA expansion, which the United States was considering. When Kissinger asked whether Tokyo's posture would be influenced by American plans to extend NAFTA southward, Hashimoto answered, "Yes, that is what would happen":

> As a member of the cabinet I do not highly regard the Mahathir plan. But if the United States strengthens its posture towards forming a protectionist bloc by extending NAFTA and closing off South America and North America, then Japan will have to emphasize its position as an Asia-Pacific country. This will inevitably alter the Japan-U.S. relationship. ... So please do not force us into such a corner.

In the years since that blunt advice, Japan's posture has moved substantially along the lines of Hashimoto's warning, as two recent developments suggest. The first is the reemergence of what Hashimoto called Japan's "position as an Asia-Pacific country." In part this revival stems from Japan's perennial debate about whether it is truly "Western," and in part it derives from the passing of the generation that directly (and usually favorably) experienced the American occupation. Equally important, however, are the views of Japan's most senior and sophisticated observers, in which a central strand holds that U.S. primacy has become somewhat suffocating and must be loosened. A good example is Ogura Kazuo, one of Japan's most senior Foreign Ministry officials, and hardly an elderly right-wing "nationalist." Now ambassador to France, he has a graduate degree in economics from Cambridge, was ambassador to both South Korea

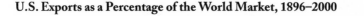

U.S. Exports as a Percentage of the World Market, 1896–2000

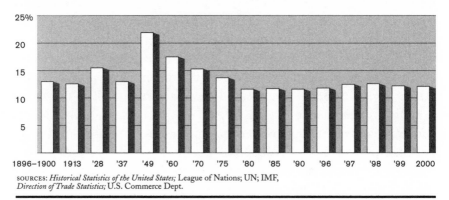

SOURCES: *Historical Statistics of the United States;* League of Nations; UN; IMF, *Direction of Trade Statistics;* U.S. Commerce Dept.

and Vietnam, and has been his ministry's director-general for economic affairs. He writes often on Asian affairs in influential Japanese journals, and in a 1999 essay titled "Creating a New Asia," Ogura argued that it is "necessary for a united Asia, along with Western Europe, to be prepared to check America. Asia must act in a unified way and … Japan must shoulder a large part of the leadership needed to achieve that. One reason has to do with America's world dominance, the concentration of power in the hands of the United States."

Hashimoto's prediction has also come to pass in Japan's decision to end its exclusive reliance on the GATT-WTO system. The Japanese government's 2000 white paper on trade signaled the change, and China's announcement of its ASEAN free trade plan prompted an immediate Japanese response. Within weeks of Beijing's initiative, Prime Minister Junichiro Koizumi went to Southeast Asia to stake out Japan's claim. In Singapore, he conceded that "China is an attractive market" but insisted nevertheless that Japan's trade approach is better: "Cooperation among Japan, China, and South Korea is essential; and in the future, it would only be natural to add Australia and New Zealand." The prime minister's rhetoric led quickly to action: Tokyo signed its first-ever free trade agreement, with Singapore, and in early 2002, Japan and South Korea announced they too were talking about an FTA.

In practice, and because of the power of Japan's agricultural interests, both steps will result in less than meets the eye. The agreement with Singapore, for example, excludes agriculture, even though Singapore has no pastureland and its "agricultural" exports are mainly its tropical fish. An agreement with South Korea will face similar hurdles. Even so, Japan is engaged in ongoing talks with both New Zealand and Mexico, and elsewhere in the region other FTA negotiations are in progress. They include talks between Thailand and China, between New Zealand and Singapore, and reportedly even between the United States and Thailand and Japan.

It is certainly true that this flurry of activity does not mean imminent change, as Beijing acknowledged with its ten-year ASEAN time frame. But more important is the question of whether Asia should be moving in this direction at all. Today's competing Chinese and Japanese models remind us why, thanks largely to Cordell Hull, U.S. secretary of state from 1933 to 1944, the early postwar vision of regions and economic blocs promoted by Winston Churchill was rejected, and why multilateralism was adopted instead. Political rivalries inevitably develop within and among the blocs, and protectionist walls, by whatever name, necessarily rise between them.

A good example is Northeast Asia today, where an FTA is being actively discussed by specialists and governments, and where its advocates expect it to result in a "huge trading bloc." That outcome, which implies a dividing line in the Pacific, would hardly be in the interests either of the global economy or of the United States. It is tempting to believe that, given the history and consequences of regional blocs between the two world wars, no policymaker today would deliberately repeat such folly, but the historical record provides no such assurance or comfort.

A WINNING RECORD

MUCH OF THE CURRENT trade dilemma and its U.S. foreign policy consequences stem from a widespread American belief that the United States has not been a successful player in world trade. This perception is found both at the local level and in Washington, and it is rooted in a long-standing mercantile tradition, which teaches that exports are better than imports. That lesson is regularly reinforced when monthly trade figures are released because they are always accompanied by reports of the nation's "growing trade deficit." The genuine importance of that deficit is debated among economists, but what is not in doubt is that Americans commonly believe that they are a "soft touch" on trade and that the United States has not done too well as an exporter.

Nothing could be further from the truth. A long look back at the record of the last 100 years, illustrated on page 116, shows that the United States has largely held a steady 12–13 percent share of world exports. That was the case at the beginning of the twentieth century, when farm products and commodities dominated U.S. exports (and Europe dominated global exports), and at the century's very end, when U.S. exports of aircraft, jet engines, medical equipment, and other high-technology and industrial products had replaced those earlier commodities.

Only in the periods that followed the two world wars did America's exports account for more than their rock-steady 12–13 percent. In those years, as a result of wartime devastation, few other nations were left on the trade scene, and American suppliers briefly and very temporarily had the export field to themselves. In all other periods, 12–13 percent was the norm; indeed it is remarkable that both in 1913 and 1998, two years that are worlds apart in almost every other respect, the U.S. share of world exports was the same: 12.6 percent.

The years since 1980 are worth a second look because that period witnessed an explosion in world trade and the arrival of major new economic actors. Both factors are essential for understanding America's role in world trade because most of those new actors either simply did not exist as independent players when the century began or—as in Japan's case—had just entered global export markets. In 1913, Japan's share of world exports was just 2 percent; since then it has more than tripled. The other new actors—Singapore, South Korea, Taiwan, and Hong Kong—played no separate role at all as export economies before World War II, but today their combined global share is more than 10 percent. Add to that China, the newest major Asian exporter, and the global share of these newcomers becomes more than 13 percent. Japan's inclusion brings the figure to more than 20 percent.

The meaning of this arithmetic is that more than a fifth of today's global export market is now held by economies that had little or no international significance when the century began. Yet despite those new arrivals, and in the face of the overall explosion in world trade, America has continued to hold a steady global share. That has been the one constant factor in a world of otherwise enormous change; it should help demonstrate that the United States, far from having been "disadvantaged" in world trade, instead has a clear winning record.

Believing the opposite, that the field is not level but is tilted against the United States, has led to two troublesome consequences. One is the kind of protectionist "safeguards" the United States is often led to adopt: antidumping measures and countervailing duties, spurred by the self-serving demands for Washington's protection that regularly come from America's steel, textile, and farming sectors. The second and now more dangerous consequence is the belief that the United States needs to build special bilateral or regional FTAs. The reality is that the United States not only does not need any such special FTAs, but is precisely in the opposite situation: because it has the world's most evenly distributed pattern of exports, U.S. interests would be harmed were regional FTAs to flourish.

To avoid that outcome, Washington should take two main steps. One is to end the promotion of regional blocs. For the United States that will mean recognizing that its own trade policies, especially its quixotic insistence on a western hemisphere FTA, have helped bring about what it cannot want: the emergence of an East Asian economic bloc. The FTAA has long been in trouble in any case, especially and increasingly with Brazil, and its aims would best be met at the WTO. Second, the United States must resume in practice as well as in rhetoric its postwar role as world trade leader. It must reject, and be seen to reject, whatever short-term advantages regionalism or bilateralism might seem to offer. That will be no easy task for an administration now in serial FTA mode: witness Australia, which was moved to the top of the list of FTA candidates following its support for the United States in Iraq, and the president's recent call for a "Free Trade Area for the Middle East." Instead, the United States must act intensively and single-mindedly to champion the multilateral system of trade, which means principally to ensure that the U.S.-inspired WTO and its Doha Round offshoot are vigorously maintained and strengthened.

Many will argue that because of its recent actions on steel, textiles, and timber, the United States cannot now enter that fray with clean hands. Paradoxically, however, since the United States clearly is not about to reverse those actions, and has already been subjected to worldwide criticisms for them, its situation contains an important tactical and strategic advantage, namely that any positive trade steps it now takes will be welcomed as acts aimed at redemption. The United States has already begun to seize that advantage with its call for the elimination of all tariffs on industrial goods traded among the nations of the Organization for Economic Cooperation and Development. More broadly, however, what is called for is a trade-policy initiative that will restore to center stage the multilateral trading system represented by the WTO.

Such an initiative will mean sparing no effort to complete, by its scheduled 2005 date, the WTO's Doha Development Round, and to meet its important milestones before then. One opportunity has already slipped by, when negotiators failed in March to agree on agricultural "modalities." The next test will be the September ministerial meeting in Cancun, Mexico, and if that chance too is missed, the prospects for 2005 will be bleak indeed. The administration should therefore now concentrate its energies on Cancun and on the core agricultural and market-access issues. In the overlapping trading format represented by the WTO's 146 members, the onus will be on several key actors: the EU, Japan, South Korea, Brazil, India, and of course the United States. All stand to gain, as the GATT's 50-year trade explosion has shown, but all will have to give in order to get.

For that reason, Zoellick—acutely sensitive to Congress' constitutional power in trade matters and already an avid counter of congressional votes—will need to hear from business, agriculture, and industry, along with consumers, that their interests require success in the Doha Round. The WTO is not as strong as it needs to be, but from the perspective of American national interests it is better than any realistic alternative. It is time, in other words, to recall that in the 1930s and 1940s, the massive contribution of U.S. policymakers was to aim for a world not of regional economic blocs, but a single world trade system. That is what we now have, and that is what could now be lost.

How Should the United States Handle Rogues?

Iraq and the Arabs' Future

Fouad Ajami

THE ROAD TO MODERNITY

THERE SHOULD BE no illusions about the sort of Arab landscape that America is destined to find if, or when, it embarks on a war against the Iraqi regime. There would be no "hearts and minds" to be won in the Arab world, no public diplomacy that would convince the overwhelming majority of Arabs that this war would be a just war. An American expedition in the wake of thwarted UN inspections would be seen by the vast majority of Arabs as an imperial reach into their world, a favor to Israel, or a way for the United States to secure control over Iraq's oil. No hearing would be given to the great foreign power.

America ought to be able to live with this distrust and discount a good deal of this anti-Americanism as the "road rage" of a thwarted Arab world—the congenital condition of a culture yet to take full responsibility for its self-inflicted wounds. There is no need to pay excessive deference to the political pieties and givens of the region. Indeed, this is one of those settings where a reforming foreign power's simpler guidelines offer a better way than the region's age-old prohibitions and defects.

Above and beyond toppling the regime of Saddam Hussein and dismantling its deadly weapons, the driving motivation of a new American endeavor in Iraq and in neighboring Arab lands should be modernizing the Arab world. The great indulgence granted to the

FOUAD AJAMI is director of the Middle East studies program at the School for Advanced International Studies at Johns Hopkins University. This article originally appeared in the January/February 2003 issue of *Foreign Affairs*.

ways and phobias of Arabs has reaped a terrible harvest—for the Arabs themselves, and for an America implicated in their affairs. It is cruel and unfair but true: the fight between Arab rulers and insurgents is for now an American concern.

In the 1970s and the 1980s, the political and economic edifice of the Arab world began to give way. Explosive demographic trends overwhelmed what had been built in the postindependence era, and then a furious Islamism blew in like a deadly wind. It offered solace, seduced the young, and provided the means and the language of resentment and refusal. For a while, the failures of that world were confined to its own terrain, but migration and transnational terror altered all that. The fire that began in the Arab world spread to other shores, with the United States itself the principal target of an aggrieved people who no longer believed that justice could be secured in one's own land, from one's own rulers. It was September 11 and its shattering surprise, in turn, that tipped the balance on Iraq away from containment and toward regime change and "rollback."

A reforming zeal must thus be loaded up with the baggage and the gear. No great apologies ought to be made for America's "unilateralism." The region can live with and use that unilateralism. The considerable power now at America's disposal can be used by one and all as a justification for going along with American goals. The drapery of a unanimous Security Council resolution authorizing Iraq's disarmament—signed by the Syrian regime, no less—will grant the Arab rulers the room they need to claim that they had simply bowed to the inevitable, and that Saddam had gotten the war he had called up.

In the end, the battle for a secular, modernist order in the Arab world is an endeavor for the Arabs themselves. But power matters, and a great power's will and prestige can help tip the scales in favor of modernity and change. "The Americans are coming," the Islamists proclaimed after the swift defeat of the Taliban. They scrambled for cover as their "charities," their incitement, and their networks of finance and recruitment came under new scrutiny.

The Islamists' apparent resurgence in recent months was born of their hope that the United States may have lost the sense of righteous violation that drove it after September 11, and that the American push in the region may have lost its steam. These Islamists are supremely political and calculating people; they probe the resolve of their enemies. The "axis of evil" speech of President George W. Bush last January had caused among the Islamists genuine panic. A measure of relief came in the months that followed. They drew new courage from the bureaucratic struggles in Washington and from the attention that the fight between Israel and the Yasir Arafat regime attracted some months later.

A successful war in Iraq would be true to this pattern. It would embolden those who wish for the Arab world deliverance from retrogression and political decay. Thus far, the United States has been simultaneously an agent of political reaction and a promoter of social revolution in the Arab-Muslim world. Its example has been nothing short of revolutionary, but from one end of the Arab world to the other, its power has invariably been on the side of political reaction and a stagnant status quo. A new war should come with the promise that the United States is now on the side of reform.

America's open backers will be Kuwait and Qatar—the first because of the trauma and violation it endured in 1990–91 at the hands of Iraq, the second because it has taken a generally assertive and novel approach in diplomacy as well as a willingness to associate openly with American power. In the main, however, the ruling order in the Arab world will duck for cover and hope to be spared. Rather than Desert Storm, the Arab rulers will want the perfect storm: a swift war, few casualties, as little exposure by themselves as possible, and the opportunity to be rid of Saddam without riding in broad daylight with the Americans or being brought to account by their people.

The political world rarely grants this kind of good fortune, but such is the dilemma of hugely unpopular rulers who have never taken their populations into their confidence, who have lived with American patronage while winking at the most malignant strands of anti-Americanism. Those rulers know that a war against Iraq would be the first war in their midst waged in the era of the satellite channels, at a time when everyone is "wired" and choices are difficult to conceal.

A new campaign against Iraq would find a deeply divided verdict in the region on the Iraqi menace. There are those who, if only out of feelings of historical inadequacy about the Arabs' technical skills, will doubt that the ruler in Baghdad and his military apparatus have at their disposal weapons of mass destruction. Others will see Iraq's weapons as proof that Arabs have come of age in the modern world, and that the powers beyond are bent on subjugating them, stripping them of the same weapons that represent modernity and scientific and military advance in a Hobbesian world of hierarchy and inequality.

Given the belligerence and self-pity in Arab life, its retreat from modernist culture, and its embrace of conspiracy theories, there are justifiable grounds for believing there are no native liberal or secular traditions to embrace the United States and use its victory to build an alternative to despotic rule. Few Arabs would believe this effort to be a Wilsonian campaign to spread the reign of liberty in the Arab world. They are to be forgiven their doubts, for American power, either by design or by default, has been built on relationships with military rulers and monarchs without popular mandates. America has not known or trusted the middle classes and the professionals in these lands. Rather, it has settled for relationships of convenience with the autocracies in the saddle, tolerating the cultural and political malignancies of the Arab world. A new American role in the region will have to break with this history.

LONELY AT THE TOP

THE SOLITUDE of the United States is more acute than it was during the Persian Gulf War in 1990–91. In that expedition, there was local cover for what was in truth an imperial campaign against an Iraqi state that threatened to shred the balance of power in the gulf. There were even Muslim jurists in Saudi Arabia and Egypt who issued *fatwa*s that sanctioned the expedition of the foreign power.

The three powers of consequence—Egypt, Syria, and Saudi Arabia—were arrayed against Saddam Hussein. The last was directly menaced, while Egypt and Syria were given substantial economic rewards for covering the flanks of the gulf states, denying the Iraqi ruler the chance to depict the struggle as a standoff between the haves and the have-nots in the Arab world. Saddam had been particularly obtuse: he had broken the code of the ruling Arab order for which he had posed as a trusted warrior against the Iranian revolutionary state. But for the vast majority of Arabs, Operation Desert Storm was an Anglo-American campaign of hegemony. A predator had risen in the region and a great foreign power, the inheritor of Pax Britannica in the Persian Gulf, had checked his bid for hegemony.

Saddam had sacked a country, but there was an odd popular identification with him, and crowds saw him as the bearer of a lofty Arab endeavor. The gullible saw him as a Robin Hood, an avenging Saladin fighting "the Franks" and their local collaborators, erasing the colonial boundaries imposed after World War I. It may be heretical to suggest it, but the Iraqi ruler would have won a "free" election among Arabs in 1990–91. The dynasties he was warring against were unloved in their world. From Amman to Nablus to Casablanca, the crowds gave their approval to the night of terror that he unleashed on the region. He was a revisionist at odds with the order around him, and in a thwarted world the bandit acts out the yearnings of subdued but resentful crowds.

No great Arab hopes are pinned on the Iraqi ruler this time around. This is the other side of the ledger, for the fickle crowd makes and breaks these kinds of attachments with brigands and false redeemers with great frequency. Saddam had lost his bid; he had treated a world steeped in defeats to yet another calamity. The crowd that had fallen for Osama bin Laden was the same floating crowd that had once trusted its scores with the world would be settled by the Iraqi ruler. The struggle against him is a different matter now. The crowd may shout itself hoarse against the Americans, but its bonds with the Iraqi ruler have been weakened.

One particular but pivotal Arab realm is calmer this time around. In 1990–91, all the currents of political revisionism, the envy of the poorer Arab lands toward the oil states, the bitter sense that history has dealt the Arabs a terrible hand, seemed to converge on Jordan. It was in that country, more than in any other in the Arab world, that the Iraqi dictator was both an avenger and would-be redeemer. He had *rujula* (manhood), he had money to throw around, and he held out the promise that the oil dynasties would be brought down. It was that radicalism that had forced King Hussein to stay a step ahead of the crowd, breaking with the Persian Gulf powers and the United States to side with Iraq. A group of religious scholars, the Conference of the Ulama of the Sharia (an offshoot of the Muslim Brotherhood), has issued a *fatwa* banning any assistance to the Americans, such as "opening airports and harbors to them, providing their planes and vehicles with fuel, offering them intelligence for their war against Muslims." It is impermissible, the *fatwa* added, "to sell the American aggressor a piece of bread or to offer him a drink of water." This time, however, the monarchy has drawn a line, and wise Jordanians have put the word out that a short war and a reconstructed Iraq would work to the advantage of their poorer and smaller domain.

For American power, there are two ways in the Arab world. One is restraint, pessimistic about the possibility of changing that stubborn world, reticent about the uses of American power. In this vision of things, the United States would either spare the Iraqi dictator or wage a war with limited political goals for Iraq and for the region as a whole. The other choice, more ambitious, would envisage a more profound American role in Arab political life: the spearheading of a reformist project that seeks to modernize and transform the Arab landscape. Iraq would be the starting point, and beyond Iraq lies an Arab political and economic tradition and a culture whose agonies and failures have been on cruel display.

The first option would hark back to Desert Storm. After a campaign imbued with high moral purpose came reticence. There was no incentive to push deeper into Iraq or into Arab politics. The balance of power had been restored, and the internal order of the Arab states did not concern George H.W. Bush. Indeed, Bush appeared to have a kind of benign affection for the Arab monarchies. His attitude toward the gulf states resembled what the British took to distant realms of their empire before "reform" caught up: love of pageantry, a fascination with exotic style, and a tolerance for time-honored traditions of rule.

The authority that the United States gained in the aftermath of Desert Storm was used to bring together Arabs and Israelis at Madrid in 1991. George H.W. Bush had resisted "linkage" between the Persian Gulf and the Israeli-Palestinian conflict, but he was to make it the cornerstone of U.S. strategy after the guns had fallen silent. The internal order of the House of Saud and the governance of Kuwait were left to the rulers of those lands. True, some liberal secularists there had thought that the United States would press for internal reforms—in Kuwait in particular. But democracy is not a foreigner's gift, nor was its export a prospect that Bush ever entertained.

For Iraq itself, there was to be no Wilsonian redemption. Bush had called upon the Iraqis to "take matters into their own hands." His call had been answered in the hills of Kurdistan and in the southern part of the country, where rebellion erupted in Basra, then spreading into the Shi`ite holy cities of Najaf and Karbala. For a brief moment, the mastery of the regime cracked as prisons were emptied, and the insurgents were joined by soldiers straggling in from the front. But with the help of the regime's helicopter gunships, the rebellions were crushed with unspeakable cruelty.

Some key players within the Bush administration were eager for a "clean break" from the war. This was particularly true of the then chairman of the Joint Chiefs of Staff, Colin Powell. "Neither revolt had a chance," Powell would later write of the Kurdish and Shi`a rebellions. "Nor, frankly, was their success a goal of our policy." It was a cruel ending for a campaign billed as the opening act of a new international order. The reordering of Iraq had not been a goal of the war.

In the intervening years, however, the ground has shifted in the Arab world, and the stakes for the United States have risen. The Iraqi dictator has hung on, outlasting and mocking his countless obituaries. And the familiar balance of power in the region sent America's way the terror of September 11. The United States has been caught in the crossfire between the regimes in the saddle and the Islamic insurgents. These insurgents could not win in Algeria, Egypt, Tunisia, or Syria, or on the Arabian Peninsula. So they took to the road and targeted the United States, and they were brutally candid about their motives. They did not strike at America because it was a patron of Israel; rather, they drew a distinction between the "near enemy" (their own rulers) and the "far enemy," the United States.

Those entrenched regimes could not be beaten at home. Their power, as well as their people's resigned acceptance that their rulers' sins would be dwarfed by the terrors that Islamists would unleash were they to prevail, had settled the fight in favor of the rulers. The targeting of America came out of this terrible political culture of Arab lands. If the leader of the Egyptian Islamic Jihad, the physician Ayman al-Zawahiri, could not avenge himself against the military regime of Hosni Mubarak for the torture he endured at the hands of his country's security services, why not target Mubarak's U.S. patrons?

A similar motivation propelled the Saudi members of al Qaeda. These men could not sack the House of Saud. The dynasty's wealth, its political primacy, and the conservative religious establishment gave the rulers a decided edge in their struggle with the Islamists; the war against America was the next best thing. The great power was an easier target: it was more open, more trusting, and its liberties more easily subverted by a band of jihadists. The jihadists and their leader, bin Laden, aimed at the dynasty's carefully nurtured self-image. The children of Arabia who had boarded those planes on September 11 and the countless young men held at the Guantanamo Bay military base could not be disowned. Bin Laden got the crisis in Saudi-American relations he aimed for. Those 15 young Saudis were put on those planes to challenge the old notions about the stability of the monarchy. Grant the devil his due: bin Laden knew the premium the dynasty placed on its privileged relationship with the United States. He had an exquisite feel for the regime's cultural style, its dread of open disagreements and of scrutiny. He treated the House of Saud to its worst nightmare, puncturing the official narrative of a realm at peace.

That veneer of Saudi-American harmony was destined to crack. The Saudi population had changed; it was younger, poorer, and more disgruntled. Its airwaves crackled with bitter anti-Americanism, and a younger breed of radicalized preachers had challenged the standard Wahhabi doctrine of obedience to the rulers. As the winds of anti-Americanism and antimodernism blew at will, the rulers stepped aside. The royal family was cautious: it rode with America but let the anti-Americanism have its play.

CASUS BELLI

THE CASE FOR WAR must rest in part on the kind of vision the United States has for Iraq. The dread of "nation-building" must be cast aside. It is too late in the annals of nations for outright foreign rule. But there will have to be a sustained American presence if the new order is to hold and take root. Iraq is a society with substantial social capital and the region's second-largest reserves of oil. It has traditions of literacy, learning, and technical competence. It can draw on the skills of a vast diaspora of means and sophistication, waves of people who fled the country's turbulent politics and the heavy hand of its rulers. If Iraq's pain has been great in the modern era, so too, has been its betrayed promise. There were skills and hope that the polity could be made right, that the abundance of oil and water and the relative freedom from an overbearing religious tradition would pave the way toward modernity and development.

For Pax Americana, Iraq may be worth the effort and the risks. America has been on the ground in Saudi Arabia for nearly six decades now, in Egypt for three. In both realms, there is wrath and estrangement toward America. What has been built in Arabia appears in serious jeopardy. The aid and help granted to Egypt has begotten nothing other than ingratitude and a deep suspicion among frustrated middle-class Egyptians that the United States wishes for them subjugation and dependence. There is an unfathomable anti-Americanism in Egypt—even among those professionals who have done well by the American connection.

There appears to be no liberal option for Egypt, no economic salvation. This country of outward tranquility and seething internal radicalism is in the grip of deep frustration. Egyptian history has stalled; the military ruler is supreme, but he offers no way out for his country. As the political life of the land has atrophied, anti-Americanism has taken hold, offering absolution and a way of airing the rage of a proud population that has fallen short of its own idea of itself and its place among the nations. Iraq may offer a contrast, a base in the Arab world free of the poison of anti-Americanism. The country is not hemmed in by the kind of religious prohibitions that stalk the U.S. presence in the Saudi realm. It may have a greater readiness for democracy than Egypt, if only because it is wealthier and is free of the weight of Egypt's demographic pressures and the steady menace of an Islamist movement.

Iraq should not be burdened, however, with the weight of great expectations. This is the Arab world, after all, and Americans do not know it with such intimacy. Iraq could disappoint its American liberators. There has been heartbreak in Iraq, and vengeance and retribution could sour Americans on this latest sphere of influence in the Muslim world.

But America could still be more daring in Iraq than it was after Desert Storm. To begin with, the bogeyman of a Shi`ite state emerging in Iraq as a satrapy of the Iranian clerical regime—the fear that paralyzed American power back in 1991—should be laid to rest. The Iranian Revolution's promise has clearly faded. The clerics there are in no position to export their "revolutionary happiness," for they would find no takers anywhere. Then, too, the Shi`a of Iraq must be seen for what they are: Arabs and Iraqis through and through.

Shi`ism was a phenomenon of Iraq centuries before it crossed to Iran, brought to that land by the Safavid rulers as a state religion in the opening years of the sixteenth century. But even long before that, it had been an Arab religious-political dispute. Moreover, the sacred geography of Shi`ism had brought Shi`a religious scholars and seminarians from India, Lebanon, and Persia to Iraq. Thanks to geographic proximity, the Persian component had been particularly strong: it had used the shrine cities of Iraq as sanctuary, checking the power of their own country's leaders in the ceaseless tug-of-war between rulers and religious scholars. But in their overwhelming numbers, the adherents of Shi`ism were drawn from Arab tribesmen. Arab nationalism, which came to Iraq with the Hashemite rulers and the officers and ideologues who rode their coattails, covered up Sunni dominion with a secular garb. As Iran was nearby, larger and more powerful, it became convenient for the ruling stratum of Iraq to disenfranchise its own Shi`a majority, claiming that they were a Persian fifth column of Iran.

This invented history took on a life of its own under Saddam Hussein. But before the Tikriti rulers terrorized the Shi`ite religious establishment and shattered its autonomy, a healthy measure of competition was always the norm between the Shi`ite seminaries of Iraq and those of Iran. Few Iraqi Shi`ites are eager to cede their own world to Iran's rulers. As the majority population of Iraq, they have a vested interest in its independence and statehood. Over the last three decades, they have endured the regime's brutality yet fought its war against Iran in 1980–88. Precious few among them dream of a Shi`a state. The majority of them are secularists who understand that the brutalized country will have to be shared among its principal communities if it is to find a way out of fear and terror.

There is a religiously based Shi`a movement, the Supreme Council for the Islamic Revolution in Iraq (SCIRI), based in Iran, led by Ayatollah Mohamed Baqir al-Hakim. The choice of Iran as sanctuary by the al-Hakim family was dictated by the brutality of the Iraqi regime and by the lack of an Arab sanctuary where the Shi`a opposition could survive and function. Iran gave the clerics and laymen of SCIRI the resources and proximity for their war against the regime. What such men could bring to a new order is difficult to forecast with any confidence, but it is hard to see them building the necessary bridges to the Kurds and the Sunni remnants willing and able to break with the Tikriti legacy.

A more likely outcome would be the rise to power of a different kind of Shi`ism: more at home in the secular world, granting the clerics a political and cultural role of their own while subordinating them to secular authorities, as is the case in Lebanon. In the scheme of historical development of the Shi`a tradition, the triumph of clerics has been a relatively recent phenomenon—more a feature of Iran since 1979 than of the Arab world.

FAREWELL TO PAN-ARABISM?

A NEW REGIME in Iraq might be willing to bid farewell to virulent pan-Arabism. The passion for a Palestinian vocation in a new Iraq may subside, if only because the Palestinians have been such faithful supporters of Saddam Hussein. The norm has been for Iraq, the frontier Arab land far away from the Mediterranean, to stoke the fires of anti-Zionism knowing that others closer to the fire—Jordanians, Palestinians, Egyptians, Syrians, and Lebanese—would be the ones consumed. A new Iraqi political order might find within itself the ability to recognize that Palestine and the Palestinians are not an Iraqi concern. A new ruling elite that picks up the pieces in Iraq might conclude that offering a bounty to the families of Palestinian suicide "martyrs" is something that a burdened country can do without.

A new Iraqi political arrangement would also empower the Shi`a
and the Kurds, and neither population owes fidelity to the pieties of
Arabism. The Iraqi Kurds owe the Arab world little. The Iraqi
opposition's solitude in the wider politics of the Arab world has
been deep and searing. Saddam's opponents have had no Egyptian
or Saudi sponsorship, nor have the Arab nationalists and "the street"
embraced them. They have worked alone from London and Iran,
and more recently, with American patronage. They are free to
fashion a world with relative indifference to Arab claims.

A respected Kuwaiti thinker, Muhammad al-Rumaihi, has
recently observed that the talk of Iraq as a model for other Arabs is
overdone, that Iraq has never enjoyed such primacy in modern
Arab life, either under the monarchy or under the radical regimes
that have held sway since the revolution of 1958. There may be
truth in what he says, for the country is idiosyncratic and lacks the
cultural accessibility to other Arabs, such as those in Cairo,
Damascus, or Beirut. But herein lies the prospect of Iraq's deliverance: freedom from the deadly legends of Arabism, from the lure
of political roles that have wrecked Arab regimes that succumbed
to them. Think of Cairo under the weight of its Arab calling and
the undoing of the bright hopes of its Nasserist era. No country
should wish for itself this sort of captivity.

The pan-Arabism that has played upon Iraq and infected its
political life has been a terrible simplification of that checkered country's history, a whip in the hands of a minority bent on dominating
the polity and dispossessing the other communities of their rightful
claims. Iraq had been a country of Kurdish highlanders, Marsh
Arabs, Sunnis, Shi`ites, Turkmen, Assyrians, Jews, and Chaldeans.
But only the Sunni Arabs came into power—the city people, the
privileged community of the (Sunni) Ottoman state.

British rule had worked through the Sunnis, for the British had
rightly assumed that a ruling community that included 20 percent
of the population would be easily subordinated to foreign tutelage.
In a cruel historical irony, the Sunni Arabs emerged with the best
of alternatives: they were at once the colonial power's proxies and
the bearers of a strident, belligerent ideology of Arab nationalism.
The state remained external to the body politic, an alien imposition.

Oil and terror gave that state freedom from the society and the means to destroy all potential challengers. The regime grew more clannish, more relentless, more Sunni, and more Arab by the day. The Assyrians were destroyed in a military campaign in 1933. Then the Jews were dispossessed and expelled. There remained the Shi`ites, the Kurds, and the Turkmen to contend with.

The state also grew in power. The dominance of Saddam Hussein's fellow townspeople, the Tikritis, led to the gradual hardening that separated the regime from the larger society around it. In earlier, more benign days, the Tikritis had lived off the making of rafts of inflated goatskins. The steamships broke that industry. By happenstance, the Tikritis made their way into the military academies and the security services. There, they found a brand-new endeavor: state terror. Their rule had to be given ideological pretense, and pan-Arabism proved to be a perfect instrument of exclusion, a modern cover for tribalism.

The Fertile Crescent has always been a land of rival communities and compact minorities. Arab nationalism, the creed of Iraq's rulers, escaped from all that ambiguity into an unyielding doctrine of Arabism. The radicalism of that history wrecked the Arab world and gave the politics of the Fertile Crescent a particularly rancid and violent temper. Saddam did not descend from the sky; he emerged out of his world's sins of omission and commission. The murderous zeal with which he went about subduing the Kurds and the Shi`a was a reflection of the deep atavisms of Arab life. There, on the eastern flank of the Arab world, Iraq and its "maximum leader" offered the fake promise of a pan-Arab Bismarck who would check the Persians to the east and, in time, head west to take up Israel's challenge.

AN OPENING FOR DEMOCRACY

AN ARAB WORLD rid of this kind of ruinous temptation might conceivably have a chance to rethink the role of political power and the very nature of the state. It has often seemed in recent years that the Arab political tradition is immune to democratic stirrings. The sacking of a terrible regime with such a pervasive cult of terror may offer Iraqis and Arabs a break with the false gifts of despotism.

If and when it comes, that task of repairing—or detoxifying—Iraq will be a major undertaking. The remarkable rehabilitation of Japan between its surrender in 1945 and the restoration of its sovereignty in 1952 offers a historical precedent. Indeed, the Japanese example has already turned up, in both American and Arab discussions, as a window onto the kind of work that awaits the Americans and the Iraqis once the dictatorship is overthrown. Granted, no analogy is perfect: Iraq, with its heterogeneity, differs from Japan. America, too, is a radically different society than it was in 1945—more diverse, more given to doubt, and lacking the sense of righteous mission that drove it through the war years and into the work in Japan.

Yet for all these differences, the Japanese precedent is an important one. In the space of a decade, imperial Japan gave way to a more egalitarian, modern society. A country poisoned by militarism emerged with a pacifist view of the world. It was the victors' justice that drove the new monumental undertaking and powered the twin goals of demilitarization and democratization. The victors tinkered with the media, the educational system, and the textbooks. Those are some of the things that will have to be done if a military campaign in Iraq is to redeem itself in the process. The theatrics and megalomania of Douglas MacArthur may belong to a bygone age, but Iraq could do worse than having the interim stewardship of a modern-day high commissioner who would help usher it toward a normal world.

At a minimum, Iraq would be lucky to have the semidemocratic politics of its neighbors. Turkey and Jordan come to mind, and even Iran is a more merciful land than the large prison that Iraq has become under its terrifying warden. The very brutality that the Iraqis have endured under Saddam may be Iraq's saving grace if redemption comes its way. There may come relief after liberation—and a measure of realism.

The deference to the wider Arab phobias about the Shi`a or the Kurds coming into new power in Iraq should be cast aside. A liberal power cannot shore up ethnic imperiums of minority groups. The rule of a Sunni minority, now well below 20 percent of Iraq's population, cannot be made an American goal. The Arabs around Iraq are not owed that kind of indulgence. It is with these sorts of phobias and biases that the Arab world must break. A culture that looks squarely at its own troubles should think aloud about the rage that is summoned on behalf of the Palestinians while the pain of the Kurds, or the Berbers in North Africa, or the Christians in the southern Sudan, is passed over in silence.

This righteous sense of Arab victimhood—which overlooks what Arab rulers do to others while lamenting its own condition—emanates from a political tradition of belligerent self-pity. The push should be for an Arab world that acknowledges its own economic and political retrogression and begins to find a way out of those crippling sectarian atavisms.

From the Kurds, there are now proposals for a federal, decentralized polity that would keep the country intact while granting that minority the measure of autonomy they were promised when they were herded into a Baghdad-based Arab government in the early 1920s. That federalism would look different in an Iraqi setting, but there may lie Iraq's salvation. It would be a departure from the command states dominant in the Arab world and in the centralized oil states in particular. In their modern history, the Kurds have been repeatedly betrayed, and that terrible history has bred in them habits of fratricide and sedition. But the Kurds ought to be given credit for what they have built over the last decade in their ancestral land in northern Iraq, albeit under the protection of Anglo-American air power.

Kurdistan has thrived, and the perennial struggle between its dominant warlords, Masoud Barzani and Jalal Talabani, appears to have subsided. An attempt is being made at parliamentary life. This achievement is fragile and could crack, but under the gaze of two watchful and hostile powers, Iran and Turkey, the Kurds appear to control the zone they rule, which consists of 10 percent of Iraq's land and 15 percent of its population. Arabs are not given to charitable views of the Kurds, but the Kurds could bring to the debate about a new Iraq the experience and the poise gained during self-rule.

It is not decreed that the Kurds, or the Shi`a for that matter, will want sectarian republics of their own. The convenience that created Iraq in the 1920s may still hold, but it would have to be a different Iraq. A country of genuine pluralism, a culture that has traffic with Iran, Turkey, Syria, and the Arabian Peninsula, and the inheritance of four decades of British tutelage, has treated the Arab world to a cruel idea of Arabism, racial belonging, and merciless clan rule as well. This duality would be tested and played out if Iraq's different communities could arrive at a tolerable public order. The "ownership" of a new Iraq would have to be shared; its vocation would have to be a new social and political contract between state and society and among the principal communities of the land.

But Iraq would also provide, as it did under British tutelage, a mirror for American power as well. A new American primacy in Iraq would play out under watchful eyes. There will be Arabs convinced that their world is being recolonized. There will be pan-Arabists sure that Iraq has been taken out of "Arab hands," given over to the minorities within, and made more vulnerable to Turkey and Iran, the two non-Arab powers nearby. There will be Europeans looking for cracks in the conduct of the distant great power. The judgment that matters will be made at home, in the United States itself, as to the costs and returns of imperial burden. The British Empire's moment in Iraq came when it was exhausted; on the eve of its occupation of Iraq, the United Kingdom's GDP was 8 percent of the world product, when the comparable figure for America today is at least three times as large. America can afford a big role in Iraq, and beyond. Whether the will and the interest are there is an entirely different matter.

The Arab world could whittle down, even devour, an American victory. This is a difficult, perhaps impossible, political landscape. It may reject the message of reform by dwelling on the sins of the American messenger. There are endless escapes available to that Arab world. It can call up the fury of the Israeli-Palestinian violence and use it as an alibi for yet more self-pity and rage. It can shout down its own would-be reformers, write them off as accomplices of a foreign assault. It can throw up its defenses and wait for the United States to weary of its expedition. It is with sobering caution, then, that a war will have to be waged. But it should be recognized that the Rubicon has been crossed. Any fallout of war is certain to be dwarfed by the terrible consequences of America's walking right up to the edge of war and then stepping back, letting the Iraqi dictator work out the terms of another reprieve. It is the fate of great powers that provide order to do so against the background of a world that takes the protection while it bemoans the heavy hand of the protector. This new expedition to Mesopotamia would be no exception to that rule.✪

Suicide From Fear of Death?

Richard K. Betts

SNAKE FIGHT

WITH WAR in the Middle East imminent, it is clear that the United States has painted itself—as well as Iraq—into a corner. The Bush administration's success in engineering international support for a preventive war in the Persian Gulf is impressive, both politically and diplomatically. But Washington's case rests on two crucial errors. It understates the very real risk that an assault on Iraq will trigger a counterattack on American civilians. And even when that risk is admitted, the pro-war camp conflates it with the threat of unprovoked attack by Iraq in the future.

Many Americans still take for granted that a war to topple Saddam Hussein can be fought as it was in 1991: on American terms. Even when they recognize that the blood price may prove greater than the optimists hope, most still assume it will be paid by the U.S. military or by people in the region. Until very late in the game, few Americans focused on the chance that the battlefield could extend back to their own homeland. Yet if a U.S. invasion succeeds, Saddam will have no reason to withhold his best parting shot—which could be the use of weapons of mass destruction (WMD) inside the United States. Such an Iraqi attack on U.S. civilians could make the death toll from September 11 look small. But Washington has done little to prepare the country for this possibility and seems to have forgotten Bismarck's characterization of preventive war as "suicide from fear of death."

RICHARD K. BETTS is Director of the Institute of War and Peace Studies and the International Security Policy program at Columbia University. This article originally appeared in the January/February 2003 issue of *Foreign Affairs*.

America's political leaders have not just lost faith in deterrence as a means to contain Iraq, they have also lost sight of the fact that, when it comes to a showdown between two countries that both possess WMD, deterrence can work both ways. The United States is about to poke a snake out of fear that the snake might strike sometime in the future, while virtually ignoring the danger that it may strike back when America pokes it. True, not everyone demanding an American attack ignores the immediate threat such an attack might raise—but even this camp misreads that threat, thinking it reinforces the urgency of preventive war. The consequences, they argue, will only get worse if Washington waits. This argument may seem like common sense at first. But it dangerously confuses two sets of odds: the chance that Iraq will eventually challenge America even without being provoked, and the risk that Baghdad will retaliate against Washington if struck first.

The probability that Iraq could bring off a WMD attack on American soil may not be high, but even a modest probability warrants concern. By mistakenly conflating the immediate and long-term risks of Iraqi attack and by exaggerating the dangers in alternatives to war, the advocates of a preventive war against Saddam have miscast a modest probability of catastrophe as an acceptable risk.

COUNTERSTRIKE

AN INVASION to get rid of Saddam would represent an American attempt to do what no government has ever done before: destroy a regime that possesses WMD. Countries with WMD have fought each other twice before, but these events (when China and the Soviet Union came to blows on the Ussuri River in 1969, and when India and Pakistan fought over Kargil in 2000) were mere skirmishes. In both of those limited clashes, neither side's leadership was truly threatened. The opposite is true this time, and yet the difference has not been digested by pro-war strategists.

During Congress' debate over whether to authorize the war, for example, the danger that a preventive assault might provoke Iraqi retaliation against the American heartland went almost unmentioned. In an October letter, Director of Central Intelligence George Tenet stated that Saddam would be more likely to attempt a WMD

attack against the United States as "his last chance to exact vengeance" if he believed he could no longer deter an American onslaught—but this comment received scant notice. Attention focused instead on less immediate, less likely, and less dangerous threats. Hawks argued that Iraq will get nuclear weapons in the future. But the fact is that the biological weapons Iraq already has are dangerous enough to do tremendous damage—even if the worst estimates of U.S. vulnerability are excessive.

A 1993 study by the Office of Technology Assessment concluded that one plane, delivering anthrax by aerosol under good weather conditions over the Washington, D.C., area, could kill between one million and three million people. That figure is probably far too pessimistic even for an efficiently executed attack, since among other things, the medical response would be quicker and more effective today than it would have been a decade ago. So discount this estimate by, say, 90 percent. Even then, fatalities could still exceed 100,000. This reduced figure may still be excessive, since clandestine Iraqi operations to infect U.S. cities might be crude and inefficient. Yet if you reduce the death toll by another

90 percent, fatalities would still be more than triple those of September 11. Multiple attacks, even clumsy ones, could yield tens of thousands of casualties. Worst of all, Iraq may have bioengineered new pathogens for which no defense is available. Chemical weapons, although less destructive than biological ones, could also exact a dramatic toll.

But is an Iraqi counterattack on U.S. soil really plausible? Hawks argue that Saddam must be eliminated because he may decide to use WMD in the future or give them to terrorists—even if the United States threatens him with devastating retaliation. This argument assumes that Saddam would be prepared to cut his own throat without provocation. If that is true, it certainly follows that he will lash out with anything he has if Washington goes for his jugular and puts his back against the wall.

Yet Washington now seems determined to push him to that wall. Few are proposing that Saddam be retired to a villa on the Riviera next to "Baby Doc" Duvalier's. The option of a golden parachute should be considered, but it is unlikely to be accepted. Saddam would demand protection from extradition so that he could avoid joining Milosevic in court. And even Saddam knows he has too many bitter enemies to survive for long outside Iraq. Regime change in Baghdad, therefore, probably means an end to Saddam Hussein. And he will not go gently if he has nothing left to lose. If a military assault to overthrow the Iraqi regime looks likely to succeed, there is no reason to doubt Saddam will try to use biological weapons where they would hurt Americans the most.

Instead of considering the chances of a strike on the American heartland, however, war planners have tended to focus on the vulnerability of U.S. invasion forces, or on local supporters such as Israel, Saudi Arabia, and Kuwait—as if they are the only likely targets of an Iraqi WMD attack. Awful as attacks on these targets would be, the consequences would be nowhere near as large from the American perspective as those of a strike on the United States itself. The only remaining question, then, is whether Saddam would have the capability to carry out such an attack.

Maybe he won't. Saddam may not be crafty enough to figure out how to strike the American homeland. Iraqi intelligence may be too incompetent to smuggle biological weapons into the United States and set them off. Or Saddam's underlings might disobey orders to do so. The terrorists to whom Iraq subcontracts the job might bungle it. Or perhaps American forces could find and neutralize all of Iraq's WMD before they could be detonated. But it would be reckless to bank on maybes. Washington has given Saddam more than enough time to concoct retaliation, since he has had months of notice that the Americans are coming. The Bush administration has made this war the most telegraphed punch in military history.

Is it alarmist to emphasize the danger of an Iraqi counterattack on American soil? The odds may be low—perhaps as low as the odds were on September 10, 2001, that 19 Arab civilians would level the World Trade Center and tear a chunk out of the Pentagon. Even if the odds are as high as one out of six, however, that makes the risks inherent in overthrowing Saddam look like Russian roulette. It would be one thing for Americans to hope that they can wage war without triggering effective retaliation. But it would be altogether different to blithely assume that outcome; such unwarranted optimism represents the kind of "best case" planning that should shame any self-respecting hawk.

Taking the threat of retaliation seriously means two big things: preparing to cope with it, and reconsidering the need to start the war that could bring it on. If war on Iraq is deemed necessary despite the risk of mass destruction, Washington is dangerously far behind in preparing the home front. The United States must not wait until the war begins to put homeland defense into high gear. Studies and plans to prepare for future biological or chemical attack should be implemented in advance, not left on the drawing board until American tanks start rolling into Baghdad. The American people deserve immediate, loud, clear, and detailed instructions about how to know, what to do, where to go, and how to cope if they encounter anthrax, ricin, smallpox, vx, or other pathogens or chemicals Iraq might use against them. It is already too late now to do what should have been done much earlier—to cut through the production problems and other complications in making anthrax vaccines available to civilians (much of the military has already been vaccinated). At least there should be a crash program to test and put in place mechanisms for detecting anthrax attacks promptly and dispensing antibiotics on a massive scale; these are the minimum steps the Bush administration should take before it pokes the snake. Smallpox is a less likely threat, and much planning has been done for mass vaccination in an emergency. But at a minimum, health-care workers should be immunized in advance. Until the U.S. government is ready to do all these things, it will not be ready to start a war.

HOW TO FIGHT A COLD WAR

ALTHOUGH it is already terribly late in the day, the risk of Iraqi retaliation also underlines the need to reconsider the alternative to provoking it. Why are containment and deterrence—the strategies that worked for the four decades of the Cold War—suddenly considered more dangerous than poking the snake? Proponents of war against Iraq have provided an answer—but they are wrong.

Deterrence rests on the assumption that a rational actor will not take a step if the consequences of that action are guaranteed to be devastating to him. The United States can therefore deter Iraqi aggression unless or until Saddam deliberately chooses to bring on his own demise, when he could otherwise continue to survive, scheme, and hope for an opportunity to improve his hand. Of course, Saddam's record is so filled with rash mistakes that many now consider him undeterrable. But there is no good evidence to prove that is the case. Reckless as he has been, he has never yet done something Washington told him would be suicidal.

It is true that Saddam has a bad record of miscalculation and risk-taking. But he made his worst mistake precisely because Bush the Elder did not try to deter him. In fact, Washington effectively gave Baghdad a green light prior to its 1990 invasion of Kuwait. Ambassador April Glaspie was never instructed to warn Saddam that the United States would go to war if he grabbed Kuwait. During the ensuing war, in contrast, American leaders did issue a deterrent threat, warning Saddam against using biological or chemical weapons. And that deterrent worked. (The threat in that case was only elliptical; to make future deterrence less uncertain, threats should be much more explicit.) Despite humiliating defeat, Saddam held back his high cards in 1991 because he was never forced to the wall or confronted with his own demise. That war, unlike the one now contemplated, was limited.

Bush the Younger has quite aptly compared Saddam to Stalin but has drawn the wrong lesson from that parallel. Like Saddam, Stalin miscalculated in approving the invasion of South Korea in 1950, because President Truman (like the elder Bush in 1990) had not tried to deter him in advance. In fact, Secretary of State Dean Acheson had indicated publicly that South Korea was outside the U.S. defense perimeter. On the other hand, Stalin never invaded Western Europe, where the NATO deterrent was clear. For his part, Saddam's record shows that he is foolishly self-destructive when the consequences of his gambles are unclear, but not when they are unmistakable.

Should Saddam be compared to terrorists instead of to Stalin? If the Iraqi regime is viewed as similar to al Qaeda (a conflation of threats that official rhetoric has encouraged), deterrence would indeed be impractical. But Saddam and his Baath Party supporters are not religious fanatics bent on martyrdom. They are secularist thugs focused on their fortunes in this world. Nor can they hide from the United States, as al Qaeda members can. The crucial difference between a rogue state and a terrorist group is that the state has a return address.

None of this is meant to imply that containment and deterrence are risk-free strategies. They are simply less risky than would be starting a war that could precipitate the very danger it aims to prevent. Besides, what makes hawks so sure that long-term deterrence is more dangerous than immediate provocation? Saddam could be a greater threat in five years than he is today. But he could also be dead. He is now 65, and although he has so far been adept at foiling coups and assassination attempts, his continued success is hardly guaranteed. His stocks of WMD will grow more potent over time, but why should Saddam suddenly decide in the future that they afford him options he now lacks? And at what point in the growth of his arsenal would he plausibly choose to bring down a decisive American assault on himself and all his works?

It is also worth remembering that briefs made for preventive war in the past have proved terribly wrong. Truman, for example, did not buy arguments for attacking the Soviet Union—despite the fact that, as the historian Paul Schroeder wrote recently in *The American Conservative*, "Stalin had nuclear weapons, was a worse sociopath than Hussein ... and his record of atrocities against his own people was far worse than Hussein's." Moreover, within a few years of Navy Secretary Francis Matthews' and others' having recommended preventive war against him, Stalin was dead. In 1968, similarly, Robert Lawrence and William Van Cleave (who served a dozen years later as head of Reagan's Pentagon transition team) published a detailed rationale in *National Review* for attacks on China's nascent nuclear facilities. It is easy today to forget that at that time, Mao was considered as fanatically aggressive and crazy as Saddam is today. But within a few years of Lawrence and Van Cleave's article, Washington and Beijing had become tacit allies. How history could have turned out had either of these preventive wars actually been fought is a sobering thought, and one that the White House should now consider.

BEST IN A BAD SITUATION

RELYING ON DETERRENCE indefinitely is not foolproof. Unfortunately, international politics is full of cases where the only policy choices are between risky options and even riskier ones. In the current era of U.S. primacy, Americans often forget this fact, mistakenly assuming that the only problems they cannot solve satisfactorily are those about which they are inattentive or irresolute. Overconfident in U.S. capacity to eliminate Saddam without disastrous side effects, leaders in Washington have also become curiously pessimistic about deterrence and containment, which sustained U.S. strategy through 40 years of Cold War against a far more formidable adversary. Why has Washington lost its faith?

One explanation is psychological and moral. Many people think of deterrence as something the good guys do to the bad, not the reverse. To use the current danger of Iraqi retaliation as a reason not to attack seems dishonorable, like taking counsel from fear, a wimpy submission to blackmail. Moreover, it strikes Americans as presumptuous for a country such as Iraq to aspire to paralyze U.S. power. And it is a matter of American honor not to be deterred from suppressing evil. The cold logic of deterrence, however, has nothing to do with which side is good or evil. Deterrence depends only on the hard facts of capability, which should constrain the good as well as the bad.

Some Americans also become indignant when it is suggested that an Iraqi counterattack could be considered the fault of American initiative. This stance, they argue, is like blaming the victim. But this argument again confuses moral and material interests. If the snake strikes back when you poke it, you may blame the snake rather than yourself for being bitten. But you will still wish that you had not poked it.

Of course, Iraq has undermined its own deterrent potential by not making it explicit. Because he always denies that he possesses prohibited WMD, Saddam cannot declare a deterrent capability or doctrine. Iraq's bugs in the basement should work like Israel's bomb in the basement—as an undeclared deterrent, known about by those who need to know. But Iraq's WMD have not worked like Israel's, because, despite their potentially comparable killing power, biological weapons just do not instill the same fear as their nuclear equivalents.

At this late date, it would be awkward for Washington to step back from war—an embarrassing retreat, unless it was cushioned by apparent success in imposing inspections. (Administration leaders are correct in believing that genuinely successful inspections are nearly impossible. To work, they would have to prove a negative— that Saddam has not stashed WMD somewhere in his vast country that inspectors have not been clued in to search.) The only thing worse than such embarrassment, however, would be to go ahead with a mistaken strategy that risks retaliation against American civilians, extraordinarily bloody urban combat, and damage to the war on terrorism. No good alternatives to war exist at this point, but there are several that are less bad.

The first such option is to squeeze the box in which Saddam is currently being contained. This means selectively tightening sanctions—

not those that allegedly harm civilians, but the prohibitions on imports of materials for military use and the illicit export of oil. More monitors could be deployed, and the inspection of cargoes could be increased. The squeeze would continue at least until absolutely unimpeded disarmament inspections—anytime, anywhere, undelayed, and institutionalized until the regime changes—had been under way for a long period. There would be no international enthusiasm for more serious sanctions, but reluctant allies would embrace such a course if it were offered as the alternative to war. The crumbling of sanctions was one of the motives for the Bush administration's move toward war; stepping back from the war will reinvigorate containment and disabuse Saddam of the hope that he can wriggle away from it.

Second, Washington should continue to foment internal over-throw of Iraq's regime. Saddam seems immune to covert action, but even long-shot possibilities sometimes pan out.

Third, the Bush administration could consider quasi war. U.S. forces might occupy the Kurdish area of northern Iraq (where Saddam has not exercised control for years) and build up the wherewithal to move quickly against him at some unspecified future date—to enforce inspections, to protect Iraqi garrisons that revolt against his rule, or, ultimately, to invade Baghdad.

As the noose tightens, Washington or its allies should offer Saddam safe haven if he and his henchmen step down. Of course, he is not likely to accept, and if he does, it would lead to an international chorus of clucking tongues as a heinous criminal escaped justice. But it would not hurt to leave open a bad alternative that remains better than unlimited war.

In pondering Bismarck's line about preventive war, it helps to recall the consequences of the Prussian's passing. He was soon replaced by leaders who saw more logic and necessity in the course Bismarck had derided. In 1914, such European leaders thought they had no alternative but to confront current threats with decisive preventive war, and they believed the war would be a short one. As often happens in war, however, their expectations were rudely confounded, and instead of resolving the threat, they produced four years of catastrophic carnage.

Applying Bismarck's definition of preventive war to the current case is a bit hyperbolic. Iraqi retaliation would not destroy the United States—it might not even occur. But running even a modest risk of tens of thousands of American civilian casualties is unacceptable when compared to the exaggerated risk that Iraq will court its own suicide by using or helping others use WMD without provocation, and will do so before Saddam's regime is overthrown from within.

If war is to be, the United States must win it as quickly and decisively as possible. If no catastrophic Iraqi counterattack occurs, these warnings will be seen as needless alarmism. But before deciding on waging a war, President Bush should consider that if that war results in consequences even a fraction of those of 1914, those results will thoroughly discredit his decision to start it.✪

Securing the Gulf

Kenneth M. Pollack

ONCE MORE UNTO THE BREACH

IN 1968, the United Kingdom relinquished its security responsibilities "east of Suez," leaving the United States to pick up the pieces. Chief among the inherited obligations was ensuring the stability and security of the strategically vital Persian Gulf region. In the decades since, Washington has tried to do this job in various ways, relying on the "twin pillars" of Iran and Saudi Arabia during the 1970s, "tilting" toward Iraq during the 1980s, and pursuing the "dual containment" of Iraq and Iran during the 1990s. None of these approaches worked very well, and as a result, the United States has had to intervene directly three times in the last 16 years against regional threats—Iran in 1987–88 and Iraq in 1991 and this past spring.

The sweeping American and British military victory in Operation Iraqi Freedom has now cleared the way for the United States to try to establish a more durable framework for Persian Gulf security. Indeed, the Bush administration is already starting to do so by withdrawing the vast majority of American troops from Saudi Arabia, although this move seems more about closing an old chapter of American involvement than about opening a new one. With Saddam Hussein gone, a broad rethinking of U.S. strategy toward the region is necessary, because in some ways the security problems of the Persian Gulf are now likely to get more challenging instead of less.

KENNETH M. POLLACK is Senior Fellow and Director of Research at the Saban Center for Middle East Policy at the Brookings Institution. This article originally appeared in the July/August 2003 issue of *Foreign Affairs*.

For example, Iran's naval threat to Persian Gulf shipping in the 1980s was easy to handle, because the vast preponderance of power enjoyed by U.S. naval and air forces enabled a relatively small military campaign to achieve the desired effect. Similarly, although the air and ground threat from Saddam's Iraq eventually required a pair of much greater efforts to eliminate it, in essence it too was a relatively straightforward military problem. The threats that the United States and its allies will confront in the future, however, are unlikely to be as simple or discrete as these. The Bush administration must therefore start thinking now about how to counter them, or risk leaving the United States ill prepared for what it will encounter down the road.

IT'S THE OIL, STUPID

AMERICA'S PRIMARY INTEREST in the Persian Gulf lies in ensuring the free and stable flow of oil from the region to the world at large. This fact has nothing to do with the conspiracy theories leveled against the Bush administration during the run-up to the recent war. U.S. interests do not center on whether gas is $2 or $3 at the pump, or whether Exxon gets contracts instead of Lukoil or Total. Nor do they depend on the amount of oil that the United States itself imports from the Persian Gulf or anywhere else. The reason the United States has a legitimate and critical interest in seeing that Persian Gulf oil continues to flow copiously and relatively cheaply is simply that the global economy built over the last 50 years rests on a foundation of inexpensive, plentiful oil, and if that foundation were removed, the global economy would collapse.

Today, roughly 25 percent of the world's oil production comes from the Persian Gulf, with Saudi Arabia alone responsible for roughly 15 percent—a figure expected to increase rather than decrease in the future. The Persian Gulf region has as much as two-thirds of the world's proven oil reserves, and its oil is absurdly economical to produce, with a barrel from Saudi Arabia costing anywhere from a fifth to a tenth of the price of a barrel from Russia. Saudi Arabia is not only the world's largest oil producer and the holder of the world's largest oil reserves, but it also has a majority of the world's excess production capacity, which the Saudis use to stabilize and control the price of oil by increasing or decreasing production as needed. Because of the importance of both Saudi production and Saudi slack capacity, the sudden loss of the Saudi oil network would paralyze the global economy, probably causing a global downturn at least as devastating as the Great Depression of the 1930s, if not worse. So the fact that the United States does not import most of its oil from the Persian Gulf is irrelevant: if Saudi oil production were to vanish, the price of oil in general would shoot through the ceiling, destroying the American economy along with everybody else's.

But the United States is not simply concerned with keeping oil flowing out of the Persian Gulf; it also has an interest in preventing any potentially hostile state from gaining control over the region and is resources and using such control to amass vast power or blackmail the world. And it has an interest in maintaining military access to the Persian Gulf because of the region's geostrategically critical location, near the Middle East, Central Asia, eastern Africa, and South Asia. If the United States were denied access to the Persian Gulf, its ability to influence events in many other key regions of the world would be greatly diminished. (Much of the air war against Afghanistan, for example, was mounted from bases in the Persian Gulf.) The tragedy of September 11, 2001, finally, has demonstrated that the United States also has an interest in stamping out the terrorist groups that flourish in the region.

TRIPLE THREAT

THE THREE MAIN PROBLEMS likely to bedevil Persian Gulf security over the next several years will be Iraq's security dilemma, Iran's nuclear weapons program, and potential internal unrest in the countries of the Gulf Cooperation Council (GCC): Bahrain, Kuwait, Oman, Qatar, Saudi Arabia, and the United Arab Emirates. Unfortunately, there are no easy answers to these problems separately, let alone together, and so difficult tradeoffs will have to be made.

The paradox of Iraqi power can be put simply: any Iraq that is strong enough to balance and contain Iran will inevitably be capable of overrunning Kuwait and Saudi Arabia. This was the problem the region faced at the end of the Iran-Iraq War, when Iraq's destruction of the Iranian army and air force left it in a position to conquer Kuwait and threaten Saudi oil fields soon afterward. The recent American victory over Saddam will do little to affect this basic dynamic, because it stems less from the nature of Iraq's leadership than from simple geopolitics. Like postwar Germany and Japan, post-Saddam Iraq will almost certainly be forbidden from developing weapons of mass destruction (WMD) ever again. But it will still have to find some way of protecting itself from a real, albeit distant, threat from Iran. If Iraq is not going to be allowed to possess WMD, then it will have to obtain some kind of credible external security guarantee or maintain substantial—and threatening—conventional military capabilities.

As for Iran, according to the latest estimates of U.S. intelligence and even of the International Atomic Energy Agency, its nuclear program has gone into overdrive and unless stopped— from inside or outside—is likely to produce one or more nuclear weapons within a decade. (Of course, the mistaken estimates of Iraq's nuclear program over the last 20 years reinforce the uncertainty underlying all such assessments.) In the case of Iraq, preemptive intervention was a thinkable (and ultimately doable) option because the United States could invade and occupy the country without a massive mobilization. But that is simply not true in the case of Iran. Its population is three times the size of Iraq's, its landmass is four times the size, its terrain is difficult and would make operations a logistical nightmare, and its population has generally rallied around the regime in the face of foreign threats. Invading Iran would be such a major undertaking that the option is essentially unthinkable in all but the most extraordinary circumstances.

Of course, it is possible that the Iranian nuclear problem might solve itself. The Iranian people are deeply unhappy with the reactionary clerics who cling to power in Tehran, and since 1997, they have voted consistently and overwhelmingly against the hard-liners. Moreover, Iran's population is very young, and the Iranian youth most strongly oppose the current regime and favor a more democratic system of government. Thus time is on the side of Iran's reformers. What's more, most Iranian reformers have expressed an interest in good relations with the United States.

All this matters because although the United States preaches a policy of universal nuclear nonproliferation, in practice, Washington has consistently, and probably correctly, been much more concerned with proliferation by its enemies (such as Iraq and North Korea) than by its friends (such as Israel and, to a lesser extent, India). American fears about Iran's nuclear program might well be lessened, therefore, by the emergence of a pluralist and pro-American government in Tehran (although even then Iranian nuclear advances would cause a major headache because of their inevitable effects on proliferation elsewhere in the region).

The problem is that no one can be certain that the reformers will triumph in Iran or, if so, when. In particular, it is not clear that the hard-liners will fall before Iran has obtained nuclear weapons. It is thus only prudent to assume that Iran will acquire nuclear weapons while its hard-line clerics are still in power, and so the United States must be prepared for that contingency. But the very actions that might be indicated in such circumstances—continued diplomatic and economic pressure, an aggressive military posture on Iran's borders, even threats to use force—could easily backfire in the maelstrom of Iranian domestic politics in ways that undermine or forestall the prospects for a "velvet revolution" in Tehran. Iran's hard-liners maintain power in part by stoking popular fears that the United States seeks to rule the country and control its policies, and so aggressive containment or active counterproliferation measures could play right into their hands. The Iranian paradox, in other words, is that preparing to deal with the worst-case scenario of Iranian hard-liners possessing nuclear weapons might very well make that scenario more likely.

Tehran appears to want nuclear weapons principally to deter an American attack. Once it gets them, however, its strategic calculus might change and it might be emboldened to pursue a more aggressive foreign policy. Iran's armed forces are still too weak to contemplate either a ground advance through Iraq into the Arabian Peninsula or an amphibious operation across the Persian Gulf, and they will remain so for a while. So the risk is not so much conventional military invasion as attempts to shut down tanker traffic in the Strait of Hormuz as a method of blackmail or foment insurrections in neighboring countries. Unfortunately, the security posture that would best deter future Iranian aggression—sizable American forces dispersed throughout the Persian Gulf—is the worst option of all from the perspective of dealing with the third major problem, terrorism and internal instability in the states of the GCC.

Terrorism and internal instability in the Persian Gulf are ultimately fueled by the political, economic, and social stagnation of the local Arab states. It is true that American policies anger many Arabs and that the Palestinian issue is a matter of great popular concern. But these are not really what creates fertile ground for domestic insurrection or the recruitment efforts of radical Islamist groups such as al Qaeda. What is more important is that too many Arabs are unemployed or underemployed because of the utter failure of their economic systems. Too many feel powerless and humiliated by despotic governments that do less and less for them while preventing them from having any say in their own governance. And too many feel both threatened and stifled within a society that cannot come to grips with modernity.

Most Middle East experts think that a revolution or civil war in any of the GCC states within the next few years is unlikely, but few say so now as confidently as they once did. In fact, even the Persian Gulf regimes themselves are increasingly fearful of their mounting internal turmoil, something that has prompted all of them to announce democratic and economic reform packages at some point during the last ten years. From Crown Prince Abdullah of Saudi Arabia to the emir of Qatar to the new king of Bahrain, the Persian Gulf rulers recognize the pressure building among their populations and the need to let off some of the steam. If the reforms do not succeed and revolution or civil war ensues, the United States might face some very difficult security challenges. Widespread unrest in Saudi Arabia, for example, would threaten Saudi oil exports just as surely as an Iranian invasion.

The best way for the United States to address the rise of terrorism and the threat of internal instability in Saudi Arabia and the other GCC states would be to reduce its military presence in the region to the absolute minimum, or even to withdraw entirely. The presence of American troops fuels the terrorists' propaganda claims that the United States seeks to prop up the hated local tyrants and control the Middle East. And it is a source of humiliation and resentment for pretty much all locals—a constant reminder that the descendants of the great Islamic empires can no longer defend themselves and must answer to infidel powers. So pulling back would diminish the internal pressure on the Persian Gulf regimes and give them the political space they need to enact the painful reforms that are vital to their long-term stability. But such a withdrawal, in turn, would be the worst move from the perspective of deterring and containing Iran—or of being in a good position to respond swiftly to, say, a civil war in Saudi Arabia should one ever emerge.

Given these conundrums, finding a workable new security architecture for the Persian Gulf will be far from easy. Iraq must be kept strong but not too strong. Iran must be kept in check while being pushed to liberalize. The governments of the GCC states must be given breathing room to reform but still be protected from their external and internal enemies. Balancing these various interests, threats, and constraints will be difficult, so much so that it would not be surprising if the next American strategy for doing so ultimately failed, just as the previous ones did. Still, the situation is not entirely hopeless. There may not be a silver bullet, a perfect policy that secures every interest and counters every threat while avoiding all the strategic, political, and cultural minefields. But three broad approaches—pulling back "over the horizon," trying to form a local NATO-like defense pact, or trying to establish a security condominium—have enough merits to be considered seriously.

BACK OVER THE HORIZON

THE MOST CONSERVATIVE approach to Persian Gulf security would be to return to the initial American strategy of offshore balancing. When tried in the 1970s and 1980s, this approach failed because Iran and Iraq were still quite strong and the United States' over-the-horizon posture was not a sufficient deterrent. Today, however, Iran and Iraq are much weaker and are likely to remain so (at least until Iran acquires nuclear weapons). Washington, meanwhile, has repeatedly demonstrated that it will intervene in the Persian Gulf to protect its interests and prevent aggression. So the strategy might work better this time around.

Securing the Gulf

In this approach, the United States would dramatically reduce its military footprint in the region, leaving only the bare minimum of the current arrangements in place. The headquarters of the 5th Fleet would remain in Bahrain (where a U.S. Navy flag has been welcome for 50 years), but fewer American warships would ply the waters of the Gulf. The air force would retain its huge new base at al Udeid in Qatar, again because the Qataris seem pleased to have it there. The army might keep some prepositioned equipment in Kuwait and Qatar and might regularly rotate in battalions to train on it—if those states were comfortable with such guests. In addition, if a future Iraqi government were amenable, the United States might retain an air base and some ground presence there. Alternately, army bases in the region might be dispensed with altogether, and instead the United States could simply rely on equipment stored on container ships stationed at Diego Garcia, in the Indian Ocean.

On the political level, the United States would preserve its informal relationships with the GCC states and possibly add a similar association with a friendly new Iraqi government. It would continue to contain Iran by making clear that any Iranian aggression would be met by an American military response. And it would continue its efforts to secure European, Japanese, and Russian support in pressuring Tehran both economically and diplomatically so as to end Iran's support for terror and its unconventional weapons programs.

This smaller military footprint would go a long way toward alleviating the internal problems caused by the presence of U.S. combat forces in the Persian Gulf region—so not surprisingly, this is the strategy that the Gulf Arabs themselves favor. With Saddam gone, their overriding goal now is to minimize domestic discontent, and they believe that the United States can keep peace in the region with a minimal presence. This approach would also be popular in certain quarters of the American military, which would be glad to shed the burdens of policing an inhospitable and less than luxurious region far from home.

On the other hand, the mere fact that the Persian Gulf states are so enamored of this strategy ought to give American planners pause. With the exception of Kuwait after the Iraqi invasion, most of these countries have shown a distressing determination over the years to ignore their problems—both external and internal—rather than confront them. Although returning to a mostly over-the-horizon presence could provide the Persian Gulf states with the leeway they need to push through reforms, it is equally likely that they will see the withdrawal of U.S. forces as a panacea for all their problems and decide that internal reforms are therefore unnecessary. A reduced U.S. military and political presence, in turn, would weaken Washington's ability to press its local allies to make the tough choices they need to for their own long-term well-being.

A return to an over-the-horizon posture would also risk re-creating some of the same problems that made the strategy untenable the first time around. If Iran were to acquire nuclear weapons, a minimal American presence in the region might tempt it to new aggression. The GCC countries have often shown a willingness to accommodate powerful, aggressive neighbors, and a reduced American presence could increase their willingness to do so again—giving Iran, say, an unhealthy degree of control over oil flows. Finally, a limited American presence might tempt other outside powers—such as China—to fish in the Gulf's troubled waters at some point down the road.

A MIDDLE EASTERN NATO

A SECOND APPROACH to securing the Persian Gulf would be to create a new regional defense alliance of the kind that worked so well in Europe during the Cold War. This approach has an even worse reputation in the region than offshore balancing, but it is somewhat undeserved. In 1954, the United States convinced Iran, Iraq, Pakistan, Turkey, and the United Kingdom to sign the Baghdad Pact, pledging them to mutual defense. Four years later, Iraq withdrew, leaving Iran, Pakistan, and Turkey to form the Central Treaty Organization, which became little more than a vehicle for the United States to arm the shah of Iran for the next 20 years. These alliances performed poorly because their members had widely divergent security problems (Pakistan was concerned with India, Turkey with Russia and Greece, and Iran with the Middle East) and because of the revolutions in Iraq in 1958 and Iran in 1979, which knocked out the central players. In today's circumstances, a regional alliance would stand a better chance of succeeding.

Securing the Gulf

The idea would be for the United States to establish a formal defense alliance with the GCC states and a new government of Iraq. To paraphrase Lord Ismay's famous quip about NATO, the goal would be to keep the Americans in, the Iranians out, and the Iraqis down. A formal defense pledge would be the best way to lock in an unflinching American commitment to the security of the region; would serve as the best deterrent to outright Iranian aggression; and, by extending a security guarantee to Iraq, would effectively solve Baghdad's security dilemma as well, providing a benign framework for Iraq's conventional rearmament while obviating the need for it to acquire WMD to deter Iran. As a bonus, if Persian Gulf publics could be convinced that American forces were there as part of a community of equals, such an arrangement might also help legitimize the U.S. presence in the region. Such an alliance should be more viable than its predecessors, meanwhile, because the GCC states and Iraq share the same primary external security threat: Iran.

Still, this approach also has its drawbacks. In particular, the GCC states do not actually want a formal alliance relationship with the United States, at least not at the moment. Gcc leaders fear that far from legitimizing an American presence, such an alliance would be seen as the ultimate act of colonialism and cronyism and would thus help to delegitimize their own regimes. Even a very pro-American Iraqi government might be uneasy with a formal treaty relationship, for similar reasons. It is also unclear how such an alliance system could address the threat of domestic instability in the GCC. Because of the weakness of its armed forces, if Tehran does ever decide to pursue a more aggressive policy, it is more likely to try to undermine its neighbors from within than attack them directly from without. And despite its fearsome punching power, a Persian Gulf alliance would still be vulnerable to an enemy that hits below the belt.

A GULF SECURITY CONDOMINIUM

IF A RETURN to offshore balancing might be inadequate to deal with external aggression and a new alliance system might be inadequate to deal with internal instability, a third course offers the tantalizing prospect of handling both problems simultaneously.

This approach would have the United States pursue a security condominium for the Persian Gulf, modeled on the arms control experiences in Europe at the end of the Cold War.

Beginning in the 1970s, NATO and the Warsaw Pact engaged in a host of security engagement forums, confidence-building measures, and arms control agreements (such as the Commission on Security and Cooperation in Europe, the Mutual and Balanced Force Reductions talks, and the Treaty on Conventional Forces in Europe) that were intended to deal with all of the continent's various security issues as a whole. Negotiating these deals took over two decades of painful wrangling. But in the end, they produced a Europe that was much more stable and secure than ever before.

In the Persian Gulf, such a security condominium would entail a similar set of activities bringing together the United States, the GCC countries, Iraq, and Iran. The process would begin by establishing a regional security forum at which relevant issues could be debated and discussed, information exchanged, and agreements framed. The members could then move on to confidence-building measures, such as notification of exercises, exchanges of observers, and information swaps. Ultimately, the intention would be to proceed to eventual arms control agreements that might include demilitarized zones, bans on destabilizing weapons systems, and balanced force reductions for all parties. In particular, the group might aim for a ban on all WMD, complete with penalties for violators and a multilateral (or international) inspection program to enforce compliance.

Such an approach has a lot to recommend it. It would be the least rancorous way to handle the inevitable prohibition on Iraqi WMD, for example. Framing the ban within a larger process in which all of the regional states were working toward similar disarmament and Iraq was simply the one leading off would help the pill go down more easily in Baghdad. Likewise, for the GCC states, if a regional security condominium succeeded in eventually defanging Iran and locking in limitations on Iraq, it would address their security problems without having to rely on a heavy, destabilizing American military presence. Moreover, U.S.-GCC military relations might be more agreeable to the Persian Gulf populations if they took place within the rubric of a regionwide forum.

Another advantage would be that the Iranians might actually be willing to participate. For 20 years, Iran has demanded that the United States, Iraq, and the GCC take its security concerns seriously, and this process would grant Iran a venue and an opportunity to discuss those concerns for the first time. Inviting Iran to discuss security issues in the Persian Gulf at the same table with the United States would give Tehran the sense that it was finally getting the respect from Washington that it believes it deserves. More to the point, such a process is the only possible way that Iran could affect the military forces of its toughest opponent, the United States. For such a system to work, Washington would have to be willing, as it was in Europe, to agree to limitations on its regional deployments. Such limitations by themselves might be worth the price of admission for Iran.

Even if the hard-liners in Tehran opted not to participate, that would not be a disaster, since they would likely isolate themselves both internally and internationally as a result. At home, it would be very difficult for them to justify any action based on a supposed threat from the United States (or Iraq or the GCC) if they were unwilling to participate in a process in which they would have the opportunity to address that threat through diplomacy and arms control. To foreign audiences, meanwhile, Tehran's refusal to accept such an olive branch from the United States would demonstrate that Iran was a pariah state uninterested in peaceful means of addressing its security concerns. This, in turn, would make it easier for Washington to muster international support for tighter sanctions and other forms of pressure.

Some might oppose such a system for fear that it would legitimize the current Iranian government. But it need not do so unduly, and it would not stand in the way of regime change if that was where political development in Iran seemed to be heading. After all, a similar process did not impede regime change in Russia and Eastern Europe.

The real problem with this approach is that such a regional security condominium might be impossible to achieve. It is worth remembering that in Europe it took between 20 and 25 years of excruciating negotiations to produce a workable system. The United States has had agonizing experiences negotiating multilateral agreements in the Middle East, and there is no reason to believe this one will be any easier. All of the parties will come to the table with their own agendas and will attempt to subvert or structure the process to address only those issues that interest them. One of the dirty little secrets of the Persian Gulf is that GCC unity is a fiction: the Qataris want American military bases not to shield them from Iran or Iraq but to deter Saudi Arabia. Likewise, Bahrain wants powerful missiles not to make it an effective member of the Peninsula Shield Force but so that it can strike Qatar if it ever feels the need. A regional security forum coupled with arms control measures could bring out all of these intra-GCC insecurities, further complicating the process.

The Iranians, meanwhile, might try to scuttle the entire effort by demanding Israel's inclusion, a call that would have tremendous resonance among the Arab populations of the Persian Gulf. Bringing Israel into such a system would mean saddling the Persian Gulf security system with the additional problems and endless disputes of the Arab-Israeli peace process and the Middle East as a whole, which would clearly be impractical.

Still, if it could somehow be made to work, a regional security condominium would offer the best prospect of creating a stable, secure Persian Gulf. But making it work will be quite a feat and take years, if not decades. The United States should thus enshrine this as its ultimate goal and start moving in that direction promptly. The mere process of announcing it as Washington's intention and convening a conference on Persian Gulf security, in fact, could have powerful positive effects, legitimizing the U.S. presence in the region and discrediting those who oppose it.

A condominium, however, should not become the sole focus of American efforts to create a new security architecture in the region, because better solutions are needed for the more immediate term. In truth, the three models proposed above are not mutually exclusive and perhaps might most usefully be seen as steps in an ongoing process. The United States could make some moves today to diminish force levels in accord with the offshore balancing approach. Meanwhile, it could begin exploring the possibility of either a new alliance system in the region or the inauguration of a process to construct a security condominium. Indeed, the threat of a new U.S.-GCC-Iraqi alliance might be another powerful incentive for Iran to participate in a security condominium, whereas the articulation of such a goal might make an alliance more acceptable to the GCC states. Ultimately, if the security condominium succeeds, peace is maintained, and forces throughout the region are considerably reduced, the road may be clear for a truly over-the-horizon American presence in the Persian Gulf—a development that would be greatly welcomed by all concerned.🌀

Korea's Place in the Axis

Victor D. Cha

METHOD OR MADNESS?

ON JANUARY 29, President George W. Bush announced what seemed a new U.S. policy toward the Korean Peninsula—and threw observers worldwide into confusion. In his state of the union address that night, Bush outlined the steps to come in his administration's "war on terrorism." Among them was a tough new approach to what he termed an "axis of evil": North Korea, Iraq, and Iran.

The president's speech seemed, at first, to bring new clarity to the U.S. security agenda, signaling the high priority the administration placed on countering links between terrorists and rogue nations that seek chemical, biological, or nuclear weapons to threaten the United States and the world. The only problem was that, at least with respect to North Korea, this new posture seemed to contradict the strategy suggested by the Bush administration seven months earlier. In June 2001, a comprehensive policy review authorized by the White House had recommended that Washington hold unconditional talks with Pyongyang on a wide range of issues, including the posture of North Korea's conventional military, its ballistic missile program, and its suspected nuclear weapons program.

This recommendation, in turn, had been at odds with a previous set of Bush remarks on the subject. In March 2001, he had

VICTOR D. CHA holds the D.S. Song-Korea Foundation Chair in Asian Studies in the Department of Government and the Edmund Walsh School of Foreign Service, Georgetown University. This article originally appeared in the May/June 2002 issue of *Foreign Affairs*.

scorned the "sunshine," or engagement, policy of South Korea's president, Kim Dae Jung, and expressed skepticism about North Korea's supposedly peaceful intentions. And these remarks, finally, had broken with still another proclamation of U.S. policy—this one by Secretary of State Colin Powell, who had announced earlier the same month that the Bush administration intended to pick up negotiations with North Korea where the Clinton administration had left off.

In light of these zigzags, it is hardly surprising that Bush's state of the union address caused a lot of head-scratching. And indeed, several months afterward, for many the question remains: Does the administration know what it is doing on North Korea? Does it actually have any policy at all, or is the topic a football grabbed by whichever internal faction has the president's ear at a particular moment?

These questions are of more than bureaucratic interest, for a confluence of trends suggests that the situation on the Korean Peninsula will not remain quiet for long. U.S. relations with North Korea are currently guided by the 1994 Agreed Framework, in which Washington offered heavy fuel oil and help building nuclear energy plants in exchange for Pyongyang's promise to shut down its nuclear weapons program. This agreement is about to reach its critical implementation stages, testing the intentions of both countries and sparking debates within the United States over whether it should revise or abandon the accord. Engagement, meanwhile, has already become a hotly contested issue in South Korea, where the upcoming presidential election in December 2002 has led to acerbic criticism of Kim Dae Jung's policy by his most prominent harder-line opponent, Lee Hoi Chang. Complicating matters still further, normalization talks between Japan and North Korea have remained frozen since the winter of 2000, and Pyongyang's rhetoric about Tokyo is growing ever more aggressive. International aid workers are projecting another food shortage in North Korea, just as donor fatigue is setting in. And most ominously, North Korean leader Kim Jong Il's self-imposed moratorium on ballistic missile tests also ends this December. Experts argue that the North is most belligerent when it has nothing to lose. If they are right, some kind of crisis looks likely on the Korean Peninsula, and so having a clear and well-thought-out policy in place could be critical.

Bush's critics argue that there is a serious gap between the new "axis of evil" language and the substance of U.S. policy toward North Korea. At best, they argue, the divide reflects Bush's unwillingness to admit openly that Bill Clinton's effort to engage Kim Jong Il made sense. At worst, the "axis of evil" puts the administration on a collision course with North Korea during the second phase of the war on terror.

In fact, however, the critics are wrong on both counts. The president's speech involved neither the unceremonious dumping of the engagement strategy nor a simple desire to distinguish himself from Clinton while actually following in his footsteps. A close reading of the state of the union address and other administration moves suggests that the Bush team is stumbling, in its own peculiar way, toward an approach to North Korea that is neither the twin nor the opposite of his predecessor's, but rather a buffed-up cousin. And when the dust settles, most people—including the administration, its critics, and the general public—might just realize how well-suited this strategy is to the complex realities of North Korea.

"Hawk engagement," as one might call the administration's developing approach, differs from traditional models more in its philosophy than in its practice. It certainly stands apart from South Korea's sunshine policy, but less by its short-term execution than by its assumptions, rationales, and potential endgames. Kim Dae Jung, as well as some Clinton officials, sees engagement as a way to build transparency and confidence and reduce insecurity. Hawk engagement, on the other hand, is based on the idea that engagement lays the groundwork for punitive action. Hawks are skeptical that North Korea can be induced to cooperate but are willing to use engagement to call Pyongyang's bluff. The goal of the sunshine policy, furthermore, is limited to achieving peaceful coexistence between the two Koreas. Hawk engagement, in contrast, offers a true vision of how to shape the future of the Korean Peninsula in a way that best suits America's larger strategic interests—both during unification and beyond.

HAWK ENGAGEMENT

THE BUSH TEAM claims that there are five elements in its new policy that are distinct from Clinton's: insistence on improved implementation of the Agreed Framework; verifiable controls on the North's missile production and exports; a way to address the posture of conventional forces; a demand for reciprocal gestures in return for compromises with the North; and close coordination with allies. Only one of these components—the focus on conventional forces—is actually new. All the others had been discussed by Clinton's Korea policy blueprint (created by former Defense Secretary William Perry in October 1999) and in the Republicans' own blueprint (penned by Richard Armitage, now deputy secretary of state, in March 1999). But there are other differences between Bush's view of North Korea and Clinton's that are even more important.

Bush's emerging strategy of hawk engagement can best be understood by juxtaposing it with the standard rationale for engagement with the North, exemplified by Kim Dae Jung's sunshine policy. Kim's strategy rests on the idea that North Korea's threatening posture arises from insecurity. Abandoned by its Cold War patrons, economically bankrupt, politically isolated, and starving, North Korea sees the pursuit of nuclear weapons and ballistic missiles as its only path to security and survival. Engagement can reduce this insecurity and end the proliferation threat. Various carrots—economic aid, normalized relations, reduced security tensions—are supposed to give Kim Jong Il a stake in the status quo and persuade him that he can best serve his own interests by giving up on the pursuit of dangerous new weapons.

Hawk engagement breaks with this logic in several respects. It acknowledges that diplomacy can be helpful, but sees the real value of engagement as a way to expose the North's true, malevolent intentions—thought to include not just the desire to develop nuclear, biological, and chemical weapons, but ultimately to expel U.S. forces from the peninsula, overthrow the regime in Seoul, and reunify Korea under communist rule. Hawk engagement aims to thwart these goals by dealing with Pyongyang in the near term but also laying the groundwork for punitive actions against it later on.

Supporters of the sunshine policy view engagement as the best way to discern and improve the intentions of the reclusive Kim Jong Il today. Hawks, however, see engagement as the best practical way to build a coalition for punishment tomorrow. Such a coalition is critical to putting effective pressure on the North, but maintaining it will require its members to agree that every opportunity to resolve the problem in a nonconfrontational manner has been exhausted.

Recent history shows just how important it is to assemble and maintain such regional support for action on North Korea. In 1994, when the North refused to comply with international inspections of its nuclear facilities, the United States sought to impose sanctions on it. But the sanctions were resisted, not only by China (which would have vetoed any attempt to impose them through the UN Security Council), but also by Japan, which was reluctant to curb remittances to the North from Koreans in Japan and argued that such a coercive strategy was premature.

Hawk engagement provides a way to convince allies that noncoercive strategies have already been tried—and failed. As the Armitage report explains, "the failure of enhanced diplomacy should be demonstrably attributable to Pyongyang."

Hawk engagement would also let the United States turn today's carrots into effective sticks for tomorrow. Merely continuing to impose the more than 50-year-old embargo on North Korea, for example, is unlikely to lead to a change in its behavior. Were Washington to lift sanctions, however—letting the North get a taste for what it could gain by cooperating—then a threat to reinstate the sanctions would likely have a much more dramatic effect. Indeed, this pattern has already played out at least once. In June 1999, North Korea detained on spy charges a citizen from the South who was visiting Mount Kumgang as part of a new inter-Korean joint tourist venture conducted by Hyundai, a South Korean conglomerate. Seoul retaliated by suspending further tours. These tours, however, represented a new and substantial source of hard currency for the North. Pyongyang quickly realized that the propaganda value of capturing a supposed spy from the South was vastly outweighed by the cash these tours were generating—and sheepishly released the tourist after soliciting a token confession. The Hyundai tour, formerly a carrot to get the North to engage, had become an effective stick with which to influence Pyongyang's behavior.

HELPING HANDS

HAWK ENGAGEMENT not only endorses such joint ventures, albeit for different reasons than those of more optimistic North Korea watchers, but it also embraces humanitarian aid—again for its own reasons rather than the standard ones. Aid groups normally view engagement as a necessary evil: one must tolerate Kim Jong Il's regime in order to help his suffering population. Hard-liners, however, look beyond the immediate effects of providing piecemeal aid to relieve short-term hardship. Hawks recognize that aid can act as investment in the will of the North Korean people to fight their regime.

Humanitarian assistance can do this in two ways. First, it can hasten the government's demise. North Korea currently faces the same dilemma regarding reform as have other illiberal regimes in the post–Cold War era. These countries need to open up in order to survive. Yet opening up can unleash forces that the government may not be able to control, and that may ultimately lead to its overthrow. Hence aid to North Korea, provided in conjunction with engagement mechanisms like the Agreed Framework, inter-Korean trade, tourism, and investment, can all help nudge the North down the slippery slope of political reform. This strategy may seem to improve the North's economic situation in the short term, but it can also create a dangerous "spiral of expectations" among the North Korean populace. And as history has shown, revolutions in repressive states generally occur not when conditions are at their worst, but once they begin to improve.

The provision of humanitarian aid can also help prepare for Korean unification by winning over the hearts and minds of Northerners.

Hard-liners have traditionally held that hostility toward and isolation of the North is the most direct route toward ensuring its collapse and absorption. But this overlooks what will perhaps be the most important factor in the success of reunification: the North Korean people. The conventional wisdom is that after the repressive regime falls, North Koreans will look to Southerners as their saviors and elder siblings. This overly optimistic view, however, underestimates the degree of enmity, confusion, and distrust between the two countries, and the amount of blood they have shed fighting one another. A policy of hard-line coercion and isolation that drove Pyongyang into the ground would only make matters worse, frightening the populace and reinforcing decades of demonization by Pyongyang of Washington and Seoul.

Engagement and aid, on the other hand, convey a more compassionate image of Americans and South Koreans. As Bush stated at this February's summit in Seoul, although Washington despises Kim Jong Il's despotic regime, it has "great sympathy and empathy for the North Korean people. We want them to have food. And at the same time, we want them to have freedom." The presence of sacks of food scattered around North Korea imprinted with "United States," "Republic of Korea," and "Government of Japan" would reinforce that message. Although coercion has traditionally been more attractive to hawks, since it seems the fastest route to the North's capitulation, engagement will better prepare for the hawks' desired objective: the reunification of the Korean Peninsula.

PEACE THROUGH STRENGTH

ANOTHER WAY hawk engagement differs from more traditional approaches to North Korea is by being compatible with missile defense. Critics argue that the Bush administration's unswerving enthusiasm for developing and deploying ballistic-missile defense systems is wholly at odds with a policy of engaging North Korea. How, they argue, can you talk peace and prepare for war at the same time?

Such criticism ignores the fact that missile defense can actually strengthen the credibility of engagement strategies. After all, engagement is most effective when undergirded by robust defensive capabilities. This demonstrates to an adversary that the decision to engage is the choice of the strong, not the expedient of the weak—and that other, more aggressive, options exist. Progress on missile defenses would only enhance this logic by further boosting the United States' defensive power. On this point, the Armitage report was very clear: "One cannot expect North Korea to take U.S. diplomacy seriously unless we demonstrate unambiguously that the United States is prepared to bolster its ... military posture."

By pursuing both engagement and missile defense simultaneously, Washington can encourage Pyongyang's better behavior and also neutralize Kim Jong Il's one strong card: his ballistic missiles and the threat they pose to other countries in the region. Of course, questions remain as to technological feasibility and the type of defensive system that could best handle the North's missile threat while incurring the fewest negative consequences. But the larger point remains that engagement and missile defense are compatible—and complementary. Neither option is sufficient: deploying only missile defense systems would do little to solve the peninsula's tensions, whereas engagement alone would remain vulnerable to future acts of brinkmanship by Pyongyang. By pursuing missile defense, finally, the Bush administration also ensures that engagement will not be interpreted as appeasement or capitulation by critics at home or in Seoul.

The last distinct principle of hawk engagement is its insistence on the exchange of tangible compromises. This emphasis was demonstrated by Bush's inclusion of conventional force reductions on the bilateral agenda with North Korea. Although mentioned by earlier U.S. policy proposals on North Korea, the issue had never been given much attention before. By giving it much more prominence now, Bush has made clear his intent to test the seriousness of Pyongyang's supposed desire to improve relations.

Underlying the decision to put force reduction on the agenda is the hawkish belief that Pyongyang has thus far not really conceded much that it truly values. Most negotiations until now have required the North to make only potential, rather than actual, sacrifices. The missile talks at the end of the Clinton administration, for example, included a North Korean promise to give up future production, testing, and export of Taepo-Dong missiles in exchange for compensation from the United States—but would not have affected Kim Jong Il's currently deployed No-Dong missiles. Forcing Pyongyang to limit its conventional forces in exchange for engagement would truly test the regime's resolve, by targeting assets that Kim greatly values.

The emphasis on real, not hypothetical, quid pro quos can also be seen in the administration's behavior toward North Korea in the context of the new war on terror. The White House's tepid response to Pyongyang's signing of two UN antiterrorism conventions in the aftermath of September 11 offers a good example. Advocates of traditional engagement would have interpreted such moves as earnest signs of North Korea's willingness to improve ties. But hawks in the administration are holding out for more concrete and verifiable steps.

STANDING ON SHOULDERS

IF HAWK ENGAGEMENT makes such sense, why was it not employed by the Clinton administration first? The answer is not that Clinton was naive or lacked the necessary moral fortitude, as some Republicans like to argue. Proponents of engagement under Clinton understood the policy implications very well. Nonetheless, Bush, for several reasons, is in a better position than was his predecessor to wield engagement as a both a carrot and a powerful stick.

Ironically, this flexibility is largely due to the success of Clinton's engagement and South Korea's sunshine policy. These measures provided Pyongyang with new benefits (such as food, energy, and hard currency) that Bush can now implicitly threaten to withdraw. By contrast, when Clinton started making overtures to the North in 1994, there were no antecedents (in terms of tangible benefits) on which he could build or existing perks he could threaten to cut. The policy that Republicans once so vehemently criticized, in other words, has now enabled their hawkish version of engagement.

Another question is whether the Bush administration is any more ready than its predecessor was to use force against North Korea. If hawk engagement exposes the evil intentions of Pyongyang, what will follow? Bush officials, while insisting that their Korea policy is distinct from Clinton's, have so far refused to comment on what could be the greatest difference—that is, their willingness to use force if engagement fails. Given that eventuality, however, the White House would face three options.

If engagement reveals North Korea to be intractable, the most bloody and least desirable of Bush's strategies would be the actual use of force: a military campaign to coerce or terminate the regime in Pyongyang. Fighting could erupt once the North demonstrated its intention to build up its weapons despite the carrots offered, once it became clear to U.S. allies and regional powers that Washington had exhausted all avenues for cooperation, and once a coalition had been rallied for action. Responses could include preemptive military attacks, massive retaliatory strikes, the establishment of food distribution centers off North Korea's shores and borders, and guarantees of safe havens for refugees. This option implicitly assumes that early unification of the peninsula would be not a daunting cost to be avoided, but an investment in the future.

Washington's second alternative would be to face down the North with a strong show of American and allied resolve. This strategy would aim not to oust Kim Jong Il but simply to neutralize the threat posed by his weapons proliferation. Such a strategy, of course, would depend on the willingness of Pyongyang to cry uncle rather than go to war. This premise is by no means certain, however, for the North is not likely to remain passive if it decides it has nothing left to lose.

Bush's third option if Pyongyang calls his bluff would be "malign" neglect: an attempt to further isolate and contain the regime. Washington would rally Seoul, Tokyo, and other interested regional powers to push Pyongyang into a box and turn their backs on it—not relenting until Kim Jong Il gave up on his proliferation campaign. The United States and its allies would hem in North Korea militarily and intercept any vessels headed in or out of the country suspected of carrying nuclear- or missile-related material. To further weaken Pyongyang, Washington, Seoul, and Tokyo would also guarantee safe haven for refugees who made it out of the North, and would offer financial incentives to Moscow and Beijing to do the same. To ratchet up the pressure, the United States and South Korea could also reorient their military posture on the peninsula, focusing it more on long-range, deep-strike missions in the hope that this realignment would force the North into pulling back its offensive weapons so as to better defend the capital.

All three of these strategies share certain assumptions. First among them is the bet that either Pyongyang will cave in to pressure, or that Washington will have a coalition ready for coercion if it does not cave in. The second part of this wager—that the failure of a good-faith attempt to engage the North will make it easy for Washington to assemble a coalition—is plausible. The first, however, is less so. The Clinton administration seemed far more worried about it than the Bush team is, which raises the question of whether the current administration's assessment of North Korea is based on credible evidence—or merely wishful thinking.

FAST FORWARD

IF THE BUSH ADMINISTRATION is indeed set on pursuing hawk engagement, a number of implications follow. First, Washington will try to speed up the engagement process. Of course, this means getting Pyongyang to agree on an agenda for engagement, and that may not be easy. North Korea has already rejected several U.S. offers to resume talks, complaining that Washington is trying to unilaterally set the agenda and arguing that the United States should compensate it for the slow implementation of the Agreed Framework. Once negotiations do begin, however, the Americans can be expected to push for shorter timelines. Hawk engagement is more impatient than standard models. President Bush underscored this point in his state of the union speech, when he warned, "Time is not on our side. I will not wait on events while dangers gather. I will not stand by as perils draw closer and closer."

Standard engagement reasons that, with greater interaction, North Korea will slowly begin to open up and reform—and that Washington should therefore wait patiently for these changes to occur. Hawks, however, have much less faith in this outcome, and see engagement largely as an instrument for revealing Pyongyang's unreconstructed intentions. Given this lack of faith, ousting the communist regime before it can build up its arsenal further starts to seem like a much more urgent priority.

Washington can also be expected to have a low tolerance for Pyongyang's brinkmanship. This may be the biggest difference between hawk engagement and standard models in the short term. If the North decides to embark on a new round of belligerence, the United States may well choose to punish it. Standard models of engagement emphasize the importance of showing great patience for the target state and constantly sending it positive signals. This administration, however, is less likely to give Pyongyang the benefit of the doubt if it starts to misbehave..

If Pyongyang truly is intent on improving relations with Washington, it will have to bear the burden of proving its good faith—through concrete measures. North Korea will have to show skeptics in the administration that they were wrong to expect the worst. Here Japan and South Korea can play a valuable role, helping convince North Korea that it must move beyond smile summitry. Seoul can do so through the secret talks it conducts with Pyongyang. Tokyo can also help with measures such as technical assistance for international inspections of North Korea's suspected nuclear waste sites.

BEYOND THE PENINSULA

THE FINAL DIFFERENCE between hawk engagement and more traditional alternatives is that the hawkish model offers more than mere short-term policy prescriptions. Rather, it presumes a distinct view of how developments in Korea could best suit American interests, both toward reunification and beyond. Hawk engagement not only foresees reunification but accepts that it may pose real problems for the maintenance of America's long-term power and position in the region. A united Korea might be inhospitable to a continued U.S. military presence, might result in growing Chinese influence over the peninsula, and could lead to the political isolation of Japan in the region. Hawk engagement seeks to complement current Korea policy, therefore, with other policies designed to promote a more America-friendly post-unification environment. It is crucial, hawks believe, to promote stronger relations between the two main U.S. Asian allies, Japan and South Korea, and to consolidate the trilateral Washington-Tokyo-Seoul relationship.

To accomplish this goal, four tasks are necessary. The first is to use current tensions with North Korea to build security cooperation between Japan and South Korea. Throughout the 1990s, the threat of North Korean implosion or aggression drove the unprecedented security cooperation between the two nations, involving cabinet-level bilateral meetings, search-and-rescue exercises, port calls, noncombatant evacuation operations, and academic military exchanges—all despite the deep historical mistrust between Seoul and Tokyo. These formerly taboo activities (past South Korean presidents vowed never to engage in security cooperation with their one-time colonizer, Japan, even during the Cold War and despite the North Korean threat) built confidence and created an entirely new dimension to Seoul-Tokyo relations beyond political and economic ties.

The second task is to infuse the U.S.-Japan and U.S.-South Korea alliances with a meaning and identity larger than the Cold War. History shows that the most resilient alliances are those that share a common ideology that runs deeper than the shared external threats that brought the alliance into existence. Washington must therefore deepen its alliance with South Korea and Japan, moving it beyond its narrow anti–North Korea basis. Already the allies have started talking about "maintaining regional stability" as their broader purpose—but they can do better than that. A host of other shared values can be drawn on (such as common preferences for liberal democracy, open economic markets, nonproliferation, universal human rights, antiterrorism, and peacekeeping). Grounding the alliance on ideals, not just an outside threat, would not only give the relationships some permanence but would also prevent the alignments from being washed away by shifting geostrategic currents.

Washington's third long-term task is to somehow consolidate the trilateral U.S.–Japan–South Korea alliance as a way to reaffirm the U.S. presence in the region—without offering any unconditional security guarantees. The United States has always been the strongest advocate of better Japan–South Korea relations, but the likelihood of Seoul and Tokyo's responding positively to these American burden-sharing entreaties has been highest, counterintuitively, when Washington has been perceived as less interested in underwriting the region's security. The U.S. position in Asia should therefore be reduced enough to nudge the allies toward consolidating their relationship—but not reduced so much that Japan and South Korea choose self-help solutions outside the alliance framework. What this probably means in practice is a greatly reduced American troop presence but a maintenance of the nuclear umbrella over the region.

Washington's fourth task is to consolidate the trilateral alliance without irking China. Efforts at trilateral cooperation should be as low-profile and transparent to Beijing as possible. Seoul-Tokyo security cooperation, for example, should focus not on military assets, but rather on transport platforms (for preplanned disaster relief, for example). The United States, meanwhile, could also shift its military presence in the area to one based primarily on air and sea power, with less pre-positioning of materiel and fewer ground forces south of the 38th parallel.

ENDGAME

THE NORTH KOREAN regime under Kim Jong Il is despicable. Pyongyang starves its people, maintains gulags nightmarish even by Stalinist standards, and generally violates almost every value the United States and the free world claim to uphold. Given the war against terrorism, however, trying to topple Kim's regime directly would run counter to American interests. The attempt would distract the United States from its missions elsewhere, further complicate already fragile relations with China and Russia, and possibly suck the U.S. armed forces into another bloody quagmire.

But this does not mean that continuing the sunshine policy of engagement as practiced by the Kim Dae Jung and Clinton administrations is necessarily the best course to take. For all its apparent maladroitness, the Bush administration is groping toward a new version of engagement that might work better than its predecessor. This strategy would not use engagement without an exit strategy, but rather as an exit strategy. If the administration can articulate and implement its approach more coherently, it might just find that, over time, its critics will come to agree.

How to Deal With North Korea

James T. Laney and Jason T. Shaplen

MIXED MESSAGES

PROGRESS in reducing tensions on the Korean peninsula, never easy, has reached a dangerous impasse. The last six months have witnessed an extraordinary series of events in the region that have profound implications for security and stability throughout Northeast Asia, a region that is home to 100,000 U.S. troops and three of the world's 12 largest economies.

Perhaps the most dramatic of these events was North Korea's December decision to restart its frozen plutonium-based nuclear program at Yongbyon—including a reprocessing facility that separates plutonium for nuclear weapons from spent reactor fuel. Just as disturbing was the North's stunning public admission two months earlier that it had begun building a new, highly-enriched-uranium (HEU) nuclear program. And then came yet another unsettling development: a growing, sharp division emerged between the United States and the new South Korean government over how to respond.

But recent events have not been entirely negative. In the two months prior to the October HEU revelation, North Korea had, with remarkable speed, undertaken an important series of posi-

---

JAMES T. LANEY is President Emeritus of Emory University. He served as U.S. Ambassador to South Korea from 1993 to 1997. JASON T. SHAPLEN is Director of Project Renewal. This article originally appeared in the March/April 2003 issue of *Foreign Affairs*.

tive initiatives that seemed the polar opposite of its posturing on the nuclear issue. These included initiating an unscheduled meeting between its foreign minister, Paek Nam Sun, and Secretary of State Colin Powell in July—the highest-level contact between the two nations since the Bush administration took office; inviting a U.S. delegation for talks in Pyongyang; proposing the highest-level talks with South Korea in a year; agreeing to re-establish road and rail links with the South and starting work on the project almost immediately; demining portions of the demilitarized zone (DMZ) and wide corridors on the east and west coasts surrounding the rail links; sending more than 600 athletes and representatives to join the Asian Games in Pusan, South Korea (marking the North's first-ever participation in an international sporting event in the South); enacting a series of economic and market reforms (including increasing wages, allowing the price of staples to float freely, and inaugurating a special economic zone similar to those in China); restarting the highest-level talks with Japan in two years; holding a subsequent summit with Japanese Prime Minister Junichiro Koizumi, during which Pyongyang admitted abducting Japanese citizens in the 1970s and 1980s; and finally, allowing the surviving abductees to visit Japan.

Viewed individually, let alone together, North Korea's initiatives represented the most promising signs of change on the peninsula in decades. Whether by desire or by necessity, the North finally appeared to be responding to the long-standing concerns of the United States, South Korea, and Japan. Equally important, Pyongyang seemed to have abandoned its policy of playing Washington, Seoul, and Tokyo off one another by addressing the concerns of one while ignoring those of the other two. For the first time, the North was actively (even aggressively) engaging all three capitals simultaneously.

Until October, that is, when North Korea acknowledged the existence of its clandestine HEU program—ending the diplomatic progress instantly. Once the news broke, Pyongyang quickly offered to halt the HEU program in exchange for a nonaggression pact with the United States. But Washington, unwilling to reward bad behavior, initially refused to open a dialogue unless the North first abandoned its HEU effort. In November, the United States went a step further: saying that Pyongyang had violated the 1994 Agreed Framework and several other nuclear nonproliferation pacts, Washington engineered the suspension of deliveries of the 500,000 tons of heavy fuel oil sent to the North each year under the 1994 accord. The Agreed Framework had frozen the North's plutonium program—a program that had included a five-megawatt experimental reactor, two larger reactors under construction, and the reprocessing facility—narrowly averting a catastrophic war on the Korean Peninsula.

In the weeks following the suspension of fuel shipments, the United States hardened its stance against dialogue with the North—despite the fact that most U.S. allies were encouraging a diplomatic solution to the situation. North Korea responded by announcing plans to reopen its Yongbyon facilities. It immediately removed the seals and monitoring cameras from its frozen nuclear labs and reactors and, a few days later, began to move its dangerous spent fuel rods out of storage. Pyongyang subsequently announced its intention to reopen the critical reprocessing plant in February 2003. On December 31, it expelled the inspectors of the International Atomic Energy Agency (IAEA). And on January 9, it announced its withdrawal from the nuclear Nonproliferation Treaty.

Although Washington, strongly urged by Seoul and Tokyo, ultimately agreed to talks, the situation appeared to be worsening almost daily. Depending on how it is resolved, the standoff could still prove a positive turning point in resolving one the world's most dangerous flash points. But it could also lead to an even worse crisis than in 1994. The proper approach, therefore, is to now re-engage with North Korea without rewarding it for bad behavior. Working together, the major external interested parties (China, Japan, Russia, and the United States) should jointly and officially guarantee the security of the entire Korean Peninsula. But the outside powers should also insist that Pyongyang abandon its nuclear weapons program before offering it any enticements. Only when security has been established (and verified by intrusive, regular inspections) should a prearranged comprehensive deal be implemented—one that involves extensive reforms in the North, an increase in aid and investment, and, eventually, a Korean federation.

THE NORTH GOES NUCLEAR

To UNDERSTAND how the most promising signs of progress in decades quickly deteriorated into nuclear brinkmanship, it is necessary to first understand the origins and motivation behind the North's HEU program and Pyongyang's subsequent decision to restart its plutonium program. Even before North Korea admitted that it was building a new HEU program, the United States had long suspected the country of violating its relevant international commitments. Three years ago, such concerns had led to U.S. inspections of suspicious underground facilities in Kumchang-ni. Although those inspections did not reveal any actual treaty violations—in part because Pyongyang had ample time to remove evidence before the inspectors arrived—suspicions lingered. These doubts proved justified in July 2002, when the United States conclusively confirmed the existence of the North's HEU program.

It now seems likely that Pyongyang actually started its HEU program in 1997 or 1998. Although Kim Jong Il's motives for doing so will probably never be clear (his regime has a record of confounding observers), there are two plausible explanations. The first focuses on fear: namely, North Korea's fear that, having frozen its plutonium-based nuclear program in 1994, it would receive nothing in return. Such a suspicion seems unreasonable on its face, since, under the 1994 Agreed Framework negotiated with Washington, Pyongyang was to be compensated in various ways for abandoning its nuclear ambitions. But from the perspective of a paranoid, isolated regime such as North Korea's, this concern was not without justification. Almost from its inception, the provisions of the 1994 accord fell substantially behind schedule—most notably in the construction of proliferation-resistant light-water reactors in the North and improved relations with the United States.[1] North Korea may thus have started its HEU program as a hedge against the possibility that it had been duped, or, more likely, that new U.S., South Korean, or Japanese administrations would be less willing to proceed with the politically controversial program than were their predecessors.

A second, darker, and more likely explanation for Pyongyang's decision to start the HEU program holds that the North never really intended to give up its nuclear ambitions. Whether motivated by fear, honor, or aggression (the determination to stage a preemptive strike if threatened), Pyongyang views a nuclear program as its sovereign right—and a necessity.

Whichever of these theories is true, the North seems to have undertaken its HEU program slowly at first, ramping it up only in late 2000 or 2001. And it was able to hide the program until July 2002, when U.S. intelligence proved its existence. Although Bush administration officials insist otherwise, it is possible, as North Korean officials have suggested, that Pyongyang decided to step up its nuclear program in response to what it perceived as Washington's increasingly hostile attitude—a hostility demonstrated to North Koreans by President Bush's decision to include them in the "axis of evil" and to set the bar for talks impossibly high. This perceived hostility was further encouraged when the administration announced its new doctrine of preemptive defense. Notwithstanding the president's remarks to the contrary, Pyongyang views the new defense doctrine as a direct threat. After all, if Washington is willing to attack Iraq, another isolated nation with a suspected nuclear program, might it not also be willing, even likely, to do the same to North Korea?

This fear helps explain why the North decided to restart its plutonium program. Many within the senior ranks of the North Korean

---

[1] The 1994 Agreed Framework called for best efforts to be made to deliver two light-water reactors to North Korea: one in 2003 and one in 2004. Even before the North admitted to having an HEU program—which has cast the future of the Agreed Framework into doubt—it had become unlikely that the first light-water reactor would be completed before 2008 or the second before 2009. To be fair, however, responsibility for the delay is borne by both sides, and primarily by the North, since it has frequently been intransigent on practical issues related to the agreement's implementation.

military believe that if the United States attacks, Pyongyang's position will be strengthened immeasurably by the possession of several nuclear weapons. North Korean planners thus reason that they should develop such weapons as quickly as possible, prior to the American attack that may come once Washington has concluded its war with Iraq.

HIGH-STAKES POKER

THERE ARE AGAIN two plausible explanations for why the North revealed its HEU program in October 2002. Since its earliest days in office, the Bush administration has made clear that it favors a more hard-line approach to North Korea than did the Clinton team. Even prior to the North's HEU admission, Bush's support for the 1994 Agreed Framework was lukewarm at best. His administration considered the accord a form of blackmail signed by his predecessor—even though, after a long review of North Korea policy in 2001, the Bush administration found it could not justify abandoning the pact without having something better with which to replace it. In short, Washington grudgingly considered itself bound by a diplomatic process it viewed as distasteful—if not an outright scam.

When U.S. Assistant Secretary of State James Kelly visited North Korea in early October, he took with him undeniable evidence of the North's HEU program. He also took with him very narrowly defined briefing papers, hard-line marching orders that reflected the influence of the Defense Department and the National Security Council.

Anticipating isolation and a worsening of already strained relations in the face of Washington's evidence, Pyongyang opted to play one of its few remaining trump cards: open admission of its nuclear program. This openness, Kim may have hoped, would keep the Bush administration from disengaging entirely. By acknowledging its HEU effort, Pyongyang essentially sent Washington the following message: "We understand that despite everything we've done over the past several months you want to isolate or disengage from us. Well, we admit we have a uranium-based nuclear program. You say you don't want to deal with us. Too bad—you can't ignore a potential nuclear power. Deal with us."

Another hypothesis to explain the timing is that Pyongyang simply miscalculated. North Korea watchers learned long ago to expect the unexpected, but even the most jaded observers were surprised in September 2002 when Kim admitted to Koizumi that the North had abducted 13 Japanese in the 1970s and 1980s to train its spies. Kim apologized for the abductions and, with remarkable speed, subsequently authorized a visit of five of the surviving abductees to Japan. In doing so, he removed a decades-old barrier to normalization of relations between the two nations (and to the payment of billions of dollars in hoped-for war reparations from Tokyo).

Kim's gamble on coming clean about the abductions appeared at the time to have paid off. Notwithstanding the predicted public backlash in Japan, further talks between Tokyo and Pyongyang took place in October (after the HEU admission).[2] Having experienced better-than-expected results in admitting to the abductions, Kim may have hoped for the same by confessing to his HEU program. His thinking may have been that, in view of Washington's evidence, Pyongyang would eventually have had to come clean anyway. That being the case, it was better to do so sooner rather than later, thereby removing one of the primary obstacles to improved U.S.–North Korea relations. Kim may further have surmised that the timing of such a revelation in October was advantageous, given recent progress in talks with Japan and South Korea. He probably hoped that Tokyo and Seoul would pressure Washington to mitigate its response.

In the weeks immediately following Kelly's visit, Washington made it clear that it did not see a military solution to the crisis on the Korean Peninsula. This left isolation, containment, and negotiation as the only viable alternatives. A policy of isolation would seek the North's collapse but would not address the HEU problem and would likely result in the North's restarting its plutonium-based nuclear program. Containment, or economic pressure

---

[2] The visit of the surviving abductees to Japan in October was originally scheduled to last two weeks. After the North acknowledged its HEU program, Japan refused to allow their return and pressed for their North Korean relatives to be allowed to join them. Interestingly, although the dispute remains unresolved, Tokyo and Pyongyang have opted to handle it quietly—even as Japan has made clear that future progress with the North is tied to this issue.

designed to squeeze the North, would seek to punish Pyongyang while leaving the door open to future negotiation. It too would not address the HEU problem but, it was hoped, might maintain the freeze on the plutonium program. Negotiations, meanwhile, would seek to address the nuclear problem but could be viewed by some as a reward for bad behavior.

If a successful isolation or containment policy wins the day, the North will have miscalculated in coming clean. If, however, a policy of dialogue and subsequent negotiation ultimately emerges—or if isolation or containment fails (in part because Washington is unable to persuade China, South Korea, and Russia to endorse it over a sustained period)—Kim will have played his cards exceedingly well.

BEST OF A BAD SITUATION

MANY PUNDITS and policymakers in Washington, on both sides of the aisle, argue that the revelations about Pyongyang's clandestine HEU program prove that President Clinton's policy of engaging the North was a mistake. This argument maintains that giving in to blackmail leads only to more blackmail.

Although it is inherently valid, such analysis is too simple. In 1994, the United States was on the edge of war with North Korea. Washington had beefed up its forces in the theater, installed Patriot missile batteries in the South, and was reviewing detailed war plans. The White House had even begun to consider the evacuation of American citizens. The 1994 Agreed Framework, although deeply flawed, represented the best deal available at a far from ideal time. It remained so for several years. And although it has been disappointing on many levels, the agreement has not been useless.

Indeed, it averted a potentially catastrophic situation. Instead of a war (which the U.S. military commander in South Korea, General Gary Luck, estimated would have killed a million people, including 80,000 to 100,000 Americans), Northeast Asia has experienced eight years of stability. This has had vast implications beyond security. In 1994, South Korea's GDP was 323 trillion won; today, even after the 1997 financial meltdown, its GDP is approximately 544 trillion won.3 This transformation would have been unlikely in the face of imminent armed conflict. China has similarly experienced explosive growth, much of which might also have slowed had there been a major confrontation on its porous border with North Korea.

The Agreed Framework also provided the parties with critical breathing room, which has allowed new realities to emerge both within North Korea and among the United States and its allies—developments that improve the chances for a better, more comprehensive deal today. To cite one example, in 1994, Kim Jong Il had only recently succeeded his father, North Korea's founder Kim Il Sung. Viewed as weak, mentally unstable, and without a power base of his own, Kim was expected to last a mere two weeks to several months. Today, however, he is acknowledged as the only power in North Korea and has established diplomatic relations with scores of nations, including many of Washington's closest allies in NATO and the European Union. This puts him in a vastly better position to strike a deal.

For its part, the United States in 1994 could not have counted on Russia or China to support its position toward North Korea. Today, however, Washington is likely to receive baseline support—albeit not carte blanche—from both. Indeed, although there has hardly been unanimity among the outside powers, there has already been evidence of such cooperation, in the form of a joint Chinese-Russian declaration issued in early December stating that the two powers "consider it important ... to preserve the non-nuclear status of the Korean Peninsula and the regime of non-proliferation of weapons of mass destruction."

Another benefit of the breathing room created by the 1994 accord is the North's economic dependence on the South. South Korea today is North Korea's largest publicly acknowledged supplier of aid and its second-largest trading partner. Although not as successful as he would have liked, former South Korean President Kim Dae Jung's "Sunshine Policy" of engaging the North has, in conjunction

---

3 In U.S. dollar terms these figures equal a 1994 GDP of $404 billion (using the 1994 exchange rate of 800 won to the dollar) and a 2001 GDP of $422 billion (using today's much lower exchange rate of 1,290 won to the dollar).

with the North's economic collapse, given Pyongyang a strong economic interest in avoiding a crisis. (Although the numbers are much smaller, the situation is not wholly unlike that between Taiwan and China.) Should the North exacerbate current tensions, the economic fallout would be traumatic, and the loss of South Korean investment could destabilize the North.

THE WAY OUT

THE TIMING of the steps now taken to resolve the current crisis will be crucial to their success. Indeed, timing is important to understand because the North's HEU program does not pose an immediate threat. Although it has the potential to eventually produce enough uranium for one nuclear weapon per year, it has not yet reached this stage and is not expected to do so for at least two to three more years, according to administration officials and the Central Intelligence Agency.

The North's decision to reopen its plutonium-based nuclear program at Yongbyon poses a more critical and immediate threat, however. Prior to its suspension in 1994, most experts believe this program had already produced enough plutonium for one or two nuclear weapons. The 8,000 spent fuel rods from the five-megawatt reactor contained enough plutonium for an additional four to five nuclear weapons.[4] The IAEA monitored the freeze via seals, cameras, and on-site inspectors. It also canned the 8,000 existing spent fuel rods, placed them in a safe-storage cooling pond, and monitored them until its inspectors were expelled from North Korea on December 31.

The five-megawatt reactor, when operational, will produce enough plutonium for one or two additional nuclear weapons per year. But the 8,000 rods represent an even more immediate challenge. If the North follows through on its threat to reopen the reprocessing facility in February, it would take just six months to reprocess all of its spent fuel and extract enough plutonium to make four or five additional weapons. This would bring Pyongyang's

---

[4] Had the Agreed Framework not been signed in 1994, the North's plutonium-based program would by today have produced enough plutonium for up to 30 nuclear weapons. Critics of the accord should not ignore this fact.

nuclear arsenal to between five and seven weapons by the end of July. It could have enough plutonium for one to three weapons even sooner.

Thus there exists only a short window of opportunity before the North's recent action translates into additional nuclear-weapons material on the ground. The trick to unraveling the current impasse is to avoid rewarding the North for its violations of past treaties with a new, more comprehensive agreement. Blackmail cannot and should not be condoned. The starting point for future discussions should therefore be that the North must completely and immediately abandon its HEU and plutonium-based programs. This pledge must be accompanied by intrusive, immediate, and continuous inspections by the IAEA.

It is a tenet of all international negotiations, however—particularly those that involve the Korean Peninsula—that all crises create opportunity, and this one is no different. At its core—politics stripped aside—the current standoff will allow Washington to scrap the flawed Agreed Framework and replace it with a new mechanism that better addresses the concerns of the United States and its allies. In many ways, the North's HEU admission and its subsequent decision to reopen its plutonium program might therefore be viewed as a blessing in disguise. The Bush administration can finally rid itself of a deal it never liked and never truly endorsed and replace it with one that addresses all of Washington's central concerns, including the North's missile program and its conventional forces. Washington must, however, be willing to make such a deal attractive to the North as well.

Yet timing poses an immediate barrier to negotiating a new mechanism. Pyongyang has insisted it will give up its HEU and plutonium programs only after Washington signs a nonaggression pact with it. But the Bush administration, while publicly reassuring the North that it has no intention of invading, has justifiably insisted that Pyongyang give up these programs before there is any discussion of a new mechanism. The North seems unwilling to lose face by giving up this trump card without a security guarantee, and Washington is unwilling to take any action that appears to reward Pyongyang before it has fully dismantled its nuclear programs.

Those who think they can outwait Pyongyang by isolating it or pressuring it economically, as the Bush administration proposed in late December, are likely to be proved wrong. North Koreans are a fiercely proud people and have endured hardships over the last decade that would have led most other countries to implode. It would therefore be a mistake to underestimate their loyalty to the state or to Kim Jong Il. When insulted, provoked, or threatened, North Koreans will not hesitate to engage in their equivalent of a holy war. Their ideology is not only political, it is quasi-religious. Pyongyang also enjoys an inherent advantage in any waiting game: Beijing. Although China might initially support a policy of economic pressure, Beijing is afraid that it will face a massive influx of unwanted refugees across the Yalu River should the North collapse. To guard against this event, it will ultimately allow fuel and food (sanctioned or unsanctioned) to move across its border with the North. Similarly, South Korea, which also wants to avoid a massive influx of refugees, is unlikely to support a sustained, indefinite policy of squeezing the North. In mid-December, it elected by a larger margin than predicted a new president who ran specifically on a platform of expanding engagement with Pyongyang.

The way to cut the Gordian knot of who goes first is through a two-stage approach. The first stage would provide the North with the security it craves while also ensuring that Pyongyang is not rewarded for its bad behavior. To achieve this end, the four outside interested powers (the United States, Japan, China, and Russia— each of which has supported one side or the other in the past) would jointly and officially guarantee the security and stability of the entire Korean Peninsula. Washington may not be able or willing to convene a meeting of the four powers to this end. If not, back channels or unofficial initiatives should be used to encourage Moscow or Beijing to take the lead. Both Russia and China have sought to increase their influence on the Korean Peninsula in recent years. This plan would solidify their places at the table.

Once the security of the peninsula has been guaranteed by the outside powers, it will be time for stage two: a comprehensive accord, again broken into two parts. The North must completely give up its HEU and plutonium programs and allow immediate, intrusive, and continuous inspections by the IAEA; end its development, production, and testing of long-range missiles in exchange for some financial compensation; draw down its conventional troops along the DMZ (although there will be no reduction of U.S. troops at this time, and only a very limited reduction of U.S. troops in five years, should the situation permit); and, finally, continue to implement economic and market reforms.

In exchange for the above, Japan would normalize its relations with the North within 18 months of the agreement's coming into effect. This normalization would include the payment of war reparations in the form of aid, delivered on a timetable extending five to seven years. Both halves of the peninsula would also enter a Korean federation within two years of the agreement's coming into effect. And as soon as the IAEA had verified that the North has dismantled its nuclear weapons programs, Washington would sign a nonaggression pact with Pyongyang. This pact, which by prior agreement would automatically be nullified by subsequent signs that the North was not cooperating or was initiating a new nuclear program, would include the gradual lifting of economic sanctions over three years.

The United States, South Korea, Japan, and the European Union—the primary members of the Korean Peninsula Energy Development Organization (or KEDO, which was set up to administer the Agreed Framework)—would further maintain the organization and provide the two new light-water reactors stipulated in the original deal. KEDO would also resume delivery of heavy fuel oil until the first reactor was completed.

In addition to the above measures, China and Russia would agree to support the North economically via investment. All outside parties to the deal—the United States, South Korea, Japan, China, and Russia—would also contribute to the compensation the North would receive in return for ending its long-range missile program.

Finally, five years after the above accord is signed, a Northeast Asia Security Forum, consisting of the four major powers plus South and North Korea, would be created to ensure long-term peace and stability throughout the region.

The timing of the various parts of stage two will be critical to its success. To this end, the leaders of all the countries involved (or their high-ranking representatives) should meet in person to negotiate the deal. North and South Korea, Japan, China, Russia, and the United States must all sign on if the plan is to work.

Certain components of the comprehensive deal (such as the U.S.–North Korea nonaggression pact and the missile accord) should exist as separate agreements, referenced in but not attached as appendices to the main text. They should be fully agreed and initialed prior to signing the comprehensive deal. Immediately after signing the comprehensive agreement, the North would have to take the first step by fully dismantling both its HEU and its plutonium programs and allowing IAEA inspections to verify these steps. Only after the IAEA had certified the dismantling would the nonaggression and missile pacts be signed: in the case of the nonaggression pact, by Pyongyang and Washington alone, and in the case of the missile pact, by Beijing, Moscow, Pyongyang, Seoul, Tokyo, and Washington.

THE SUM OF TWO PARTS

INITIALLY, Washington's response to North Korea's HEU and plutonium programs consisted mostly of condemning Pyongyang. Then, in early January, President Bush and Secretary of State Powell took steps to ease the tension. Following a trilateral meeting with South Korea and Japan (during which Seoul and Tokyo pressed for a diplomatic approach), Washington finally agreed to open a dialogue with Pyongyang. The Bush administration, however, limited the scope of the meetings to discussion of how North Korea could abide by its international commitments. It is now time to move beyond this narrow agenda to a policy of resolution—one that addresses all concerns on the Korean Peninsula.

Such a shift is particularly important given the very serious rupture that has opened between Washington and Seoul. At precisely the time that the situation in North Korea has reached a crisis stage,

U.S.–South Korean relations have hit their lowest level ever. Korean anti-Americanism—far more than just a difference of opinion on how to deal with the North—was responsible for the election of Roh Moo Hyun as president in December. Roh beat a more hard-line rival specifically by distancing himself from Washington's position on the North and by promising to continue Kim Dae Jung's Sunshine Policy. More critically, he promised a new, more prominent role for South Korea in its relationship with the United States. America will therefore no longer be able to force its position on the more assertive and restless South Korean population.

The process above, fortunately, will address the major concerns of all the parties involved. It will assure North Korea of the underlying security it seeks, without requiring Washington to sign a nonaggression pact until after Pyongyang has dismantled its HEU and plutonium programs. If the North balks despite a security guarantee by all major outside powers and the prospect of a comprehensive accord, isolation or economic pressure by Washington and its allies will not only remain a viable alternative, it will be stronger and more fully justified than it would be otherwise, and will more easily win the unified, sustained support of major players in the region. The upside to exploring the path presented above is therefore massive, and the downside very limited. Doing nothing, meanwhile, could become the most dangerous option of all.☯

The Rogue Who
Came in From the Cold

Ray Takeyh

LIBYA MENDS ITS WAYS

As THE Bush administration struggles to define its foreign policy, with sanctions slipping on Iraq and the prospect of missile defense raising complications around the world, a new question has emerged: How should Washington handle a "rogue" state that is gradually abandoning its objectionable practices? What should the United States do when its long-standing policy toward a maverick country such as Libya starts to pay off—and that country finally begins to clean up its act? The question has recently become a pressing one as, in a surprising twist of events, the often and justifiably maligned Libyan regime of Colonel Mu'ammar Qaddafi has started to meet international demands and redress its past crimes. How the United States responds will serve as a test of Washington's ability to reintegrate a reforming "rogue" into the community of nations.

On January 31, three Scottish judges deliberating at a specially convened court in the Netherlands convicted a Libyan intelligence agent for the 1988 bombing of Pan Am flight 103. The attack, which occurred over Lockerbie, Scotland, killed 270 passengers (including 189 Americans) and passersby, dramatizing the threat that terrorism and its state sponsors pose to the United States. The recent verdict has achieved a modicum of

RAY TAKEYH is Professor and Director of Studies at Near East and South Asia Center, National Defense University. This article originally appeared in the May/June 2001 issue of *Foreign Affairs*.

justice. But it has only reconfirmed, rather than resolved, the quandary that Libya's behavior raises for U.S. foreign policy. On the one hand, the verdict seems to have validated long-held perceptions of Libya as a pariah state. But on the other hand, the very fact that Qaddafi surrendered the suspects suggests that international pressure has prompted subtle yet significant changes in his foreign policy. After decades of militancy, Libya seems to be accommodating itself to international norms.

Few have acknowledged the true dimensions of the challenge these changes pose for Washington. President George W. Bush must deal with the remaining Lockerbie-related issues—including how to force Tripoli to accept responsibility for the crime—while also figuring out how to move beyond them. Successive American administrations have proven adept at devising strategies for isolating offending regimes such as Libya's. But Washington has thus far neglected to plan what to do when it succeeds.

RADICAL SHEIK

MU'AMMAR QADDAFI came of age during the 1960s, as Libya and much of the developing world battled to escape imperial domination. This bitter struggle against colonialism shaped Qaddafi's political philosophy, infusing him with a deep suspicion of the West. It also convinced him of the inherent iniquity of the international order, and led him to the conclusion that Tripoli should be unfettered by international conventions or rules. Rather, as a vanguard revolutionary state, Libya should help liberate the rest of the Third World and reshape its political institutions.

With Libya's vast oil wealth at his disposal and a radical ideology as his guide, Qaddafi systematically attacked Western—especially American—interests, as well as conservative African and Arab leaders whom he routinely derided as "lackeys of imperialism." Libya lent its support to liberation movements, secessionists, and terrorists from the Philippines to Argentina, embarking on a course that culminated in the Pan Am explosion.

Then, in the 1990s, certain events pressed Qaddafi toward a pragmatic redefinition of his nation's interests. The collapse of the

Soviet Union deprived Libya of its main counterweight to the United States and exposed it to the kind of unified international pressure that was once impossible. As Qaddafi became isolated, his ideology and methods came to seem hopelessly anachronistic. The colonel's anti-imperialism was eclipsed as the nonaligned bloc turned its attention to securing its position in the global economy. While Qaddafi remained rigid, much of the rest of the Arab world came to terms with Israel and grudgingly accepted the need for an American security umbrella. Libya's continuous interference in the internal affairs of other African states, meanwhile, estranged Qaddafi from that continent, the liberation of which he had often trumpeted as one of his highest priorities. Qaddafi thus spent the 1990s on the sidelines while his onetime revolutionary compatriots—leaders such as Nelson Mandela and Yasir Arafat—were feted in Washington and in European capitals. To remain relevant, Qaddafi realized, he had to accept the passing of the age of revolutions and the arrival of the age of globalization.

Another reason for Qaddafi's shift was the much-derided U.N. sanctions regime imposed on Libya after the Lockerbie bombing. The colonel had long believed that Libya's oil wealth and commercial appeal would undermine any cohesive opposition to his revolutionary excesses. But the Lockerbie sanctions, enacted by the United Nations in 1992, shattered that conviction. The United States managed to convince even states with close economic ties to Libya, such as Italy and Germany, to support the sanctions as a way to force Qaddafi to hand over the bombing suspects. As a senior Libyan official admitted, "when America imposed an embargo, the whole world followed it." For the first time, Qaddafi's militancy incurred a palpable cost.

Prior attempts to coerce Libya had proven ineffective: U.S. air strikes in 1986 only enhanced Qaddafi's domestic power and led to his lionization in the developing world. But the U.N. sanctions—particularly the prohibition on the sale of oil equipment and technology and a ban on financial transfers—hit Qaddafi where it hurt the most, undermining his government's ability to extract and export its main source of revenue. Libya estimates that the sanctions have deprived its economy of $33 billion, whereas the World

Bank puts the damage at the lower but still daunting sum of $18 billion. Whatever their actual cost, the basic efficacy of the sanctions demonstrated Libya's special vulnerability to such multilateral coercion. Libya's economic vitality and its government's popularity depend on access to international petroleum markets. Thus the same resource that gave Qaddafi the power to upset the international order also let the world community undermine him.

Already, in the 1980s, low oil prices had sparked an economic recession from which Libya could not escape. The sanctions of the 1990s then exacerbated the woes of an economy that was plagued with 30 percent unemployment and 50 percent inflation rates. Tripoli embarked on an austerity program, freezing salaries and reducing subsidies, but this proved dangerous for a regime that depended for its survival on buying the population's acquiescence. Demonstrations in urban areas soon erupted, as did at least two military coup attempts and an Islamic insurgency in the eastern provinces.

As Libya approached the brink of chaos in the mid-1990s, an extraordinary dispute broke out in the higher echelons of the regime. The pragmatists in the bureaucracy—led by the late General Secretary Umar al-Muntasir and Energy Minister Abdallah Salim al-Badri—stressed the need for structural economic reforms and international investments to ensure Libya's long-term economic vitality and political stability. The hard-liners—including long-time Qaddafi confidant Abdelssalem Jalloud—wanted to continue defying the West, for they saw Libya's past radicalism as the basis of the regime's legitimacy.

As the debate raged, Qaddafi at first remained strangely silent, unwilling or unable to make a decision. But in 1998, the colonel seemed to resolve the debate in favor of the pragmatists. A series of articles in the official daily *Al-Jamahiriya* began to criticize the intransigence of the hard-liners and their inability to recognize prevailing global realities. The Revolutionary Committees—informal groups of zealots, drawn from the lower echelons of Libyan society and indoctrinated in radical ideology, that served as the hard-liners' power base and had dominated Libyan politics since their creation in the late 1970s— were purged and relegated to the margins of society. Meanwhile, the pragmatists were granted an all-important advantage: proximity to the colonel. "We cannot stand in the way of progress," announced Qaddafi. "No more obstacles between human beings are accepted. The fashion now is the free market and investments." In April 1999, Qaddafi accepted U.N. demands for the trial of the Lockerbie suspects in the Netherlands, announcing shortly thereafter that "the world has changed radically and drastically. The methods and ideas should change, and being a revolutionary and a progressive man, I have to follow this movement."

In the last few years, Qaddafi has begun to offer a new vision for Libya. In a September 2000 speech commemorating the Libyan Revolution, he not only proclaimed an end to his long-standing anti-imperialist struggle but also suggested that it was time for former antagonists to start cooperating with one another. In a series of seminars and speeches, the colonel outlined his new ideas to his restive constituents, declaring, "Now is the era of economy, consumption, markets, and investments. This is what unites people irrespective of language, religion, and nationalities." The hoary policies of subsidizing rebellions and plotting the overthrow of sovereign leaders have become unsustainable in the era of economic interdependence—even for oil-rich Libya. As a sign of the times, the regular procession of visitors to the colonel's tent no longer includes guerrilla leaders and terrorists, but instead features investment consultants and Internet executives.

Qaddafi has also begun to shift his international focus toward Africa. After decades of involvement in the Middle East, in March 1999 the colonel proclaimed his new orientation with a typical flourish, announcing, "I have no time to lose talking with Arabs. ... I now talk about Pan-Africanism and African unity." There is a certain logic to this new focus; after all, the Organization of African Unity (OAU) was the only regional group to defy the U.N. sanctions on Libya, and Nelson Mandela, Africa's elder statesman, was instrumental in resolving the Lockerbie crisis. While Arab politicians equivocated during the 1990s, African leaders warmly embraced Qaddafi. Mandela even hailed him as "one of the revolutionary icons of our time."

Libya's new Africa policy has become the first test of Qaddafi's evolving ideology and newfound moderation. Previously, Libya had tried to export revolution through Africa by subsidizing insurgencies and destabilizing local states. Now Qaddafi seems to have abandoned his radical heritage. He has focused on mediating crises while claiming a place at the African roundtable. The colonel has embarked on a high-profile diplomatic campaign to settle conflicts in the Democratic Republic of the Congo, the Horn of Africa, Sudan, and Sierra Leone. Libya has also signed bilateral trade and cultural pacts with Niger, Senegal, and South Africa, while extending aid to Ethiopia, the Ivory Coast, Mali, Tanzania, Uganda, and Zimbabwe. Tripoli has even demonstrated an uncharacteristic appreciation for multilateral institutions. Not only has it participated constructively in various regional forums, but it has hosted an extraordinary OAU meeting to press for the creation of a "United States of Africa" as a means to promote solidarity and economic integration. Most of these initiatives have yet to produce substantial practical results. But their importance lies in the fact that, after decades of attempting to subvert Africa's state system, Qaddafi is now making positive contributions to the continent's political cohesion and economic rehabilitation.

THE ROAD TO REDEMPTION

QADDAFI's philosophical evolution and his African endeavors have sparked some interest in the international community. But further changes must occur before rapprochement with the United States will be possible. Three problems in particular loom large: Libya's support for terrorism, its attempts to acquire weapons of mass destruction (WMD), and its opposition to the Arab-Israeli peace process.

American objectives in Libya have never been explicitly directed at toppling Qaddafi. This is explained by the fact that the colonel's adventurism, while disturbing to Americans, has never actually destabilized fundamental U.S. interests. This puts Qaddafi in a very different category from that occupied by a leader like Saddam Hussein, who twice invaded his neighbors and continues to seek hegemony over the Persian Gulf. Qaddafi has also shown himself to be more susceptible to international pressure than Saddam. Successive American administrations have stated that they would welcome resumed relations with Libya if

Qaddafi would just abandon his provocative behavior. Now he may finally be doing just that.

Although Libya has a long history of supporting outlawed organizations such as Italy's Red Brigades and the Irish Republican Army, Qaddafi has recently severed his links to his terrorist clients and abandoned terrorism as an instrument of policy. In 1999, for example, Libya expelled the Abu Nidal organization from its territory and broke its ties to other radical Palestinian groups such as the Popular Front for Liberation of Palestine–General Command and Palestinian Islamic Jihad. In addition, in accordance with an Arab League agreement, Libya has extradited Islamist militants and suspected terrorists to Egypt, Yemen, and Jordan. Once-notorious training camps have been closed down, and terror groups have been told to find other sources of arms and supplies.

Apart from terrorism, U.S. policymakers have also been concerned by Libya's attempts to acquire WMD. Here there seem to be fewer signs of improvement. Since the April 1999 suspension of the U.N. arms embargo, Libya has sought to modernize its decrepit armed forces by acquiring advanced weapons from North Korea and Russia. And the CIA recently announced that "Tripoli has not given up its goal of establishing its own offensive [chemical weapons] program."

Although Libya has made progress toward acquiring chemical weapons, it has not yet managed to become a nuclear threat. As the Pentagon describes it, Libya's nuclear project "lacks well-developed plans, expertise, consistent financial support, and adequate foreign suppliers." And Libya's nuclear infrastructure is limited to a Soviet-made research reactor operating under the auspices of the International Atomic Energy Agency.

Washington should recognize that Tripoli's attempts to acquire WMD make a certain kind of sense. After all, Libya is richer than its neighbors but is sparsely populated and has long, unsettled borders. The country's lucrative oil fields have, at various times, been coveted by neighbors such as Algeria. And Libya's unsteady relations with Egypt have caused sporadic tension on Libya's eastern flank. Little wonder, then, that Tripoli has chosen to build up its air power, missile force, and chemical weapons in order to deter potential adversaries with larger armies. Both of these factors—the rudimentary level of Libya's WMD program and the genuine basis for its regional insecurity—suggest that it might be possible to persuade Tripoli to abandon its plans for WMD. U.S. diplomacy should persuade Libya that its WMD projects will only precipitate a regional arms race that will exacerbate, rather than alleviate, its vulnerability. Even if Qaddafi remains unpersuaded, Libya's primitive facilities and poor technological infrastructure ensure that the country will not become a nuclear threat anytime soon.

A third major obstacle in U.S.-Libyan relations has been Qaddafi's ferocious rejection of efforts to settle the conflict between Israel and its neighbors. But here again Libya seems to have undergone a conversion in the past few years. Although the colonel still makes shrill calls for the "battle of the century" to end the "Zionist occupation," on a practical level Libya has yielded to American demands by terminating its support for rejectionist Palestinian groups and accepting the Palestinian Authority's right to negotiate with Israel. In the past, the kind of violence now occurring in the West Bank and Gaza would have led to the dispatch of Libyan arms and aid to Palestinian militants. This time, Qaddafi has limited himself to sporadic rhetorical fulmination and avoided tangible measures that would add further strain to an already tense situation. Qaddafi may never cross the existential barrier that some other Arab leaders have traversed by recognizing Israel. But in practice, he has already extricated Libya from Arab-Israeli confrontations.

Libya's ongoing reintegration into the world community has already started to pay off, and the rewards it has won from reclaimed trade partnerships have generated a desire within the country to come to terms with the Americans as well. Unlike Iran, which refuses official contact with the United States, Libya is eager to open a diplomatic dialogue. Abuzed Dorda, Libya's U.N. envoy, has said, "I expect that we will sit down with the Americans and put the past behind us." Even Qaddafi, in his own eccentric manner, has made overtures to the new American president, stressing, "I believe that George W. Bush will be nice. As a person he is not malicious or imperialist. I believe that he attaches importance to the United States and does not have world ambitions." A modest level of trade has already quietly developed between the two states. Last year, Libya took advantage of the newly eased sanctions on food and medicine to purchase 50,500 tons of wheat and 26,100 tons of corn from the United States. In a further, subtle signal to the United States, last November Libyan General Secretary Mubarak al-Shamikh dismissed reports that U.S. oil companies' assets in Libya have been nationalized and pledged that American investments are "protected and waiting for them to return." All of this suggests that a flexible yet determined American policy toward Libya stands a good chance of convincing Qaddafi to make further pragmatic adjustments.

NEW WINE IN NEW BOTTLES

THE CHALLENGE that Libya poses for the Bush administration is how to acknowledge Qaddafi's partial rehabilitation while continuing to press for further changes. Until now, the United States has relied on a range of unilateral and coercive measures (such as sanctions) to contain Libya. But in the aftermath of the Lockerbie trial, with U.N. sanctions having been suspended, the United States can hardly isolate Libya on its own. Unless it adds incentives to the mix, Washington will have little in the way of leverage.

Unlike the United States, Europe has responded to Libya's overtures with uncritical dialogue and greatly increased trade. But whereas U.S. policy may be too unyielding, the European model goes too far in the other direction. By warmly welcoming Libya back into the international fold, Europe has rewarded (or, at best, ignored) Qaddafi's continued refusal to accept basic responsibility for the Pan Am bombing and turned a blind eye to his noncompliance with other international demands. Still, since Europe is Libya's foremost trading partner and the market for nine-tenths of its oil exports, the success of any U.S. policy will depend on European compliance and support.

A U.S.-Libyan dialogue should start by focusing on the remaining U.N. demands relating to Lockerbie—namely, that Tripoli pay compensation to the families of the victims and formally renounce terrorism. For symbolic reasons and to deter future crimes, these two points should be made non-negotiable prerequisites to any softening of U.S. policy toward Libya. Fortunately, the chances for success on these issues are good. Despite Libya's refusal to compensate Americans for state-sponsored crimes, recent history suggests it may eventually offer restitution. In 1999, for example, after a court in France convicted six Libyan intelligence officials for the 1989 bombing of a French UTA flight over West Africa, Libya paid out $25.7 million in reparations. Now, in exchange for both direct compensation and a Libyan admission of responsibility, Washington should consider removing Tripoli from its list of state sponsors of terrorism, rescinding its ban on American citizens' travel to Libya, and unfreezing the country's assets in the United States.

A similar approach should be used to dissuade Libya from acquiring WMD. The chances that Libya will manage to assemble nuclear weapons anytime soon are remote, but Qaddafi's pursuit of chemical weapons and delivery systems remains a threat. The United States should therefore mount a concerted diplomatic campaign involving not just Libya but also Europe. The political cost of the five-year-old Iran-Libya Sanctions Act (ILSA) has been considerable and its impact on deterring investments in "rogue" states negligible. The Bush administration should thus allow ILSA to expire in August in exchange for a European ban on the export to Libya of sensitive technology.

In a similar vein, the United States should start talking to Russia about preventing arms sales to Libya. Since these sales have been stymied by long-outstanding Libyan debts for prior purchases, the Russians may be more inclined to cooperate here than they have been on arms sales to Iran. In the end, however, keeping WMD technology out of Libyan hands will require a complex, broad-based, and multilateral policy.

In addition to coordinating international measures, the United States should also use its own set of incentives to get Tripoli to acquiesce to various WMD treaties. Libya has already signed the nuclear Nonproliferation Treaty. It should be pressed to sign the Chemical Weapons Convention as well, and to permit the inspections that treaty mandates. In exchange for such compliance, the United States could stop blocking Libya's access to international capital markets, establish low-level diplomatic representation, and allow U.S. investment in Libya's non-oil sectors. The flow of investments into Libya need not be limited to the energy sector: Tripoli is also trying to refurbish its airline and financial services industries and its national infrastructure, and these projects offer lucrative opportunities for U.S. firms.

RIGHTING THE ROGUE

IT MAY TAKE a number of years before U.S.-Libyan diplomatic relations are fully restored at the ambassadorial level and American oil firms return to Libya. Until then, the United States should monitor Libya's compliance with international standards and offer concessions only after judging Tripoli's record. The current administration should aim simply to establish a framework that can be used for the gradual resumption of U.S.-Libyan ties.

American policy, furthermore, should not try to directly alter Libya's international orientation. Instead, it should provide various inducements and pressures designed to help Libya move along its own path of moderation. This incremental normalization would reward constructive Libyan conduct and punish intransigence. It would also have the advantage of reconstituting international—particularly European—cooperation, an essential part of any Libya policy.

Most important, the Bush administration ought to accept the possibility of "rogue" states' rehabilitation. U.S. policy should employ a full complement of economic, political, and diplomatic tools not just to frustrate these states' nefarious designs but also to show them that, should they temper their policies, they can be reintegrated into global society. The Libyan case can provide a model for how to deal with a revolutionary regime that has grown weary of its isolation and ostracism. The United States should not waste the opportunity. Libya—and the world—will be watching.

What Role Should the United Nations Play?

Why the Security Council Failed

Michael J. Glennon

SHOWDOWN AT TURTLE BAY

"THE TENTS have been struck," declared South Africa's prime minister, Jan Christian Smuts, about the League of Nations' founding. "The great caravan of humanity is again on the march." A generation later, this mass movement toward the international rule of law still seemed very much in progress. In 1945, the League was replaced with a more robust United Nations, and no less a personage than U.S. Secretary of State Cordell Hull hailed it as the key to "the fulfillment of humanity's highest aspirations." The world was once more on the move.

Earlier this year, however, the caravan finally ground to a halt. With the dramatic rupture of the UN Security Council, it became clear that the grand attempt to subject the use of force to the rule of law had failed.

In truth, there had been no progress for years. The UN's rules governing the use of force, laid out in the charter and managed by the Security Council, had fallen victim to geopolitical forces too strong for a legalist institution to withstand. By 2003, the main question facing countries considering whether to use force was not whether it was lawful. Instead, as in the nineteenth century, they simply questioned whether it was wise.

MICHAEL J. GLENNON is Professor of International Law at the Fletcher School of Law and Diplomacy at Tufts University. This article originally appeared in the May/June 2003 issue of *Foreign Affairs*.

The beginning of the end of the international security system had actually come slightly earlier, on September 12, 2002, when President George W. Bush, to the surprise of many, brought his case against Iraq to the General Assembly and challenged the UN to take action against Baghdad for failing to disarm. "We will work with the UN Security Council for the necessary resolutions," Bush said. But he warned that he would act alone if the UN failed to cooperate.

Washington's threat was reaffirmed a month later by Congress, when it gave Bush the authority to use force against Iraq without getting approval from the UN first. The American message seemed clear: as a senior administration official put it at the time, "we don't need the Security Council."

Two weeks later, on October 25, the United States formally proposed a resolution that would have implicitly authorized war against Iraq. But Bush again warned that he would not be deterred if the Security Council rejected the measure. "If the United Nations doesn't have the will or the courage to disarm Saddam Hussein and if Saddam Hussein will not disarm," he said, "the United States will lead a coalition to disarm [him]." After intensive, behind-the-scenes haggling, the council responded to Bush's challenge on November 7 by unanimously adopting Resolution 1441, which found Iraq in "material breach" of prior resolutions, set up a new inspections regime, and warned once again of "serious consequences" if Iraq again failed to disarm. The resolution did not explicitly authorize force, however, and Washington pledged to return to the council for another discussion before resorting to arms.

The vote for Resolution 1441 was a huge personal victory for Secretary of State Colin Powell, who had spent much political capital urging his government to go the UN route in the first place and had fought hard diplomatically to win international backing. Nonetheless, doubts soon emerged concerning the effectiveness of the new inspections regime and the extent of Iraq's cooperation. On January 21, 2003, Powell himself declared that the "inspections will not work." He returned to the UN on February 5 and made the case that Iraq was still hiding its weapons of mass destruction (WMD). France and Germany responded by pressing for more time. Tensions between the allies, already high, began to mount and divisions deepened still further when 18 European countries signed letters in support of the American position.

On February 14, the inspectors returned to the Security Council to report that, after 11 weeks of investigation in Iraq, they had discovered no evidence of WMD (although many items remained unaccounted for). Ten days later, on February 24, the United States, the United Kingdom, and Spain introduced a resolution that would have had the council simply declare, under Chapter VII of the UN Charter (the section dealing with threats to the peace), that "Iraq has failed to take the final opportunity afforded to it in Resolution 1441." France, Germany, and Russia once more proposed giving Iraq still more time. On February 28, the White House, increasingly frustrated, upped the ante: Press Secretary Ari Fleischer announced that the American goal was no longer simply Iraq's disarmament but now included "regime change."

A period of intense lobbying followed. Then, on March 5, France and Russia announced they would block any subsequent resolution authorizing the use of force against Saddam. The next day, China declared that it was taking the same position. The United Kingdom floated a compromise proposal, but the council's five permanent members could not agree. In the face of a serious threat to international peace and stability, the Security Council fatally deadlocked.

POWER POLITICS

AT THIS POINT it was easy to conclude, as did President Bush, that the UN's failure to confront Iraq would cause the world body to "fade into history as an ineffective, irrelevant debating society." In reality, however, the council's fate had long since been sealed. The problem was not the second Persian Gulf War, but rather an earlier shift in world power toward a configuration that was simply incompatible with the way the UN was meant to function. It was the rise in American unipolarity—not the Iraq crisis—that, along with cultural clashes and different attitudes toward the use of force, gradually eroded the council's credibility. Although the body had managed to limp along and function adequately in more tranquil times, it proved incapable of performing under periods of great stress. The fault for this failure did not lie with any one country; rather, it was the largely inexorable upshot of the development and evolution of the international system.

Consider first the changes in power politics. Reactions to the United States' gradual ascent to towering preeminence have been predictable: coalitions of competitors have emerged. Since the end of the Cold War, the French, the Chinese, and the Russians have sought to return the world to a more balanced system. France's former foreign minister Hubert Védrine openly confessed this goal in 1998: "We cannot accept ... a politically unipolar world," he said, and "that is why we are fighting for a multipolar" one. French President Jacques Chirac has battled tirelessly to achieve this end. According to Pierre Lellouche, who was Chirac's foreign policy adviser in the early 1990s, his boss wants "a multipolar world in which Europe is the counterweight to American political and military power." Explained Chirac himself, "any community with only one dominant power is always a dangerous one and provokes reactions."

In recent years, Russia and China have displayed a similar preoccupation; indeed, this objective was formalized in a treaty the two countries signed in July 2001, explicitly confirming their commitment to "a multipolar world." President Vladimir Putin has declared that Russia will not tolerate a unipolar system, and China's former president Jiang Zemin has said the same. Germany, although it joined the cause late, has recently become a highly visible partner in the effort to confront American hegemony. Foreign Minister Joschka Fischer said in 2000 that the "core concept of Europe after 1945 was and still is a rejection of ... the hegemonic ambitions of individual states." Even Germany's former chancellor Helmut Schmidt recently weighed in, opining that Germany and France "share a common interest in not delivering ourselves into the hegemony of our mighty ally, the United States."

In the face of such opposition, Washington has made it clear that it intends to do all it can to maintain its preeminence. The Bush administration released a paper detailing its national security strategy in September 2002 that left no doubt about its plans to ensure that no other nation could rival its military strength. More controversially, the now infamous document also proclaimed a doctrine of preemption—one that, incidentally, flatly contradicts the precepts of the UN Charter. Article 51 of the charter permits the use of force only in self-defense, and only "if an armed attack occurs against a Member of the United Nations." The American policy, on the other hand, proceeds from the premise that Americans "cannot let our enemies strike first." Therefore, "to forestall or prevent ... hostile acts by our adversaries," the statement announced, "the United States will, if necessary, act preemptively"—that is, strike first.

Apart from the power divide, a second fault line, one deeper and longer, has also separated the United States from other countries at the UN. This split is cultural. It divides nations of the North and West from those of the South and East on the most fundamental of issues: namely, when armed intervention is appropriate. On September 20, 1999, Secretary-General Kofi Annan spoke in historic terms about the need to "forge unity behind the principle that massive and systematic violations of human rights—wherever they take place—should never be allowed to stand." This speech led to weeks of debate among UN members. Of the nations that spoke out in public, roughly a third appeared to favor humanitarian intervention under some circumstances. Another third opposed it across the board, and the remaining third were equivocal or noncommittal. The proponents, it is important to note, were primarily Western democracies. The opponents, meanwhile, were mostly Latin American, African, and Arab states.

The disagreement was not, it soon became clear, confined merely to humanitarian intervention. On February 22 of this year, foreign ministers from the Nonaligned Movement, meeting in Kuala Lumpur, signed a declaration opposing the use of force against Iraq. This faction, composed of 114 states (primarily from the developing world), represents 55 percent of the planet's population and nearly two-thirds of the UN's membership.

As all of this suggests, although the UN's rules purport to represent a single global view—indeed, universal law—on when and whether force can be justified, the UN's members (not to mention their populations) are clearly not in agreement.

Moreover, cultural divisions concerning the use of force do not merely separate the West from the rest. Increasingly, they also separate the United States from the rest of the West. On one key subject in particular, European and American attitudes diverge and are moving further apart by the day. That subject is the role of law in international relations. There are two sources for this disagreement. The first concerns who should make the rules: namely, should it be the states themselves, or supranational institutions?

Americans largely reject supranationalism. It is hard to imagine any circumstance in which Washington would permit an international regime to limit the size of the U.S. budget deficit, control its currency and coinage, or settle the issue of gays in the military. Yet these and a host of other similar questions are now regularly decided for European states by the supranational institutions (such as the European Union and the European Court of Human Rights) of which they are members. "Americans," Francis Fukuyama has written, "tend not to see any source of democratic legitimacy higher than the nation-state." But Europeans see democratic legitimacy as flowing from the will of the international community. Thus they comfortably submit to impingements on their sovereignty that Americans would find anathema. Security Council decisions limiting the use of force are but one example.

DEATH OF A LAW

ANOTHER general source of disagreement that has undermined the UN concerns when international rules should be made. Americans prefer after-the-fact, corrective laws. They tend to favor leaving the field open to competition as long as possible and view regulations as a last resort, to be employed only after free markets have failed. Europeans, in contrast, prefer preventive rules aimed at averting crises and market failures before they take place. Europeans tend to identify ultimate goals, try to anticipate future difficulties, and then strive to regulate in advance, before problems develop. This approach suggests a preference for stability and predictability; Americans, on the other hand, seem more comfortable with innovation and occasional chaos. Contrasting responses across the Atlantic to emerging high-technology and telecommunications industries are a prime example of these differences in spirit. So are divergent transatlantic reactions to the use of force.

More than anything else, however, it has been still another underlying difference in attitude—over the need to comply with the UN's rules on the use of force—that has proved most disabling to the UN system. Since 1945, so many states have used armed force on so many occasions, in flagrant violation of the charter, that the regime can only be said to have collapsed. In framing the charter, the international community failed to anticipate accurately when force would be deemed unacceptable. Nor did it apply sufficient disincentives to instances when it would be so deemed. Given that the UN's is a voluntary system that depends for compliance on state consent, this short-sightedness proved fatal.

This conclusion can be expressed a number of different ways under traditional international legal doctrine. Massive violation of a treaty by numerous states over a prolonged period can be seen as casting that treaty into desuetude—that is, reducing it to a paper rule that is no longer binding. The violations can also be regarded as subsequent custom that creates new law, supplanting old treaty norms and permitting conduct that was once a violation. Finally, contrary state practice can also be considered to have created a *non liquet,* to have thrown the law into a state of confusion such that legal rules are no longer clear and no authoritative answer is possible. In effect, however, it makes no practical difference which analytic framework is applied. The default position of international law has long been that when no restriction can be authoritatively established, a country is considered free to act. Whatever doctrinal formula is chosen to describe the current crisis, therefore, the conclusion is the same. "If you want to know whether a man is religious," Wittgenstein said, "don't ask him, observe him." And so it is if you want to know what law a state accepts. If countries had ever truly intended to make the UN's use-of-force rules binding, they would have made the costs of violation greater than the costs of compliance.

But they did not. Anyone who doubts this observation might consider precisely why North Korea now so insistently seeks a nonaggression pact with the United States. Such a provision, after all, is supposedly the centerpiece of the UN Charter. But no one could seriously expect that assurance to comfort Pyongyang. The charter has gone the way of the Kellogg-Briand Pact, the 1928 treaty by which every major country that would go on to fight in World War II solemnly committed itself not to resort to war as an instrument of national policy. The pact, as the diplomatic historian Thomas Bailey has written, "proved a monument to illusion. It was not only delusive but dangerous, for it ... lulled the public ... into a false sense of security." These days, on the other hand, no rational state will be deluded into believing that the UN Charter protects its security.

Surprisingly, despite the manifest warning signs, some international lawyers have insisted in the face of the Iraq crisis that there is no reason for alarm about the state of the UN. On March 2, just days before France, Russia, and China declared their intention to cast a veto that the United States had announced it would ignore, Anne-Marie Slaughter (president of the American Society of International Law and dean of Princeton's Woodrow Wilson School) wrote, "What is happening today is exactly what the UN founders envisaged." Other experts contend that, because countries have not openly declared that the charter's use-of-force rules are no longer binding, those rules must still be regarded as obligatory. But state practice itself often provides the best evidence of what states regard as binding. The truth is that no state—surely not the United States—has ever accepted a rule saying, in effect, that rules can be changed only by openly declaring the old rules to be dead.

States simply do not behave that way. They avoid needless confrontation. After all, states have not openly declared that the Kellogg-Briand Pact is no longer good law, but few would seriously contend that it is.

Still other analysts worry that admitting to the death of the UN's rules on the use of force would be tantamount to giving up completely on the international rule of law. The fact that public opinion forced President Bush to go to Congress and the UN, such experts further argue, shows that international law still shapes power politics. But distinguishing working rules from paper rules is not the same as giving up on the rule of law. Although the effort to subject the use of force to the rule of law was the monumental internationalist experiment of the twentieth century, the fact is that that experiment has failed. Refusing to recognize that failure will not enhance prospects for another such experiment in the future.

Indeed, it should have come as no surprise that, in September 2002, the United States felt free to announce in its national security document that it would no longer be bound by the charter's rules governing the use of force. Those rules have collapsed. "Lawful" and "unlawful" have ceased to be meaningful terms as applied to the use of force. As Powell said on October 20, "the president believes he now has the authority [to intervene in Iraq] ... *just as we did in Kosovo.*" There was, of course, no Security Council authorization for the use of force by NATO against Yugoslavia. That action blatantly violated the UN Charter, which does not permit humanitarian intervention any more than it does preventive war. But Powell was nonetheless right: the United States did indeed have all the authority it needed to attack Iraq— not because the Security Council authorized it, but because there was no international law forbidding it. It was therefore impossible to act unlawfully.

HOT AIR

THESE, THEN, were the principal forces that dismasted the Security Council. Other international institutions also snapped in the gale, including NATO—when France, Germany, and Belgium tried to block it from helping to defend Turkey's borders in the event of a war in Iraq. ("Welcome to the end of the Atlantic alliance," said François Heisbourg, an adviser to the French foreign ministry).

Why did the winds of power, culture, and security overturn the legalist bulwarks that had been designed to weather the fiercest geopolitical gusts? To help answer this question, consider the following sentence: "We have to keep defending our vital interests just as before; we can say no, alone, to anything that may be unacceptable." It may come as a surprise that those were not the words of administration hawks such as Paul Wolfowitz, Donald Rumsfeld, or John Bolton. In fact, they were written in 2001 by Védrine, then France's foreign minister. Similarly, critics of American "hyperpower" might guess that the statement, "I do not feel obliged to other governments," must surely have been uttered by an American. It was in fact made by German Chancellor Gerhard Schröder on February 10, 2003. The first and last geopolitical truth is that states pursue security by pursuing power. Legalist institutions that manage that pursuit maladroitly are ultimately swept away.

A corollary of this principle is that, in pursuing power, states use those institutional tools that are available to them. For France, Russia, and China, one of those tools is the Security Council and the veto that the charter affords them. It was therefore entirely predictable that these three countries would wield their veto to snub the United States and advance the project that they had undertaken: to return the world to a multipolar system. During the Security Council debate on Iraq, the French were candid about their objective. The goal was never to disarm Iraq. Instead, "the main and constant objective for France throughout the negotiations," according to its UN ambassador, was to "strengthen the role and authority of the Security Council" (and, he might have added, of France). France's interest lay in forcing the United States to back down, thus appearing to capitulate in the face of French diplomacy. The United States, similarly, could reasonably have been expected to use the council—or to ignore it—to advance Washington's own project: the maintenance of a unipolar system. "The course of this nation," President Bush said in his 2003 State of the Union speech, "does not depend on the decisions of others."

The likelihood is that had France, Russia, or China found itself in the position of the United States during the Iraq crisis, each of these countries would have used the council—or threatened to ignore it—just as the United States did. Similarly, had Washington found itself in the position of Paris, Moscow, or Beijing, it would likely have used its veto in the same way they did. States act to enhance their own power—not that of potential competitors. That is no novel insight; it traces at least to Thucydides, who had his Athenian generals tell the hapless Melians, "You and everybody else, having the same power as we have, would do the same as we do." This insight involves no normative judgment; it simply describes how nations behave.

The truth, therefore, is that the Security Council's fate never turned on what it did or did not do on Iraq. American unipolarity had already debilitated the council, just as bipolarity paralyzed it during the Cold War. The old power structure gave the Soviet Union an incentive to deadlock the council; the current power structure encourages the United States to bypass it. Meanwhile, the council itself had no good option. Approve an American attack, and it would have seemed to rubber-stamp what it could not stop. Express disapproval of a war, and the United States would have vetoed the attempt. Decline to take any action, and the council would again have been ignored. Disagreement over Iraq did not doom the council; geopolitical reality did. That was the message of Powell's extraordinary, seemingly contradictory declaration on November 10, 2002, that the United States would not consider itself bound by the council's decision—even though it expected Iraq to be declared in "material breach."

It has been argued that Resolution 1441 and its acceptance by Iraq somehow represented a victory for the UN and a triumph of the rule of law. But it did not. Had the United States not threatened Iraq with the use of force, the Iraqis almost surely would have rejected the new inspections regime. Yet such threats of force violate the charter. The Security Council never authorized the United States to announce a policy of regime change in Iraq or to take military steps in that direction. Thus the council's "victory," such as it was, was a victory of diplomacy backed by force—or more accurately, of diplomacy backed by the threat of unilateral force in violation of the charter. The unlawful threat of unilateralism enabled the "legitimate" exercise of multilateralism. The Security Council reaped the benefit of the charter's violation.

As surely as Resolution 1441 represented a triumph of American diplomacy, it represented a defeat for the international rule of law. Once the measure was passed after eight weeks of debate, the French, Chinese, and Russian diplomats left the council chamber claiming that they had not authorized the United States to strike Iraq—that 1441 contained no element of "automaticity." American diplomats, meanwhile, claimed that the council had done precisely that. As for the language of the resolution itself, it can accurately be said to lend support to both claims. This is not the hallmark of great legislation. The first task of any lawgiver is to speak intelligibly, to lay down clear rules in words that all can understand and that have the same meaning for everyone. The UN's members have an obligation under the charter to comply with Security Council decisions. They therefore have a right to expect the council to render its decisions clearly. Shrinking from that task in the face of threats undermines the rule of law.

The second, February 24 resolution, whatever its diplomatic utility, confirmed this marginalization of the security council. Its vague terms were directed at attracting maximal support but at the price of juridical vapidity. The resolution's broad wording lent itself, as intended, to any possible interpretation. A legal instrument that means everything, however, also means nothing. In its death throes, it had become more important that the council say something than that it say something important. The proposed compromise would have allowed states to claim, once again, that private, collateral understandings gave meaning to the council's empty words, as they had when Resolution

1441 was adopted. Eighty-five years after Woodrow Wilson's Fourteen Points, international law's most solemn obligations had come to be memorialized in winks and nods, in secret covenants, secretly arrived at.

APOLOGIES FOR IMPOTENCE

STATES AND COMMENTATORS, intent on returning the world to a multipolar structure, have devised various strategies for responding to the council's decline. Some European countries, such as France, believed that the council could overcome power imbalances and disparities of culture and security by acting as a supranational check on American action. To be more precise, the French hoped to use the battering ram of the Security Council to check American power. Had it worked, this strategy would have returned the world to multipolarity through supranationalism. But this approach involved an inescapable dilemma: what would have constituted success for the European supranationalists?

The French could, of course, have vetoed America's Iraq project. But to succeed in this way would be to fail, because the declared American intent was to proceed anyway—and in the process break the only institutional chain with which France could hold the United States back. Their inability to resolve this dilemma reduced the French to diplomatic ankle-biting. France's foreign minister could wave his finger in the face of the American secretary of state as the cameras rolled, or ambush him by raising the subject of Iraq at a meeting called on another subject. But the inability of the Security Council to actually stop a war that France had clamorously opposed underscored French weakness as much as it did the impotence of the council.

Commentators, meanwhile, developed verbal strategies to forestall perceived American threats to the rule of law. Some argued in a communitarian spirit that countries should act in the common interest, rather than, in the words of Védrine, "making decisions under [their] own interpretations and for [their] own interests." The United States should remain engaged in the United Nations, argued Slaughter, because other nations "need a forum ... in which to ... restrain the United States." "Whatever became," asked *The New Yorker's* Hendrik Hertzberg, "of the conservative suspicion of untrammeled power ... ? Where is the conservative belief in limited government, in checks and balances? Burke spins in his grave. Madison and Hamilton torque it up, too." Washington, Hertzberg argued, should voluntarily relinquish its power and forgo hegemony in favor of a multipolar world in which the United States would be equal with and balanced by other powers.

No one can doubt the utility of checks and balances, deployed domestically, to curb the exercise of arbitrary power. Setting ambition against ambition was the framers' formula for preserving liberty. The problem with applying this approach in the international arena, however, is that it would require the United States to act against its own interests, to advance the cause of its power competitors—and, indeed, of power competitors whose values are very different from its own. Hertzberg and others seem not to recognize that it simply is not realistic to expect the United States to permit itself to be checked by China or Russia. After all, would China, France, or Russia—or any other country—voluntarily abandon preeminent power if it found itself in the position of the United States? Remember too that France now aims to narrow the disparity between itself and the United States—but not the imbalance between itself and lesser powers (some of which Chirac has chided for acting as though "not well brought-up") that might check France's own strength.

There is, moreover, little reason to believe that some new and untried locus of power, possibly under the influence of states with a long history of repression, would be more trustworthy than would the exercise of hegemonic power by the United States. Those who would entrust the planet's destiny to some nebulous guardian of global pluralism seem strangely oblivious of the age-old question: Who guards that guardian? And how will that guardian preserve international peace—by asking dictators to legislate prohibitions against weapons of mass destruction (as the French did with Saddam)?

In one respect James Madison is on point, although the communitarians have failed to note it. In drafting the U.S. Constitution, Madison and the other founders confronted very much the same dilemma that the world community confronts today in dealing with American hegemony. The question, as the framers posed it, was why the powerful should have any incentive to obey the law. Madison's answer, in the Federalist Papers, was that the incentive lies in an assessment of future circumstances—in the unnerving possibility that the strong may one day become weak and then need the protection of the law. It is the "uncertainty of their condition," Madison wrote, that prompts the strong to play by the rules today. But if the future were certain, or if the strong believed it to be certain, and if that future forecast a continued reign of power, then the incentive on the powerful to obey the law would fall away. Hegemony thus sits in tension with the principle of equality. Hegemons have ever resisted subjecting their power to legal constraint. When Britannia ruled the waves, Whitehall opposed limits on the use of force to execute its naval blockades—limits that were vigorously supported by the new United States and other weaker states. Any system dominated by a "hyperpower" will have great difficulty maintaining or establishing an authentic rule of law. That is the great Madisonian dilemma confronted by the international community today. And that is the dilemma that played out so dramatically at the Security Council in the fateful clash this winter.

BACK TO THE DRAWING BOARD

THE HIGH DUTY of the Security Council, assigned it by the charter, was the maintenance of international peace and security. The charter laid out a blueprint for managing this task under the council's auspices. The UN's founders constructed a Gothic edifice of multiple levels, with grand porticos, ponderous buttresses, and lofty spires—and with convincing façades and scary gargoyles to keep away evil spirits.

In the winter of 2003, that entire edifice came crashing down. It is tempting, in searching for reasons, to return to the blueprints and blame the architects. The fact is, however, that the fault for the council's collapse lies elsewhere: in the shifting ground beneath the construct. As became painfully clear this year, the terrain on which the UN's temple rested was shot through with fissures. The ground was unable to support humanity's lofty legalist shrine. Power disparities, cultural disparities, and differing views on the use of force toppled the temple.

Law normally influences conduct; that is, of course, its purpose. At their best, however, international legalist institutions, regimes, and rules relating to international security are largely epiphenomenal—that is, reflections of underlying causes. They are not autonomous, independent determinants of state behavior but are the effects of larger forces that shape that behavior. As the deeper currents shift and as new realities and new relations (new "phenomena") emerge, states reposition themselves to take advantage of new opportunities for enhancing their power. Violations of security rules occur when that repositioning leaves states out of sync with fixed institutions that cannot adapt. What were once working rules become paper rules.

This process occurs even with the best-drafted rules to maintain international security, those that once reflected underlying geopolitical dynamics. As for the worst rules—those drafted without regard to the dynamics—they last even less time and often are discarded as soon as compliance is required. In either case, validity ultimately proves ephemeral, as the UN's decline has illustrated. Its Military Staff Committee died almost immediately. The charter's use-of-force regime, on the other hand, petered out over a period of years. The Security Council itself hobbled along during the Cold War, underwent a brief resurgence in the 1990s, and then flamed out with Kosovo and Iraq.

Some day policymakers will return to the drawing board. When they do, the first lesson of the Security Council's breakdown should become the first principle of institutional engineering: what the design *should* look like must be a function of what it *can* look like. A new international legal order, if it is to function effectively, must reflect the underlying dynamics of power, culture, and security. If it does not—if its norms are again unrealistic and do not reflect the way states actually behave and the real forces to which they respond—the community of nations will again end up with mere paper rules. The UN system's dysfunctionality was not, at bottom, a legal problem. It was a geopolitical one. The juridical distortions that proved debilitating were effects, not causes. "The UN was founded on the premise," Slaughter has observed in its defense, "that some truths transcend politics." Precisely—and therein lay the problem. If they are to comprise working rules rather than paper ones, legalist institutions—and the "truths" on which they act—must flow from political commitments, not vice versa.

A second, related lesson from the UN's failure is thus that rules must flow from the way states actually behave, not how they ought to behave. "The first requirement of a sound body of law," wrote Oliver Wendell Holmes, "is that it should correspond with the actual feelings and demands of the community, whether right or wrong." This insight will be anathema to continuing believers in natural law, the armchair philosophers who "know" what principles must control states, whether states accept those principles or not. But these idealists might remind themselves that the international legal system is, again, voluntarist. For better or worse, its rules are based on state consent. States are not bound by rules to which they do not agree. Like it or not, that is the Westphalian system, and it is still very much with us. Pretending that the system can be based on idealists' own subjective notions of morality won't make it so.

Architects of an authentic new world order must therefore move beyond castles in the air—beyond imaginary truths that transcend politics—such as, for example, just war theory and the notion of the sovereign equality of states. These and other stale dogmas rest on archaic notions of universal truth, justice, and morality. The planet today is fractured as seldom before by competing ideas of transcendent truth, by true believers on all continents who think, with Shaw's Caesar, "that the customs of his tribe and island are the laws of nature." Medieval ideas about natural law and natural rights ("nonsense on stilts," Bentham called them) do little more than provide convenient labels for enculturated preferences—yet serve as rallying cries for belligerents everywhere.

As the world moves into a new, transitional era, the old moralist vocabulary should be cleared away so that decision-makers can focus pragmatically on what is really at stake. The real questions for achieving international peace and security are clear-cut: What are our objectives? What means have we chosen to meet those objectives? Are those means working? If not, why not? Are better alternatives available? If so, what tradeoffs are required? Are we willing to make those tradeoffs? What are the costs and benefits of competing alternatives? What support would they command?

Answering those questions does not require an overarching legalist metaphysic. There is no need for grand theory and no place for self-righteousness. The life of the law, Holmes said, is not logic but experience. Humanity need not achieve an ultimate consensus on good and evil. The task before it is empirical, not theoretical. Getting to a consensus will be accelerated by dropping abstractions, moving beyond the polemical rhetoric of "right" and "wrong," and focusing pragmatically on the concrete needs and preferences of real people who endure suffering that may be unnecessary. Policymakers may not yet be able to answer these questions. The forces that brought down the Security Council—the "deeper sources of international instability," in George Kennan's words—will not go away. But at least policymakers can get the questions right.

One particularly pernicious outgrowth of natural law is the idea that states are sovereign equals. As Kennan pointed out, the notion of sovereign equality is a myth; disparities among states "make a mockery" of the concept. Applied to states, the proposition that all are equal is belied by evidence everywhere that they are not—neither in their power, nor in their wealth, nor in their respect for international order or for human rights. Yet the principle of sovereign equality animates the entire structure of the United Nations—and disables it from effectively addressing emerging crises, such as access to WMD, that derive precisely from the presupposition of sovereign equality. Treating states as equals prevents treating individuals as equals: if Yugoslavia truly enjoyed a right to nonintervention equal to that of every other state, its citizens would have been denied human rights equal to those of individuals in other states, because their human rights could be vindicated only by intervention. This year, the irrationality of treating states as equals was brought home as never before when it emerged that the will of the Security Council could be determined by Angola, Guinea, or Cameroon—nations whose representatives sat side by side and exercised an equal voice and vote with those of Spain, Pakistan, and Germany. The equality principle permitted any rotating council member to cast a de facto veto (by denying a majority the critical ninth vote necessary for potential victory). Granting a de jure veto to the permanent five was, of course, the charter's intended antidote to unbridled egalitarianism. But it didn't work: the de jure veto simultaneously undercorrected and overcorrected for the problem, lowering the United States to the level of France and raising France above India, which did not even hold a rotating seat on the council during the Iraq debate. Yet the de jure veto did nothing to dilute the rotating members' de facto veto. The upshot was a Security Council that reflected the real world's power structure with the accuracy of a fun-house mirror—and performed accordingly. Hence the third great lesson of last winter: institutions cannot be expected to correct distortions that are embedded in their own structures.

STAYING ALIVE?

THERE IS LITTLE REASON to believe, then, that the Security Council will soon be resuscitated to tackle nerve-center security issues, however the war against Iraq turns out. If the war is swift and successful, if the United States uncovers Iraqi WMD that supposedly did not exist, and if nation-building in Iraq goes well, there likely will be little impulse to revive the council. In that event, the council will have gone the way of the League of Nations. American decision-makers will thereafter react to the council much as they did to NATO following Kosovo: Never again. Ad hoc coalitions of the willing will effectively succeed it.

If, on the other hand, the war is long and bloody, if the United States does not uncover Iraqi WMD, and if nation-building in Iraq falters, the war's opponents will benefit, claiming that the United States would not have run aground if only it had abided by the charter. But the Security Council will not profit from America's ill fortune. Coalitions of adversaries will emerge and harden, lying in wait in the council and making it, paradoxically, all the more difficult for the United States to participate dutifully in a forum in which an increasingly ready veto awaits it.

The Security Council will still on occasion prove useful for dealing with matters that do not bear directly on the upper hierarchy of world power. Every major country faces imminent danger from terrorism, for example, and from the new surge in WMD proliferation. None will gain by permitting these threats to reach fruition. Yet even when the required remedy is nonmilitary, enduring suspicions among the council's permanent members and the body's loss of credibility will impair its effectiveness in dealing with these issues.

However the war turns out, the United States will likely confront pressures to curb its use of force. These it must resist. Chirac's admonitions notwithstanding, war is not "always, always, the worst solution." The use of force was a better option than diplomacy in dealing with numerous tyrants, from Milosevic to Hitler. It may, regrettably, sometimes emerge as the only and therefore the best way to deal with WMD proliferation. If judged by the suffering of noncombatants, the use of force can often be more humane than economic sanctions, which starve more children than soldiers (as their application to Iraq demonstrated). The greater danger after the second Persian Gulf War is not that the United States will use force when it should not, but that, chastened by the war's horror, the public's opposition, and the economy's gyrations, it will not use force when it should. That the world is at risk of cascading disorder places a greater rather than a lesser responsibility on the United States to use its power assertively to halt or slow the pace of disintegration.

All who believe in the rule of law are eager to see the great caravan of humanity resume its march. In moving against the centers of disorder, the United States could profit from a beneficent sharing of its power to construct new international mechanisms directed at maintaining global peace and security. American hegemony will not last forever. Prudence therefore counsels creating realistically structured institutions capable of protecting or advancing U.S. national interests even when military power is unavailable or unsuitable. Such institutions could enhance American preeminence, potentially prolonging the period of unipolarity.

Yet legalists must be hard-headed about the possibility of devising a new institutional framework anytime soon to replace the battered structure of the Security Council. The forces that led to the council's undoing will not disappear. Neither a triumphant nor a chastened United States will have sufficient incentive to resubmit to old constraints in new contexts. Neither vindicated nor humbled competitors will have sufficient disincentives to forgo efforts to impose those constraints. Nations will continue to seek greater power and security at the expense of others. Nations will continue to disagree on when force should be used. Like it or not, that is the way of the world. In resuming humanity's march toward the rule of law, recognizing that reality will be the first step.☯

Response

Stayin' Alive

The Rumors of the UN's Death
Have Been Exaggerated

THE END OF AN ILLUSION
Edward C. Luck

IN "WHY THE SECURITY COUNCIL FAILED" (May/June 2003), Michael J. Glennon provides a singular service by insisting that our understanding of international law should take historical practice and prevailing security and power realities fully into account. His commonsense approach offers a refreshing contrast to the tendentious claim (too often heard during the Iraq debate) that the proper role of the UN Security Council is to pass judgment on when member states can or cannot use force in defense of their national security.

Such a definition of the council's job is based on an overly narrow and selective reading of the UN Charter. The charter's provisions limiting the use of force were adopted as part of a larger system of collective security that the Security Council was meant to enforce. By repeatedly failing over the past decade to take effective action against Iraq, those

EDWARD C. LUCK is Director of the Center on International Organization at the School of International and Public Affairs at Columbia University. ANNE-MARIE SLAUGHTER is Dean of the Woodrow Wilson School of Public and International Affairs at Princeton University. IAN HURD is assistant professor of political science at Northwestern University. This article originally appeared in the July/August 2003 issue of *Foreign Affairs*.

permanent members now claiming to be the guardians of international law have, in fact, done the most to undermine it.

Up to this point, Glennon's analysis is right on track. But his commendable effort to apply the cold logic of political realism goes too far: what we are witnessing today is not the death of the actual Security Council, as he suggests, but of the illusion that it is meant to function like a court. Glennon takes three wrong turns in reaching the overly dramatic conclusion that the council is finished.

First, to conclude as he does that the council's failure to act as a global legal arbiter will leave the body unemployed and irrelevant requires adopting the absolutist standards of the legal purists, standards that Glennon elsewhere rejects. In fact, abandoning a maximalist view of what the council is meant to do will have a positive impact, allowing its members to refocus their energies on seeking common ground and on identifying joint projects for maintaining international peace and security. There are plenty of these missions to go around: the successful completion of the UN's 14 existing peacekeeping operations and the amelioration of the continuing violence in western Africa, Congo, and Sudan should provide the council with ample challenges in the months ahead.

No doubt the council faces an acute identity crisis. As Glennon aptly points out, the efforts of medium powers to employ it to counterbalance American primacy have debilitated the already weakened body. Neither Paris, Moscow, nor Washington, however, is ready to drop the council from its political tool kit. France wants its help in Côte d'Ivoire, the United States wants to use it for North Korea and the larger war on terrorism, and the whole council recently embarked on a fact-finding trip to western Africa. Chances are that a wounded, and hopefully chastened, Security Council will find a way to muddle through, as it has so often in the past.

Second, in seeking to draw a sharp distinction between the normative and political dimensions of world affairs, Glennon fails to take account of the critical ways in which the two interact. The fact that power politics predominates does not mean that norms, values, and even legal rules are not also relevant in shaping both the ends to which the powerful give priority and the means by which they choose to pursue them. Power gives a state capacity, but these other factors help determine what the state will do with that capacity. It is hardly coincidental that both sides in the Security Council debate on Iraq sought to invoke legal as well as political symbolism. They recognized the pull that such claims, however cynical or superficial, have on both domestic and international constituencies.

Third, Glennon, again like the legal purists, asserts that one must choose between realism and multilateralism, between power and the council. They argue for the latter, he for the former. But this is a false dichotomy, one that has been promoted by those most resistant to invoking the muscular enforcement provisions of Chapter VII of the charter. The UN's founders had quite the opposite worry: that U.S. power, already predominant in 1945, would not be sufficiently integrated into the UN's structures and capacities. This fear was based on a stark realism forged by world war, not on vague pieties or abstract ideals.

Glennon's trenchant arguments, although they ultimately miss the mark, serve as a pointed reminder of just how far the UN community has drifted from that founding calculus. Rebuilding the bridges between power and law could prove to be a daunting task, but it beats a premature burial for such a promising partnership.

MISREADING THE RECORD
Anne-Marie Slaughter

Michael J. Glennon makes four fallacious arguments to support his claim that the Security Council has failed. First is his historical claim that the establishment of the UN represented a triumph of legalism in foreign policy. As early as 1945, *Time* magazine, reporting from the UN's founding conference in San Francisco, concluded that the UN Charter is "written for a world of power, tempered by a little reason." Or as Arthur Vandenberg, the Michigan senator whose switch from isolationism to internationalism was indispensable to U.S. ratification of the UN Charter, described it, "this is anything but a wild-eyed internationalist dream of a world state. ... It is based virtually on a four-power alliance." Such comments make clear that the UN always was, and remains today, a legal framework for political bargaining. Glennon's central insight—that the UN's effectiveness depends on the power and will of its members—was in fact the world body's point of departure.

Second, Glennon argues that the political context in which the UN operates has changed fundamentally and permanently. The United States has become a hyperpower and is determined to preserve that status; therefore, the other permanent members of the Security Council will inevitably try to use the body to thwart the United States. Glennon concludes that for Washington to use the UN today will thus only "advance the cause of its power competitors." But while Glennon is right about the power shift and the incentives of some other powers (although he ignores the role of the United Kingdom), his definition of U.S. self-interest is too crude. The United States has long had a strong interest in allowing itself to be constrained—to the extent of playing by rules that offer predictability and reassurance to its allies and potential adversaries. As Harvard's Joseph Nye has pointed out, such behavior maximizes America's "soft power" (to persuade) as well as its "hard power" (to coerce).

Third, Glennon offers legal analysis, asserting that the charter should no longer be thought of as law because it has been violated so many times. It is certainly true that states have often used force without Security Council authorization since 1945. But in any legal system, international or domestic, breaking the law does not make the law disappear. We all must live with imperfect compliance, and that is as true at the World Trade Organization as it is at the UN. Furthermore, even during the Iraq crisis, the United States acknowledged the force of the charter as law by relying on it as justification for its actions.

Finally, Glennon dismisses any moral claims for upholding the framework of the charter, dismissing "archaic notions of universal truth, justice, and morality" and insisting that "medieval ideas about natural law and natural rights ... do little more than provide convenient labels for enculturated preferences." But such ideals are not "imaginary truths"; they are goals that can never be fully achieved but that exist in all the world's countries, cultures, and religions. And the debate over their proper role in legal practice remains very much alive today.

Equally surprising is that Glennon is so eager to pronounce a death sentence on the Security Council *today*. As he admits, states routinely used force without UN authorization during the Cold War, when the U.S.-Soviet conflict froze the world body. But by lumping together the Security Council's stalemate this past March with its Cold War paralysis, Glennon completely ignores the UN's actions throughout the 1990s—in the first Gulf War, Bosnia, East Timor, Haiti, Rwanda, Somalia, and, after the fact, Kosovo. Some of these crises were indeed shameful failures for the entire international community and particularly for its most powerful states. But in all save Kosovo, those states used the Security Council to frame their common response.

And consider the nearly two years since September 11, during which we witnessed the repayment of American UN dues and unanimous Security Council resolutions condemning terrorism, supporting the reconstruction of Afghanistan, and demanding the disarmament of Saddam Hussein. From November to March, Americans from Wall Street to Main Street actively watched the Security Council's every move—the same people who, ten years ago, would not have known what the council was. Even today, the principal point of debate among the council's permanent members has become whether the UN will play a "vital" or merely a "central" role in Iraq. On the ground, meanwhile, the UN presence there increases daily through myriad agencies.

Glennon argues that looking at what Washington tried to achieve during the Iraq crisis rather than what it did achieve is naive—that the Bush administration was determined from the beginning to go to war regardless of what the UN said or did. That is a fashionable view in many circles, and one that can never be disproved. But it requires believing, among other things, that the administration would have preferred sending possibly hundreds of young Americans and thousands of Iraqis to their deaths rather than genuinely trying to oust Saddam through coercive diplomacy. It requires overlooking French President Jacques Chirac's decision, for his own political reasons, to focus the world on the threat of U.S. power. And it requires listening to Richard Perle, former chair of the Defense Policy Board, who has written openly of his hope that the war in Iraq will indeed be "the end of the UN," but ignoring Secretary of State Colin Powell, who has written and spoken of U.S. determination to continue working with and through it.

I agree with Glennon that we are once again in an era in which threats to international peace and security may increasingly require the use of force. But if so, genuinely recommitting the United States to a multilateral decision-making framework is America's only hope of ensuring that its fellow nations—including its closest allies—do not form coalitions to balance against it, as if the United States were the real problem. Pursuing such a strategy requires a blueprint for reforming the UN, not one for abandoning it.

TOO LEGIT TO QUIT
Ian Hurd

Michael J. Glennon's article is a useful introduction to the politics of the second Gulf War. But his analysis of the Security Council rests on a faulty reading of its original powers and purposes.

Glennon is right to suggest that the Security Council lies at the core of the UN's international security system, but he mischaracterizes its purpose. The council was never intended as a "grand attempt to subject the use of force to the rule of law," nor as a "legalist institution" in opposition to "geopolitical forces." It did not, as he claims, enshrine faith in "a single global view."

Instead, the council represents a political compromise to manage the competing interests of the great powers. The UN Charter clearly grants the council power to intervene in the domestic affairs of states, but its five permanent members can each block any such intervention using their veto. There was no expectation at San Francisco that the council's contribution to world order would be to regulate the foreign adventures of the permanent members. The veto meant that these states were deliberately shielded from all accountability to the council; and without such protection, they would never have agreed to the UN in the first place. The council compromise was not primarily intended to protect the security of the small states; it was intended to avoid great-power war. At this, it has succeeded quite well.

The power that the council wields over the strong comes not from its ability to block their military adventures (which it is not empowered to do) but rather from the fact that the council is generally seen as legitimate. This legitimacy functions by raising the costs of unilateral action in the eyes of many countries and their citizens.

The legitimacy granted by the council helps explain the pattern of recent U.S. diplomacy, charted by Glennon. Washington clearly would have preferred to act with council approval rather than without it, as was demonstrated by the first round of talks, which resulted in Resolution 1441. The impact of the council's ability to convey legitimacy is also demonstrated by the fact that many countries, including Turkey, waited to see which way it would turn before deciding whether to support the U.S. action in Iraq.

In ultimately rebuffing the United States, the Security Council signaled its view that a military solution to the crisis was the wrong approach. This disapproval was not enough to stop the American operation, but that isn't the point. It raised the costs of unilateralism, and this is the most that the council can do when the great powers clash.

Partnership or Hegemony?

Toward a Neo-Reaganite Foreign Policy

William Kristol and Robert Kagan

THE TEPID CONSENSUS

IN FOREIGN policy, conservatives are adrift. They disdain the Wilsonian multilateralism of the Clinton administration; they are tempted by, but so far have resisted, the neoisolationism of Patrick Buchanan; for now, they lean uncertainly on some version of the conservative "realism" of Henry Kissinger and his disciples. Thus, in this year's election campaign, they speak vaguely of replacing Clinton's vacillation with a steady, "adult" foreign policy under Robert Dole. But Clinton has not vacillated that much recently, and Dole was reduced a few weeks ago to asserting, in what was heralded as a major address, that there really are differences in foreign policy between him and the president, appearances to the contrary notwithstanding. But the fault is not Dole's; in truth, there has been little attempt to set forth the outlines of a conservative view of the world and America's proper role in it.

Is such an attempt necessary, or even possible? For the past few years, Americans, from the foreign policy big-thinker to the man on the street, have assumed it is not. Rather, this is supposed to be a time for unshouldering the vast responsibilities the United States acquired at the end of the Second World War and for concentrating its energies at home. The collapse of the Soviet Empire has made possible a "return to normalcy" in American foreign and

WILLIAM KRISTOL is editor of the *Weekly Standard*. ROBERT KAGAN is Senior Associate at the Carnegie Endowment for International Peace. This article originally appeared in the July/August 1996 issue of *Foreign Affairs*.

defense policy, allowing the adoption of a more limited definition of the national interest, with a commensurate reduction in overseas involvement and defense spending.

Republicans and conservatives at first tended to be wary of this new post–Cold War consensus. But they joined it rapidly after 1992, in the wake of the defeat of the quintessential "foreign policy president" by a candidate who promised to focus "like a laser" on the domestic economy. Now conservatives tailor their foreign and defense policies to fit the presumed new political reality: an American public that is indifferent, if not hostile, to foreign policy and commitments abroad, more interested in balancing the budget than in leading the world, and more intent on cashing in the "peace dividend" than on spending to deter and fight future wars. Most conservatives have chosen to acquiesce in rather than challenge this public mood.

In a way, the current situation is reminiscent of the mid-1970s. But Ronald Reagan mounted a bold challenge to the tepid consensus of that era—a consensus that favored accommodation to and coexistence with the Soviet Union, accepted the inevitability of America's declining power, and considered any change in the status quo either too frightening or too expensive. Proposing a controversial vision of ideological and strategic victory over the forces of international communism, Reagan called for an end to complacency in the face of the Soviet threat, large increases in defense spending, resistance to communist advances in the Third World, and greater moral clarity and purpose in U.S. foreign policy. He championed American exceptionalism when it was deeply unfashionable. Perhaps most significant, he refused to accept the limits on American power imposed by the domestic political realities that others assumed were fixed.

Many smart people regarded Reagan with scorn or alarm. Liberal Democrats still reeling from the Vietnam War were, of course, appalled by his zealotry. So were many of Reagan's fellow Republicans, especially the Kissingerian realists then dominant in foreign affairs. Reagan declared war on his own party, took on Gerald Ford for the 1976 Republican presidential nomination (primarily over issues of foreign policy), and trained his guns on Kissinger, whose stewardship of U.S. foreign policy, he charged, had "coincided precisely with the loss of U.S. military supremacy." Although Reagan lost the battle to unseat Ford, he won the fight at the Republican convention for a platform plank on "morality in foreign policy." Ultimately, he succeeded in transforming the Republican party, the conservative movement in America, and, after his election to the presidency in 1980, the country and the world.

BENEVOLENT HEGEMONY

TWENTY YEARS later, it is time once again to challenge an indifferent America and a confused American conservatism. Today's lukewarm consensus about America's reduced role in a post–Cold War world is wrong. Conservatives should not accede to it; it is bad for the country and, incidentally, bad for conservatism. Conservatives will not be able to govern America over the long term if they fail to offer a more elevated vision of America's international role.

What should that role be? Benevolent global hegemony. Having defeated the "evil empire," the United States enjoys strategic and ideological predominance. The first objective of U.S. foreign policy should be to preserve and enhance that predominance by strengthening America's security, supporting its friends, advancing its interests, and standing up for its principles around the world.

The aspiration to benevolent hegemony might strike some as either hubristic or morally suspect. But a hegemon is nothing more or less than a leader with preponderant influence and authority over all others in its domain. That is America's position in the world today. The leaders of Russia and China understand this. At their April summit meeting, Boris Yeltsin and Jiang Zemin joined in denouncing "hegemonism" in the post–Cold War world. They meant this as a complaint about the United States. It should be taken as a compliment and a guide to action.

Consider the events of just the past six months, a period that few observers would consider remarkable for its drama on the world stage. In East Asia, the carrier task forces of the U.S. Seventh Fleet helped deter Chinese aggression against democratic Taiwan, and the 35,000 American troops stationed in South Korea helped deter a possible invasion by the rulers in Pyongyang. In Europe, the United States sent 20,000 ground troops to implement a peace agreement in the former Yugoslavia, maintained 100,000 in Western Europe as a symbolic commitment to European stability and security, and intervened diplomatically to prevent the escalation of a conflict between Greece and Turkey. In the Middle East, the United States maintained the deployment of thousands of soldiers and a strong naval presence in the Persian Gulf region to deter possible aggression by Saddam Hussein's Iraq or the Islamic fundamentalist regime in Iran, and it mediated in the conflict between Israel and Syria in Lebanon. In the Western Hemisphere, the United States completed the withdrawal of 15,000 soldiers after restoring a semblance of democratic government in Haiti and, almost without public notice, prevented a military coup in Paraguay. In Africa, a U.S. expeditionary force rescued Americans and others trapped in the Liberian civil conflict.

These were just the most visible American actions of the past six months, and just those of a military or diplomatic nature. During the same period, the United States made a thousand decisions in international economic forums, both as a government and as an amalgam of large corporations and individual entrepreneurs, that shaped the lives and fortunes of billions around the globe. America influenced both the external and internal behavior of other countries through the International Monetary Fund and the World Bank. Through the United Nations, it maintained sanctions on rogue states such as Libya, Iran, and Iraq. Through aid programs, the United States tried to shore up friendly democratic regimes in developing nations. The enormous web of the global economic system, with the United States at the center, combined with the pervasive influence of American ideas and culture, allowed Americans to wield influence in many other ways of which they were were entirely unconscious. The simple truth of this era was stated last year by a Serb leader trying to explain Slobodan Milošević's decision to finally seek rapprochement with Washington. "As a pragmatist," the Serbian politician said, "Milošević knows that all satellites of the United States are in a better position than those that are not satellites."

And America's allies are in a better position than those who are not its allies. Most of the world's major powers welcome U.S. global involvement and prefer America's benevolent hegemony to the alternatives. Instead of having to compete for dominant global influence with many other powers, therefore, the United States finds both the Europeans and the Japanese—after the United States, the two most powerful forces in the world—supportive of its world leadership role. Those who anticipated the dissolution of these alliances once the common threat of the Soviet Union disappeared have been proved wrong. The principal concern of America's allies these days is not that it will be too dominant but that it will withdraw.

Somehow most Americans have failed to notice that they have never had it so good. They have never lived in a world more conducive to their fundamental interests in a liberal international order, the spread of freedom and democratic governance, an international economic system of free-market capitalism and free trade, and the security of Americans not only to live within their own borders but to travel and do business safely and without encumbrance almost anywhere in the world. Americans have taken these remarkable benefits of the post–Cold War era for granted, partly because it has all seemed so easy. Despite misguided warnings of imperial overstretch, the United States has so far exercised its hegemony without any noticeable strain, and it has done so despite the fact that Americans appear to be in a more insular mood than at any time since before the Second World War. The events of the last six months have excited no particular interest among Americans and, indeed, seem to have been regarded with the same routine indifference as breathing and eating.

And that is the problem. The most difficult thing to preserve is that which does not appear to need preserving. The dominant strategic and ideological position the United States now enjoys is the product of foreign policies and defense strategies that are no longer being pursued. Americans have come to take the fruits of their hegemonic power for granted. During the Cold War, the strategies of deterrence and containment worked so well in checking the ambitions of America's adversaries that many American liberals denied that our adversaries had ambitions or even, for that matter, that America had adversaries. Today the lack of a visible threat to U.S. vital interests or to world peace has tempted Americans to absentmindedly dismantle the material and spiritual foundations on which their national well-being has been based. They do not notice that potential challengers are deterred before even contemplating confrontation by their overwhelming power and influence.

The ubiquitous post–Cold War question—where is the threat?—is thus misconceived. In a world in which peace and American security depend on American power and the will to use it, the main threat the United States faces now and in the future is its own weakness. American hegemony is the only reliable defense against a breakdown of peace and international order. The appropriate goal of American foreign policy, therefore, is to preserve that hegemony as far into the future as possible. To achieve this goal, the United States needs a neo-Reaganite foreign policy of military supremacy and moral confidence.

THREE IMPERATIVES

SETTING FORTH the broad outlines of such a foreign policy is more important for the moment than deciding the best way to handle all the individual issues that have preoccupied U.S. policymakers and analysts. Whether or not the United States continues to grant most-favored-nation status to China is less important than whether it has an overall strategy for containing, influencing, and ultimately seeking to change the regime in Beijing. Whether NATO expands this year or five years from now is less important than whether NATO remains strong, active, cohesive, and under decisive American leadership. Whether America builds 20 B-2 bombers or 30 is less important than giving its military planners enough money to make intelligent choices that are driven more by strategic than by budget requirements. But it is clear that a neo-Reaganite foreign policy would have several implications.

The defense budget. Republicans declared victory last year when they added $7 billion to President Clinton's defense budget. But the hard truth is that Washington—now spending about $260 billion per year on defense—probably needs to spend about $60-$80 billion more each year in order to preserve America's role as global hegemon. The United States currently devotes about three percent of its GNP to defense. U.S. defense planners, who must make guesses about a future that is impossible to predict with confidence, are increasingly being forced to place all their chips on one guess or another. They are being asked to predict whether the future is likely to bring more conflicts like the Gulf War or peacekeeping operations like those in Bosnia and Haiti, or more great-power confrontations similar to the Cold War. The best answer to these questions is: who can tell? The odds are that in the coming decades America may face all these kinds of conflict, as well as some that have yet to be imagined.

For the past few years, American military supremacy has been living off a legacy, specifically, the legacy of Ronald Reagan. As former Chairman of the Joint Chiefs of Staff General Colin Powell once noted, it was Reagan's military, built in the 1980s to deter the Soviet Union, that won the war against Iraq. No serious analyst of American military capabilities today doubts that the defense budget has been cut much too far to meet America's responsibilities to itself and to world peace. The United States may no longer have the wherewithal to defend against threats to America's vital interests in Europe, Asia, and the Middle East, much less to extend America's current global preeminence well into the future.

The current readiness of U.S. forces is in decline, but so is their ability to maintain an advantage in high-technology weapons over the coming decades. In the search for some way to meet extensive strategic requirements with inadequate resources, defense planners have engaged in strategic fratricide. Those who favor current readiness have been pitted against those who favor high-tech research and development; those who favor maintaining American forward deployment at bases around the world have been arrayed against those who insist that for the sake of economizing the job be accomplished at long range without bases. The military is forced to choose between army combat divisions and the next generation of bombers, between lift capacities and force projection, between short-range and long-range deterrence. Constructing a military force appropriate to a nation's commitments and its resources is never an easy task, and there are always limits that compel difficult choices. But today's limits are far too severe; the choices they compel are too dramatic; and because military strategy and planning are far from exact sciences, the United States is dangerously cutting its margin for error.

The defense budget crisis is now at hand. Chairman of the Joint Chiefs General John Shalikashvili has complained that the weapons procurement budget has been reduced to perilously low levels, and he has understated the problem. Since 1985, the research and development budget has been cut by 57 percent; the procurement budget has been cut 71 percent. Both the Clinton administration and the Republican Congress have achieved budget savings over the next few years by pushing necessary procurement decisions into the next century. The Clinton administration's so-called "Bottom-Up Review" of U.S. defense strategy has been rightly dismissed by Democrats like Senate Armed Services Committee member Joseph Lieberman (D-Conn.) as "already inadequate to the present and certainly to the future." Both the General Accounting Office and the Congressional Budget Office have projected a shortfall of $50 billion to $100 billion over the next five years in funding just for existing force levels and procurement plans.

These shortfalls do not even take into account the development of new weapons, like a missile defense system capable of protecting American territory against missiles launched from rogue states such as North Korea or shielding, say, Los Angeles from nuclear intimidation by the Chinese during the next crisis in the Taiwan Strait. Deployment of such a system could cost more than $10 billion a year.

Add together the needed increases in the procurement budget called for by the Joint Chiefs of Staff and the justifiable increases in funding for existing forces to make up the shortfalls identified by the GAO and the CBO, and it becomes obvious that an increase in defense spending by $60 billion to $80 billion is not a radical proposal. It is simply what the United States will require to keep the peace and defend its interests over the coming decades.

If this number sounds like a budget-buster, it should not. Today, defense spending is less than 20 percent of the total federal budget. In 1962, before the Vietnam War, defense spending ran at almost 50 percent of the overall budget. In 1978, before the Carter-Reagan defense buildup, it was about 23 percent. Increases of the size required to pursue a neo-Reaganite foreign policy today would require returning to about that level of defense spending—still less than one-quarter of the federal budget.

Toward a Neo-Reaganite Foreign Policy

These days, some critics complain about the fact that the United States spends more on defense than the next six major powers combined. But the enormous disparity between U.S. military strength and that of any potential challenger is a good thing for America and the world. After all, America's world role is entirely different from that of the other powers. The more Washington is able to make clear that it is futile to compete with American power, either in size of forces or in technological capabilities, the less chance there is that countries like China or Iran will entertain ambitions of upsetting the present world order. And that means the United States will be able to save money in the long run, for it is much cheaper to deter a war than to fight one. Americans should be glad their country's defense capabilities are as great as those of the next six powers combined. Indeed, they may even want to enshrine this disparity in U.S. defense strategy. Great Britain in the late nineteenth century maintained a "two-power standard" for its navy, insisting that at all times the British navy should be as large as those of the next two naval powers combined. Perhaps the United States should inaugurate such a two- (or three-, or four-) power standard of its own, which would preserve its military supremacy regardless of the near-term global threats.

Citizen involvement. A gap is growing, meanwhile, between America's professional military, uncomfortable with some of the missions that the new American role requires, and a civilian population increasingly unaware of or indifferent to the importance of its military's efforts abroad. U.S. military leaders harbor justifiable suspicions that while they serve as a kind of foreign legion, doing the hard work of American-style "empire management," American civilians at home, preoccupied with the distribution of tax breaks and government benefits, will not come to their support when the going gets tough. Weak political leadership and a poor job of educating the citizenry to the responsibilities of global hegemony have created an increasingly distinct and alienated military culture. Ask any mechanic or mess boy on an aircraft carrier why he is patrolling the oceans, and he can give a more sophisticated explanation of power projection than 99 percent of American college graduates. It is foolish to imagine that the United States can lead the world effectively while the overwhelming majority of the population neither understands nor is involved, in any real way, with its international mission.

The president and other political leaders can take steps to close the growing separation of civilian and military cultures in our society. They can remind civilians of the sacrifices being made by U.S. forces overseas and explain what those sacrifices are for. A clear statement of America's global mission can help the public understand why U.S. troops are deployed overseas and can help reassure military leaders of public support in difficult circumstances. It could also lay the groundwork for reasserting more comprehensive civilian control over the military.

There could be further efforts to involve more citizens in military service. Perhaps the United States has reached the point where a return to the draft is not feasible because of the high degree of professionalization of the military services. But there are other ways to lower the barriers between civilian and military life. Expanded forms of reserve service could give many more Americans experience of the military and an appreciation of military virtues. Conservatives preach that citizenship is not only about rights but also about responsibilities. There is no more profound responsibility than the defense of the nation and its principles.

Moral clarity. Finally, American foreign policy should be informed with a clear moral purpose, based on the understanding that its moral goals and its fundamental national interests are almost always in harmony. The United States achieved its present position of strength not by practicing a foreign policy of live and let live, nor by passively waiting for threats to arise, but by actively promoting American principles of governance abroad—democracy, free markets, respect for liberty. During the Reagan years, the United States pressed for changes in right-wing and left-wing dictatorships alike, among both friends and foes—in the Philippines, South Korea, Eastern Europe and even the Soviet Union. The purpose was not Wilsonian idealistic whimsy. The policy of putting pressure on authoritarian and totalitarian regimes had practical aims and, in the end, delivered strategic benefits. Support for American principles around the world can be sustained only by the continuing exertion of American influence. Some of that influence comes from the aid provided to friendly regimes that are trying to carry out democratic and free market reforms. However strong the case for reform of foreign aid programs, such programs deserve to be maintained as a useful way of exerting American influence abroad. And sometimes that means not just supporting U.S. friends and gently pressuring other nations but actively pursuing policies—in Iran, Cuba, or China, for instance—ultimately intended to bring about a change of regime. In any case, the United States should not blindly "do business" with every nation, no matter its regime. Armand Hammerism should not be a tenet of conservative foreign policy.

FROM NSC-68 TO 1996

THIS SWEEPING, neo-Reaganite foreign policy agenda may seem ambitious for these tepid times. Politicians in both parties will protest that the American people will not support the burdens of such a policy. There are two answers to this criticism.

First, it is already clear that, on the present course, Washington will find it increasingly impossible to fulfill even the less ambitious foreign policies of the realists, including the defense of so-called "vital" interests in Europe and Asia. Without a broad, sustaining foreign policy vision, the American people will be inclined to withdraw from the world and will lose sight of their abiding interest in vigorous world leadership. Without a sense of mission, they will seek deeper and deeper cuts in the defense and foreign affairs budgets and gradually decimate the tools of U.S. hegemony.

Consider what has happened in only the past few years. Ronald Reagan's exceptionalist appeal did not survive the presidency of George Bush, where self-proclaimed pragmatists like James Baker found it easier to justify the Gulf War to the American people in terms of "jobs" than as a defense of a world order shaped to suit American interests and principles. Then, having discarded the overarching Reaganite vision that had sustained a globally active foreign policy through the last decade of the Cold War, the Bush administration in 1992 saw its own prodigious foreign policy successes swept into the dustbin by Clinton political adviser James Carville's campaign logic: "It's the economy, stupid." By the time conservatives took their seats as the congressional opposition in 1993, they had abandoned not only Reaganism but to some degree foreign policy itself.

Now the common wisdom holds that Dole's solid victory over Buchanan in the primaries constituted a triumphant reassertion of conservative internationalism over neoisolationism. But the common wisdom may prove wrong. On the stump during the Republican primaries this year, what little passion and energy there was on foreign policy issues came from Buchanan and his followers. Over the past four years Buchanan's fiery "America First" rhetoric has filled the vacuum among conservatives created by the abandonment of Reagan's very different kind of patriotic mission. It is now an open question how long the beleaguered conservative realists will be able to resist the combined assault of Buchanan's "isolationism of the heart" and the Republican budget hawks on Capitol Hill.

History also shows, however, that the American people can be summoned to meet the challenges of global leadership if statesmen make the case loudly, cogently, and persistently. As troubles arise and the need to act becomes clear, those who have laid the foundation for a necessary shift in policy have a chance to lead Americans onto a new course. In 1950, Paul Nitze and other Truman administration officials drafted the famous planning document NSC-68, a call for an all-out effort to meet the Soviet challenge that included a full-scale ideological confrontation and massive increases in defense spending. At first, their proposals languished. President Truman, worried about angering a hostile, budget-conscious Congress and an American public which was enjoying an era of peace and prosperity, for months refused to approve the defense spending proposals. It took the North Korean invasion of South Korea to allow the administration to rally support for the prescriptions of NSC-68. Before the Korean War, American politicians were fighting over whether the defense budget ought to be $15 billion or $16 billion; most believed more defense spending would bankrupt the nation. The next year, the defense budget was over $50 billion.

A similar sequence of events unfolded in the 1970s. When Reagan and the "Scoop" Jackson Democrats began sounding the alarm about the Soviet danger, the American public was not ready to listen. Then came the Soviet invasion of Afghanistan and the seizure of American hostages in Iran. By the time Jimmy Carter professed to have learned more about the Soviet Union than he had ever known before, Reagan and his fellow conservatives in both parties had laid the intellectual foundation for the military buildup of the 1980s.

AN ELEVATED PATRIOTISM

IN THEORY, either party could lay the groundwork for a neo-Reaganite foreign policy over the next decade. The Democrats, after all, led the nation to assume its new global responsibilities in the late 1940s and early 1950s under President Truman and Secretary of State Dean Acheson. It is unlikely, however, that they are prepared to pursue such a course today. Republicans may have lost their way in the last few years, but the Democrats are still recovering from their post-Vietnam trauma of two decades ago. President Clinton has proved a better manager of foreign policy than many expected, but he has not been up to the larger task of preparing and inspiring the nation to embrace the role of global leadership. He, too, has tailored his internationalist activism to fit the constraints of a popular mood that White House pollsters believe is disinclined to sacrifice blood and treasure in the name of overseas commitments. His Pentagon officials talk more about exit strategies than about national objectives. His administration has promised global leadership on the cheap, refusing to seek the levels of defense spending needed to meet the broad goals it claims to want to achieve in the world. Even Clinton's boldest overseas adventures, in Bosnia and Haiti, have come only after strenuous and prolonged efforts to avoid intervention.

Republicans are surely the genuine heirs to the Reagan tradition. The 1994 election is often said to have represented one last victory for Ronald Reagan's domestic agenda. But Reagan's earlier successes rested as much on foreign as on domestic policy. Over the long term, victory for American conservatives depends on recapturing the spirit of Reagan's foreign policy as well.

Indeed, American conservatism cannot govern by domestic policy alone. In the 1990s conservatives have built their agenda on two pillars of Reaganism: relimiting government to curtail the most intrusive and counterproductive aspects of the modern welfare state, and reversing the widespread collapse of morals and standards in American society. But it is hard to imagine conservatives achieving a lasting political realignment in this country without the third pillar: a coherent set of foreign policy principles that at least bear some resemblance to those propounded by Reagan. The remoralization of America at home ultimately requires the remoralization of American foreign policy. For both follow from Americans' belief that the principles of the Declaration of Independence are not merely the choices of a particular culture but are universal, enduring, "self-evident" truths. That has been, after all, the main point of the conservatives' war against a relativistic multiculturalism. For conservatives to preach the importance of upholding the core elements of the Western tradition at home, but to profess indifference to the fate of American principles abroad, is an inconsistency that cannot help but gnaw at the heart of conservatism.

Conservatives these days succumb easily to the charming old metaphor of the United States as a "city on a hill." They hark back, as George Kennan did in these pages not long ago, to the admonition of John Quincy Adams that America ought not go "abroad in search of monsters to destroy." But why not? The alternative is to leave monsters on the loose, ravaging and pillaging to their hearts' content, as Americans stand by and watch. What may have been wise counsel in 1823, when America was a small, isolated power in a world of European giants, is no longer so, when America is the giant. Because America has the capacity to contain or destroy many of the world's monsters, most of which can be found without much searching, and because the responsibility for the peace and security of the international order rests so heavily on America's shoulders, a policy of sitting atop a hill and leading by example becomes in practice a policy of cowardice and dishonor.

And more is at stake than honor. Without a broader, more enlightened understanding of America's interests, conservatism will too easily degenerate into the pinched nationalism of Buchanan's "America First," where the appeal to narrow self-interest masks a deeper form of self-loathing. A true "conservatism of the heart" ought to emphasize both personal and national responsibility, relish the opportunity for national engagement, embrace the possibility of national greatness, and restore a sense of the heroic, which has been sorely lacking in American foreign policy—and American conservatism—in recent years. George Kennan was right 50 years ago in his famous "X" article: the American people ought to feel a "certain gratitude to a Providence, which by providing [them] with this implacable challenge, has made their entire security as a nation dependent on pulling themselves together and accepting the responsibilities of moral and political leadership that history plainly intended them to bear." This is as true today—if less obviously so—as it was at the beginning of the Cold War.

A neo-Reaganite foreign policy would be good for conservatives, good for America, and good for the world. It is worth recalling that the most successful Republican presidents of this century, Theodore Roosevelt and Ronald Reagan, both inspired Americans to assume cheerfully the new international responsibilities that went with increased power and influence. Both celebrated American exceptionalism. Both made Americans proud of their leading role in world affairs. Deprived of the support of an elevated patriotism, bereft of the ability to appeal to national honor, conservatives will ultimately fail in their effort to govern America. And Americans will fail in their responsibility to lead the world.❧

U.S. Power and
Strategy After Iraq

Joseph S. Nye, Jr.

THE VIEW FROM THE TOP

THE WORLD is off balance. If anyone doubted the overwhelming nature of U.S. military power, Iraq settled the issue. With the United States representing nearly half of the world's military expenditures, no countervailing coalition can create a traditional military balance of power. Not since Rome has one nation loomed so large above the others. Indeed, the word "empire" has come out of the closet. Respected analysts on both the left and the right are beginning to refer to "American empire" approvingly as the dominant narrative of the twenty-first century. And the military victory in Iraq seems only to have confirmed this new world order.

Americans, however, often misunderstand the nature of their power and tend to extrapolate the present into the future. A little more than a decade ago, the conventional wisdom held that the United States was in decline. In 1992, a presidential candidate won votes by proclaiming that the Cold War was over and Japan had won. Now Americans are told that their unipolar moment will last and that they can do as they will because others have no choice but to follow. But focusing on the imbalance of military power among states is misleading. Beneath that surface structure, the world changed in profound ways during the last decades of the twentieth century. September 11, 2001, was like a flash of lightning on a summer evening that displayed

JOSEPH S. NYE, JR. is Dean of the John F. Kennedy School of Government at Harvard University. This article originally appeared in the July/August 2003 issue of *Foreign Affairs*.

an altered landscape, leaving U.S. policymakers and analysts still groping in the dark, still wondering how to understand and respond.

ABOUT-FACE

GEORGE W. BUSH entered office committed to a realist foreign
policy that would focus on great powers such as China and Russia
and eschew nation building in failed states of the less-developed
world. China was to be "a strategic competitor," not the "strategic
partner" of Bill Clinton's era, and the United States was to take a
tougher stance with Russia. But in September 2002, the Bush
administration issued a new national security strategy, declaring that
"we are menaced less by fleets and armies than by catastrophic technologies falling into the hands of the embittered few." Instead of
strategic rivalry, "today, the world's great powers find ourselves on the
same side—united by common dangers of terrorist violence and
chaos." Not only was Chinese President Jiang Zemin welcomed to
Bush's ranch in Crawford, Texas, but Bush's strategy embraces "the
emergence of a strong, peaceful, and prosperous China." And it
commits the United States to increasing its development assistance
and efforts to combat HIV/AIDS, because "weak states, like Afghanistan,
can pose as great a danger to our national interest as strong states."
Moreover, these policies will be "guided by the conviction that no
nation can build a safer, better world alone." How the world turned
in one year! And, between the lines, Iraq came to be viewed as the
new strategy's first test, even though another member of the "axis of
evil" was much closer to developing nuclear weapons.

The rhetoric of the new strategy attracted criticism at home
and abroad. The trumpeting of American primacy violated Teddy
Roosevelt's advice about speaking softly when you carry a big stick.
The United States will remain number one, but there was no need
to rub others' noses in it. The neo-Wilsonian promises to promote
democracy and freedom struck some traditional realists as dangerously unbounded. The statements about cooperation and coalitions
were not followed by equal discussion of institutions. And the
much-criticized assertion of a right to preempt could be interpreted
either as routine self-defense or as a dangerous precedent.

These criticisms notwithstanding, the Bush administration was correct in its change of focus. The distinguished historian John Lewis Gaddis has compared the new strategy to the seminal days that redefined American foreign policy in the 1940s. Although that comparison may be exaggerated, the new strategy does respond to the deep trends in world politics that were illuminated by the events of September 11. Globalization, for instance, has proved itself to be more than just an economic phenomenon; it has been wearing away at the natural buffers that distance and two oceans have always provided to the United States. September 11 thus dramatized how dreadful conditions in poor, weak countries halfway around the world can have terrible consequences for the United States.

The information revolution and technological change have elevated the importance of transnational issues and have empowered nonstate actors to play a larger role in world politics. A few decades ago, instantaneous global communications were out of the financial reach of all but governments or large organizations such as multinational corporations or the Catholic Church. At the same time, the United States and the Soviet Union were secretly spending billions of dollars on overhead space photography. Now inexpensive commercial satellite photos are available to anyone, and the Internet enabled 1,500 nongovernmental organizations to inexpensively coordinate the "battle of Seattle" that disrupted the World Trade Organization's meeting in December 1999.

Most worrying are the effects of these deep trends on terrorism. Terrorism itself is nothing new, but the "democratization of technology" over the past decades has been making terrorists more lethal and more agile, and the trend is likely to continue. In the twentieth century, a pathological individual—a Hitler or a Stalin—needed the power of a government to be able to kill millions of people. If twenty-first-century terrorists get hold of weapons of mass destruction, this devastating power will for the first time become available to deviant groups and individuals. Traditional state-centric analysts think that punishing states that sponsor terrorism can solve the problem. Such punitive measures might help, but in the end they cannot stop individuals who have already gained access to destructive technology. After all, Timothy McVeigh in the United States and Aum Shinrikyo in Japan were not sponsored by states. And in 2001, one surprise attack by a transnational terrorist group killed more Americans than the state of Japan did in 1941. The "privatization of war" is not only a major historical change in world politics; its potential impact on U.S. cities could drastically alter the nature of American civilization. This shifting ground is what the new Bush strategy gets right.

A STRATEGY DIVIDED

WHAT THE BUSH ADMINISTRATION has not yet sorted out is how to go about implementing its new approach. At first glance, it appears that the Iraq war settled the issue. But the war can be interpreted as the last chapter of the twentieth century rather than the first chapter of the twenty-first. Not only was it unfinished business in the minds of its planners, but it also rested on more than a decade of unfulfilled UN Security Council resolutions. A number of close observers—such as British Ambassador to the UN Sir Jeremy Greenstock—believe that with a little more patience and diplomacy, the administration could have obtained another resolution that would have focused on the sins of Saddam Hussein rather than allowing France and Russia to turn the problem into one of American power. If that close call had come out differently, the continuity with the past would be clearer today. Moreover, the administration is currently faced with another dangerous dictator who is months rather than years away from having nuclear weapons and thus fits the criteria of the new strategy even more closely than Iraq did. North Korea may prove to be the real test of how to implement the new strategy. Thus far, the Bush administration has responded cautiously and in close consultation with U.S. allies. Deterrence seems to have worked, although in this case it was North Korea's conventional capacity to wreak havoc on Seoul in the event of war that deterred U.S. military action.

There is also a larger struggle involved in the debate over how to implement the new strategy. The administration is deeply divided between those who want to escape the constraints of the post-1945 institutional framework that the United States helped to build and those who believe U.S. goals are better achieved by working within that framework. The neoconservative "Wilsonians of the right" and the "Jacksonian unilateralists" (to adapt terms coined by historian Walter Russell Mead) are pitted against the more multilateral and cautious traditional realists. The tug of war within the administration was visible both in the strategy document and in the run-up to the Iraq war. Vice President Dick Cheney and Secretary of Defense Donald Rumsfeld disparaged the UN as a "false comfort," traditional realist Republicans such as Brent Scowcroft and James Baker urged a multilateral approach, and President Bush's September 12, 2002, speech to the UN represented a temporary victory for the coalition of U.S. Secretary of State Colin Powell and British Prime Minister Tony Blair. The failure to obtain a second Security Council resolution and the success of the war, however, have ensured the ascendancy of the Jacksonians and the neo-Wilsonians.

Earlier, in 2001, the columnist Charles Krauthammer presaged their vision when he argued for a "new unilateralism," one in which the United States refuses to play the role of a "docile international citizen" and unashamedly pursues its own ends. For most analysts, unilateralism and multilateralism are simply two ends of a spectrum of diplomatic tactics; few leaders follow one or the other approach exclusively. But the new unilateralists go a step further. They believe that today Washington faces new threats of such dire nature that it must escape the constraints of the multilateral structures it helped build after World War II. In their view, the implementation of a new strategy requires more radical change. As Philip Stephens of the *Financial Times* put it, they would like to reverse Dean Acheson's famous title and be "present at the destruction." They deliberately resisted calling upon NATO after Washington's allies invoked Article 5, offering collective self-defense in the wake of the September 11 terrorist attacks. They sought to minimize the role of the UN in Iraq before and after the war, and they now talk of a "disaggregation" approach to Europe rather than traditional support for European union. In Rumsfeld's words, the issues should determine the coalitions, not vice versa. Some advocates do not shrink from an explicitly imperial approach. In the words of William Kristol, editor of *The Weekly Standard*, "if people want to say we are an imperial power, fine."

U.S. Power and Strategy After Iraq

ONE-DIMENSIONAL THINKING

ALTHOUGH THE NEW UNILATERALISTS are right that maintaining U.S. military strength is crucial and that pure multilateralism is impossible, they make important mistakes that will ultimately undercut the implementation of the new security strategy. Their first mistake is to focus too heavily on military power alone. U.S. military power is essential to global stability and is a critical part of the response to terrorism. But the metaphor of war should not blind Americans to the fact that suppressing terrorism will take years of patient, unspectacular civilian cooperation with other countries in areas such as intelligence sharing, police work, tracing financial flows, and border controls. For example, the American military success in Afghanistan dealt with the easiest part of the problem: toppling an oppressive and weak government in a poor country. But all the precision bombing destroyed only a small fraction of al Qaeda's network, which retains cells in some 60 countries. And bombing cannot resolve the problem of cells in Hamburg or Detroit. Rather than proving the new unilateralists' point, the partial nature of the success in Afghanistan illustrates the continuing need for cooperation. The best response to transnational terrorist networks is networks of cooperating government agencies.

Power is the ability to obtain the outcomes one wants, and the changes sketched out above have made its distribution more complex than first meets the eye. The agenda of world politics has become like a three-dimensional chess game in which one can win only by playing vertically as well as horizontally. On the top board of classical interstate military issues, the United States is likely to remain the only superpower for years to come, and it makes sense to speak in traditional terms of unipolarity or hegemony. However, on the middle board of interstate economic issues, the distribution of power is already multipolar. The United States cannot obtain the outcomes it wants on trade, antitrust, or financial regulation issues without the agreement of the European Union (EU), Japan, and others. It makes little sense to call this distribution "American hegemony." And on the bottom board of transnational issues, power is widely distributed and chaotically organized among state and nonstate actors. It makes no sense at all to call this a "unipolar world" or an "American empire." And, as Bush's new doctrine makes clear, this is precisely the set of issues now intruding into the world of grand strategy. Yet many of the new unilateralists, particularly the Jacksonians, focus almost entirely on the top board of classical military solutions. They mistake the necessary for the sufficient. They are one-dimensional players in a three-dimensional game. In the long term, their approach to implementing the strategy guarantees losing.

SELLING SOFT POWER SHORT

THE WILLINGNESS of other countries to cooperate in dealing with transnational issues such as terrorism depends in part on their own self-interest, but also on the attractiveness of American positions. Soft power lies in the ability to attract and persuade rather than coerce. It means that others want what the United States wants, and there is less need to use carrots and sticks. Hard power, the ability to coerce, grows out of a country's military and economic might. Soft power arises from the attractiveness of a country's culture, political ideals, and policies. When U.S. policies appear legitimate in the eyes of others, American soft power is enhanced. Hard power will always remain crucial in a world of nation-states guarding their independence, but soft power will become increasingly important in dealing with the transnational issues that require multilateral cooperation for their solution.

One of Rumsfeld's "rules" is that "weakness is provocative." In this, he is correct. As Osama bin Laden observed, it is best to bet on the strong horse. The effective demonstration of military power in the second Gulf War, as in the first, might have a deterrent as well as a transformative effect in the Middle East. But the first Gulf War, which led to the Oslo peace process, was widely regarded as legitimate, whereas the legitimacy of the more recent war was contested. Unable to balance American military power, France, Germany, Russia, and China created a coalition to balance American soft power by depriving the United States of the legitimacy that might have been bestowed by a second UN resolution. Although such balancing did not avert the war in Iraq, it did significantly raise its price. When Turkish parliamentarians regarded U.S. policy as illegitimate, they refused Pentagon requests to allow the Fourth Infantry Division to enter Iraq from the north. Inadequate attention to soft power was detrimental to the hard power the United States could bring to bear in the early days of the war. Hard and soft power may sometimes conflict, but they can also reinforce each other. And when the Jacksonians mistake soft power for weakness, they do so at their own risk.

One instructive usage of soft power that the Pentagon got right in the second Gulf War has been called the "weaponization of reporters." Embedding reporters with forward military units undercut Saddam's strategy of creating international outrage by claiming that U.S. troops were deliberately killing civilians. Whereas CNN framed the issues in the first Gulf War, the diffusion of information technology and the rise of new outlets such as al Jazeera in the intervening decade required a new strategy for maintaining soft power during the second. Whatever other issues it raises, embedding reporters in frontline units was a wise response to changing times.

ALLIANCE A LA CARTE

PROPONENTS of the neoconservative strand in the new unilateralism are more attentive to some aspects of soft power. Their Wilsonian emphasis on democracy and human rights can help make U.S policies attractive to others when these values appear genuine and are pursued in a fair-minded way. The human rights abuses of Saddam's regime have thus become a major post hoc legitimization of the war. Moreover, as indicated earlier, the Bush administration has made wise investments in American soft power by increasing development aid and offering assistance in the campaign against HIV/AIDS. But although they share Woodrow Wilson's desire to spread democracy, the neo-Wilsonians ignore his emphasis on institutions. In the absence of international institutions through which others can feel consulted and involved, the imperial imposition of values may neither attract others nor produce soft power.

Both the neo-Wilsonian and the Jacksonian strands of the new unilateralism tend to prefer alliance à la carte and to treat international institutions as toolboxes into which U.S. policymakers can reach when convenient. But this approach neglects the ways in which institutions legitimize disproportionate American power. When others feel that they have been consulted, they are more likely to be helpful. For example, NATO members are doing much of the work of keeping the peace in the Balkans and in Afghanistan. NATO works through many committees to achieve the standardization and interoperability that allow coalitions of the willing to be more than ad hoc groupings. Without regular institutional consultation, the United States may find others increasingly reluctant to put tools into the toolbox. One day the box might even be bare. American-led coalitions will become less willing and shrink in size—witness the two gulf wars.

The UN is a particularly difficult institution. The power of the veto in the Security Council has prevented it from authorizing the use of force for collective-security operations in all but three cases in the past half-century. But the council was specifically designed to be a concert of large powers that would not work when they disagreed. The veto is like a fuse box in the electrical system of a house. Better that a fuse blows and the lights go out than that the house burns down. Moreover, as UN Secretary-General Kofi Annan pointed out after the Kosovo war proceeded in 1999 without a UN resolution—but with French and German participation—the UN is torn between the strict Westphalian interpretation of state sovereignty and the rise of international humanitarian and human rights law that sets limits on what leaders can do to their citizens. To complicate matters further, politics has made the UN Charter virtually impossible to amend. Still, for all its flaws, the UN has proved useful in its humanitarian and peacekeeping roles on which states agree, and it remains an important source of legitimacy in world politics.

The latter point is particularly galling to the new unilateralists, who (correctly) point to the undemocratic nature of many of the regimes that cast votes in the UN and chair its committees—one rankling example being Libya's chairmanship of the Human Rights

Commission. But their proposed solution of replacing the UN with a new organization of democracies ignores the fact that the major divisions over Iraq were among the democracies. Rather than engage in futile efforts to ignore the UN or change its architecture, Washington should improve its underlying bilateral diplomacy with the other veto-wielding powers and use the UN in practical ways to further the new strategy. In addition to overseeing the UN's development and humanitarian agenda, the Security Council may wind up playing a background role in diffusing the crisis in North Korea; the Committee on Terrorism can help prod states to improve their procedures; and UN peacekeepers can save the United States from having to be the world's lone sheriff. If Washington uses it wisely, the UN can serve U.S. interests in a variety of practical ways. But the reverse is also true: the new unilateralists' attacks on the UN may backfire in ways that undercut American soft power.

There is considerable evidence that the new unilateralists' policies tend to squander U.S. soft power. Before the war, a Pew Charitable Trust poll found that U.S. policies (not American culture) led to less favorable attitudes toward the United States over the past two years in 19 of 27 countries, including the Islamic countries so crucial to the prosecution of the war on terrorism. Other polls showed an average drop of 30 points in the popularity of the United States in major European countries.

No large country can afford to be purely multilateralist, and sometimes the United States must take the lead by itself, as it did in Afghanistan. And the credible threat to exercise the unilateral option was probably essential to getting the UN Security Council to pass Resolution 1441, which brought the weapons inspectors back into Iraq. But the United States should incline toward multilateralism whenever possible as a way to legitimize its power and to gain broad acceptance of its new strategy. Preemption that is legitimized by multilateral sanction is far less costly and sets a far less dangerous precedent than the United States asserting that it alone can act as judge, jury, and executioner. Granted, multilateralism can be used by smaller states to restrict American freedom of action, but this downside does not detract from its overall usefulness. Whether Washington learns to listen to others and to define U.S. national interests more broadly to include global interests will be crucial to the success of the new strategy and to whether others see the American preponderance the strategy proclaims as benign or not. To implement the new strategy successfully, therefore, the United States will need to pay more attention to soft power and multilateral cooperation than the new unilateralists would like.

IMPERIAL UNDERSTRETCH

FINALLY, those of the new unilateralists who openly welcome the idea of an American empire mistake the underlying nature of American public opinion. Even if the transformation of undemocratic regimes in the Middle East would indeed reduce some of the sources of Islamic terrorism, the question remains whether the American public will tolerate an imperial role. Neoconservative writers such as Max Boot argue that the United States should provide troubled countries with "the sort of enlightened foreign administration once provided by self-confident Englishmen in jodhpurs and pith helmets," but as the British historian Niall Ferguson points out, modern America differs from nineteenth-century Britain in its chronically short attention span.

Some say the United States is already an empire and it is just a matter of recognizing reality, but they mistake the politics of primacy for those of empire. The United States may be more powerful compared to other countries than the United Kingdom was at its imperial peak, but it has less control over what occurs inside other countries than the United Kingdom did when it ruled a quarter of the globe. For example, Kenya's schools, taxes, laws, and elections—not to mention external relations—were controlled by British officials. The United States has no such control over any country today. Washington could not even get the votes of Mexico City and Santiago for a second Security Council resolution. Devotees of the new imperialism argue that such analysis is too literal, that "empire" is intended merely as a metaphor. But this "metaphor" implies a control from Washington that is unrealistic and reinforces the prevailing temptations of unilateralism.

Despite its natal ideology of anti-imperialism, the United States has intervened and governed countries in Central America and the Caribbean, as well as the Philippines. But Americans have never felt comfortable as imperialists, and only a small number of cases led directly to the establishment of democracies. American empire is not limited by "imperial overstretch" in the sense of costing an unsustainable portion of U.S. gross domestic product. Indeed, the United States devoted a much higher percentage of GDP to the military budget during the Cold War than it does today. The overstretch will come from having to police more peripheral countries than public opinion will accept. Even after the second Gulf War, polls show little taste for empire and no public inclination toward invading Syria and Iran. Instead, the American public continues to say that it favors multilateralism and using the UN.

In fact, the problem of creating an American empire might better be termed "imperial understretch." Neither the public nor Congress has proved willing to invest seriously in the instruments of nation building and governance, as opposed to military force. The entire allotment for the State Department and the U.S. Agency for International Development is only 1 percent of the federal budget. The United States spends nearly 16 times as much on its military, and there is little indication of change to come in this era of tax cuts and budget deficits. The U.S. military is designed for fighting rather than police work, and the Pentagon has cut back on training for peacekeeping operations. In practice, the coalition of neo-Wilsonians and Jacksonians may divide over this issue. The former will espouse a prolonged U.S. presence to produce democracy in the Middle East, whereas the latter, who tend to eschew "nation building," have designed a military that is better suited to kick down the door, beat up a dictator, and go home than to stay for the harder work of building a democratic polity.

Among a number of possible futures for Iraq are three scenarios that deserve some elaboration. The first is the example of Japan or Germany in 1945, in which the United States stays for seven years and leaves behind a friendly democracy. This would be the preferred outcome, but it is worth remembering that Germany and Japan were ethnically homogeneous societies, ones that also did not produce any terrorist responses to the presence of U.S. troops and could boast significant middle classes that had already experienced democracy in the 1920s. A second scenario is akin to that of Ronald Reagan in Lebanon or Bill Clinton in Somalia, where some of the people who cheered U.S. entry wound up protesting its presence six months later. In this scenario, terrorists kill U.S. soldiers, and the American public reacts by saying, "Saddam is gone, Iraq has no weapons of mass destruction, they don't want our democracy, let's pull out." If this scenario left Iraq in conflict, dictatorship, or theocracy, it would undercut the major post hoc legitimization for the war. The third scenario would be reminiscent of Bosnia or Kosovo. The United States would entice NATO allies and other countries to help in the policing and reconstruction of Iraq, a UN resolution would bless the force, and an international administrator would help to legitimize decisions. The process would be long and frustrating, but it would reduce the prominence of the United States as a target for anti-imperialists and would probably best ensure that America did not pull out prematurely. Ironically, the neo-Wilsonians of the new unilateralist coalition might have to make common cause with the multilateral realists to achieve their objectives. They might find that the world's only superpower can't go it alone after all.

THE PARADOX OF PRIMACY

THE BUSH ADMINISTRATION'S new national security strategy correctly identified the challenges growing out of the deep changes in world politics that were illuminated on September 11. But the administration has still not settled on how to implement the new strategy most effectively. Rather than resolving the issue, the second Gulf War leaves the divisions in place, and the real tests still await.

The problem for U.S. power in the twenty-first century is that more and more continues to fall outside the control of even the most powerful state. Although the United States does well on the traditional measures of hard power, these measures fail to capture the ongoing transformation of world politics brought about by globalization and the democratization of technology. The paradox of American power is that world politics is changing in a way that makes it impossible for the strongest world power since Rome to achieve some of its most crucial international goals alone. The United States lacks both the international and the domestic capacity to resolve conflicts that are internal to other societies and to monitor and control transnational developments that threaten Americans at home. On many of today's key issues, such as international financial stability, drug trafficking, the spread of diseases, and especially the new terrorism, military power alone simply cannot produce success, and its use can sometimes be counterproductive. Instead, as the most powerful country, the United States must mobilize international coalitions to address these shared threats and challenges. By devaluing soft power and institutions, the new unilateralist coalition of Jacksonians and neo-Wilsonians is depriving Washington of some of its most important instruments for the implementation of the new national security strategy. If they manage to continue with this tack, the United States could fail what Henry Kissinger called the historical test for this generation of American leaders: to use current preponderant U.S. power to achieve an international consensus behind widely accepted norms that will protect American values in a more uncertain future. Fortunately, this outcome is not preordained.⊛

Striking a New Transatlantic Bargain

Andrew Moravcsik

BACK ON TRACK

THE RECENT WAR in Iraq has triggered the most severe transatlantic tensions in a generation, dividing Europeans and Americans from each other and themselves. Pundits proclaim daily the imminent collapse of three vital pillars in the institutional architecture of world politics: NATO, the UN, and even the EU. And yet some form of transatlantic cooperation clearly remains essential, given the vast mutual interests at stake. Where, then, should the Western alliance go now?

The Iraq crisis offers two basic lessons. The first, for Europeans, is that American hawks were right. Unilateral intervention to coerce regime change can be a cost-effective way to deal with rogue states. In military matters, there is only one superpower—the United States—and it can go it alone if it has to. It is time to accept this fact and move on.

The second lesson, for Americans, is that moderate skeptics on both sides of the Atlantic were also right. Winning a peace is much harder than winning a war. Intervention is cheap in the short run but expensive in the long run. And when it comes to the essential instruments for avoiding chaos or quagmire once the fighting stops—trade, aid, peacekeeping, international monitoring, and multilateral legitimacy—Europe remains indispensable. In this respect, the unipolar world turns out to be bipolar after all.

ANDREW MORAVCSIK is Professor of Government and Director of the European Union program at Harvard University. This article originally appeared in the July/August 2003 issue of *Foreign Affairs*.

Given these truths, it is now time to work out a new transatlantic bargain, one that redirects complementary military and civilian instruments toward common ends and new security threats. Without such a deal, danger exists that Europeans—who were rolled over in the run-up to the war, frozen out by unilateral U.S. nation building, disparaged by triumphalist American pundits and politicians, and who lack sufficiently unified regional institutions—will keep their distance and leave the United States to its own devices. Although understandable, this reaction would be a recipe for disaster, since the United States lacks both the will and the institutional capacity to follow up its military triumphs properly—as the initial haphazard efforts at Iraqi reconstruction demonstrate.

To get things back on track, both in Iraq and elsewhere, Washington must shift course and accept multilateral conditions for intervention. The Europeans, meanwhile, must shed their resentment of American power and be prepared to pick up much of the burden of conflict prevention and postconflict engagement. Complementarity, not conflict, should be the transatlantic watchword.

THE DEATH OF ATLANTICISM?

THERE ARE TWO conflicting views about the seriousness of the current crisis in transatlantic relations. Pessimists maintain that differences in power, threat perceptions, and values are forcing an inexorable divergence in European and American interests. Optimists see recent troubles as the product of rigid ideologies, domestic politics, and missed diplomatic opportunities. Both views are partly right.

The pessimists emphasize the radically new distribution of power in the international system. The United States is less militarily dependent on allies than at any time in the past half-century. U.S. defense spending now surpasses that of China, France, Germany, India, Japan, Russia, and the United Kingdom combined, and the disparity will only grow, since the United States outspends Europe by a ratio of 5 to 1 on military research and development. Washington can now wage war confident of quick victory, low casualties, and little domestic fallout, and its ambitions have expanded accordingly. Two decades ago, the Reagan administration pursued "regime change" only in small countries and by proxy; today, the Bush administration feels free to conquer a midsize power across the globe directly, with little allied participation.

American and European threat perceptions, meanwhile, have also diverged. The terrorist attacks on the World Trade Center and the Pentagon, combined with existing U.S. commitments involving oil and Israel, have led many Americans to view the war against rogue regimes, terrorism, and weapons of mass destruction (WMD) as a matter of vital national interest. But since the attacks were not directed at them, Europeans find the threat less pressing—and with large Muslim minorities at home and Islamic neighbors next door, they worry more about the spillover of Middle East instability. For Europe, the defining moment of the contemporary era remains the collapse of the Soviet empire, symbolized by the fall of the Berlin Wall on November 9, 1989; 11/9 is thus more important to Europeans than 9/11. Without major direct threats to their security, Europeans have felt free to disarm, cultivate their unique postmodern polity, and criticize the United States.

Europeans and Americans disagree about not only power and threats, but also means. As Robert Kagan and other neoconservatives argue, U.S. military power begets an ideological tendency to use it. In Europe, by contrast, weak militaries coexist with an aversion to war. Influenced by social democratic ideas, the legacy of two world wars, and the EU experience, Europeans prefer to deal with problems through economic integration, foreign aid, and multilateral institutions. These differences have become embedded in bureaucracy: the best and brightest American diplomats specialize in unilateral politico-military affairs, whereas their European counterparts focus on civilian multilateral organizations such as the EU.

These structural shifts do mark an important, and perhaps epochal, transformation in world politics. The heyday of Atlanticism, when the protection of Europe by U.S. strategic and European conventional forces was the centerpiece of the Western alliance, is gone for good. Americans and Europeans must accept new realities: the rise of new extra-European threats that are of varied concern to the allies, the American military ability to force regime change, and the deep European commitment to multilateral institutions and civilian power.

UNNECESSARY ENMITY

TRANSATLANTIC OPTIMISTS are also right when they argue that the recent shifts need not lead inexorably to the collapse of NATO, the UN, or the EU. Historically, they note, transatlantic crises have been cyclical events, arising most often when conservative Republican presidents pursued assertive unilateral military policies. During the Vietnam era and the Reagan administration, as today, European polls recorded 80–95 percent opposition to U.S. intervention, millions of protesters flooded the streets, NATO was deeply split, and European politicians compared the United States to Nazi Germany. Washington went into "opposition" at the UN, where, since 1970, it has vetoed 34 Security Council resolutions on the Middle East alone, each time casting the lone dissent.

In the recent crisis, a particularly radical American policy combined with a unique confluence of European domestic pressures— German Chancellor Gerhard Schröder's political vulnerability and French President Jacques Chirac's Gaullist skepticism of American power—to trigger the crisis.

Most Europeans—like most Americans—rejected the neoconservative claim that a preemptive war against Iraq without multilateral support was necessary or advisable. Sober policy analysis underlay the concerns of the doubters, who felt that the war in Iraq, unlike the one in Afghanistan, was not really connected to the "war on terrorism." Skeptics were also wary of the difficulties and costs likely to attend postwar reconstruction. No surprise, then, that most foreign governments sought to exhaust alternatives to war before moving forward and refused to set the dangerous precedent of authorizing an attack simply because the United States requested it.

In spite of these doubts about the Bush administration's policies, however, underlying U.S. and European interests remain strikingly convergent. It is a cliché but nonetheless accurate to assert that the Western relationship rests on shared values: democracy, human rights, open markets, and a measure of social justice. No countries are more likely to agree on basic policy, and to have the power to do something about it. Even regarding a sensitive area such as the

Middle East, both sides recognize Israel's right to exist, advocate a Palestinian state, oppose tyrants such as Saddam Hussein, seek oil security, worry about radical Islamism, and fear terrorism and the proliferation of WMD.

Indeed, these shared interests and values help explain why the trend over the past two decades has been toward transatlantic harmony. Europeans are hardly doctrinaire pacifists or myopic regionalists; the recent Iraq war is the first U.S. military action since the Reagan years to trigger significant European opposition. In the first Gulf War, for example, UN authorization unlocked European support, participation, and cofinancing. And the Kosovo intervention, although "preventive" and conducted without UN authorization, was unanimously backed by NATO.

The September 11 attacks themselves did little to change this situation. The celebrated *Le Monde* headline on September 13 proclaiming "Nous sommes tous Américains" ("We are all Americans") and Schöder's simultaneous pledge of "unconditional solidarity" were not just rhetoric. Diplomats invoked NATO's Article 5 (its mutual defense clause) for the first time, and when the United States invaded Afghanistan in hot pursuit of al Qaeda, European governments lent their unanimous support. Since then, Europeans have provided more financial and peacekeeping support to Afghanistan than has the United States. The shared commitment to peacekeeping operations in Bosnia, Côte d'Ivoire, East Timor, Kosovo, Rwanda, and Sierra Leone suggests a consensus on humanitarian intervention, and the unanimous passage of Security Council Resolution 1441 regarding Iraq in November suggests that a similar consensus may exist on counterproliferation.

Even in the recent crisis, the vigorous rhetoric of some European governments was balanced by more tempered action. Many NATO members backed the United States outright. Setting aside a few regrettable episodes, such as the brief attempt to delay NATO defensive assistance to Turkey (easily overcome in a few days), it is misleading to portray France and Germany as having attempted to balance American power. Neither state took material action against Washington, nor even proposed multilateral condemnation of the U.S. position, as has happened many times in decades past.

(Indeed, Germany and other countries informally aided the war effort.) Paris and Berlin simply withheld multilateral legitimacy and bilateral assistance for what they considered a rushed war, and encouraged others to do likewise.

Rigid positions, unfortunate rhetoric, and misguided diplomatic tactics on both sides, however, unnecessarily exacerbated the crisis. The Bush administration offered a variety of shifting rationales for the war, some of them dubious, and engaged in little of the patient, painstaking diplomacy that had underpinned the broad coalition of the first Gulf War. In the end, the U.S. case for war rested on an open-ended assertion of U.S. security interests, unconstrained by explicit doctrinal constraints, a firm commitment to multilateral procedures, or widespread trust in the American president. Given the Bush administration's flagrant repudiation of a series of multilateral agreements over the previous two years and its apparent lack of concern for foreign interests, other governments were loath to grant it a free hand.

Despite all this, a Security Council majority of 13 or 14 states could have been mustered to support a second war resolution had the Bush administration been willing to wait until June or September and then advance a procedurally proper case for war based on completed inspections. Even French military participation would have been likely under such conditions. Yet Washington declined to make any substantive concessions on either its timetable or alternatives to war. Meanwhile, France, backed by Germany and Russia, seemed determined to oppose any hasty compromise as a matter of principle, only softening its position when it was too late.

The evidence of so much rigidity, bungling, and pique gives the optimists heart, since it suggests that the ultimate outcome was avoidable—and thus that future crises could be handled more smoothly. By going it alone, the United States lost the tens of billions of dollars in financial support that it managed to attract in the first Gulf War and complicated its military operations by missing a chance to create a second front. Postwar reconstruction is proving an embarrassing burden rather than a prized opportunity, and Iraq's future remains unclear. For France, meanwhile, the crisis undermined the two institutions in which it holds the greatest influence—the

UN and the EU—and perhaps NATO as well. French opposition failed to slow the American move to war and thus undermined France's transatlantic and cross-Channel relations with little to show in return.

THREE PATHS

THE PESSIMISTS are right to note that the Iraq crisis highlighted the need for a new set of arrangements, structures that can deal with global issues but are appropriate to a world in which the United States and Europe possess different means, perceive different threats, and prefer different procedures. For their part, however, the optimists are right to argue that such crises are still manageable and that Western governments have a strong incentive to manage them. Wiser leadership on both sides, backed by solid institutional cooperation, could have avoided the transatlantic breakdown in the first place.

To prevent future ruptures, both sides must recognize that they benefit from the active participation of the other in most ventures. Only a frank recognition of complementary national interests and mutual dependence will elicit moderation, self-restraint, and a durable willingness to compromise. To this end, the allies could follow one of three paths. They can simply agree to disagree about certain issues, cordoning off areas of dispute from areas of consensus; they can begin to part ways militarily, with Europe developing its own, more autonomous force projection capabilities; or they can negotiate a new bargain, in which American military power and European civilian power are deployed together at targets of mutual concern. The first option is the simplest and least costly solution, but the last promises the greatest returns.

DECENT DIPLOMACY

THE EASIEST WAY to overcome the recent troubles would be for the United States and Europe to manage controversial high-stakes issues delicately while continuing to work together on other subjects that matter to both sides. This is how the Western alliance has functioned for most of its history—protecting core cooperation in

European and nonmilitary matters, while disagreeing about "out of area" intervention and, sometimes, nuclear strategy. Today this lowest-common-denominator policy should still unite nearly all Western leaders.

The transatlantic partnership remains the most important diplomatic relationship in the world, and so the allies have much to protect. Together, the United States and Europe account for 70 percent of world trade. The success of the Doha Round of global trade negotiations—which promises much for the developing world—could contribute greatly to long-term global security. Ongoing cooperation on intelligence and law enforcement is indispensable to successful counterterrorism. An expanded NATO is now widely recognized as a force for democracy and stability. Western governments have unanimously authorized a dozen humanitarian interventions over the last ten years. They work together on many other issues, including human rights, environmental policy, disease control, and financial regulation. Failure to cauterize and contain disputes such as that over Iraq threatens all of this cooperation, as would any deliberate U.S. strategy of trying to weaken or divide international organizations like the UN, the EU, or NATO.

The challenge that remains, of course, is just how to depoliticize controversial high-stakes issues such as preventive intervention. The simplest way to do so would be for the United States to adopt a less aggressively unilateral approach, trying to persuade or compromise with its allies rather than simply issuing peremptory commands. Fortunately, since this policy would appeal to any centrist U.S. administration, American strategy is likely to move in this direction over the long term. Unless senior officials of the Bush administration undergo a radical conversion on the road to Damascus, however, such a course is unlikely to emerge anytime soon.

Restoring diplomatic decency would be an easier first step. The transatlantic partners should commit to consulting quietly and comprehensively before launching public attacks in the media. Similarly, reprisals, whether they take the form of U.S. threats against Europe or French threats against small central European democracies, are ineffective and inflammatory, particularly when a domestic majority supports the offending policy.

More fundamentally, the Iraq crisis suggests that both sides harbored unreasonable expectations about the UN Security Council, fueling an escalating spiral of rhetoric and diplomatic threats. Contrary to what many Europeans wish, the Security Council was not initially designed, and cannot function today, to block a permanent member's military action against a perceived security threat. And contrary to what some Americans wish, U.S. military assistance to Europe (whether in World War II, in the Cold War, or today) does not oblige Europeans to offer blanket authorizations for unlimited U.S. military activity anywhere. Were the Security Council to find itself deadlocked again, therefore, the prudent (and, arguably, normatively appropriate) course would be to drop the matter and allow discussions to move ahead in other forums, as was done with the debate over Kosovo. Absent a clearer threat, however, this implies that the United States would act almost alone—likely failing to persuade even staunch allies such as Blair's United Kingdom.

FROM EUROPE TO MARS

MANY WILL FEEL that mere diplomatic flexibility is an insufficient response to the problems at hand. A parade of pundits—American neoconservatives, traditional NATO analysts, European federalists, and French Gaullists alike—have recently promulgated a new conventional wisdom: that the rearming of Europe is the alliance's only hope. Their logic is simple. To get the United States to listen to its concerns, Europe needs to develop true power projection capabilities. Only an alliance of equals can work, and military power is the only coin that matters.

Interestingly, given their supposedly "Venusian" tendencies, many Europeans find defense cooperation attractive. Nearly 75 percent of the European public favor the notion, and politicians from Tony Blair to Jacques Chirac and German Foreign Minister Joschka Fischer have reasons to advocate it. The governments of Belgium, France, Germany, and Luxembourg—the same group that impeded NATO support to Turkey—recently called a summit to discuss the creation of a group to coordinate European defense procurement, establish a common military headquarters, and construct a unified force.

Little has come of schemes for a powerful European military, however—and little will. A common European force with the capacity to wage high-intensity, low-casualty war around the globe remains a pipe dream. Whatever they may tell pollsters, European publics will not tolerate the massive increases in military spending required to come anywhere near the American level, and more efficient use of current European resources, although desirable, will achieve only modest gains.

Even if Europeans could agree on the funding and the mission for such a unified force, moreover, new transport aircraft, satellites, and soldiers would not add up to a viable European alternative to U.S. unilateralism. For what would the Europeans do with their new power? Deploy it against the United States? Launch pre-preventive interventions? Even if they sought simply to reduce European dependency on U.S. security guarantees, the result would only be to encourage the redeployment of even more American forces outside of Europe. In the end, the best way for Europe to play a world role is to play with, not against, the United States.

A more pragmatic variant of remilitarization would be to develop a European high-intensity power projection capability within NATO. The alliance's members have already pledged to create a response force: a European expeditionary unit of 21,000 troops capable of executing a full range of high-intensity missions. If European troops are able to fight alongside Americans, it is argued, their political leaders will get more of a say in U.S. grand strategy. Some foresee such a force, increased in size tenfold, as the Germans and others have proposed, as suitable for intervention in areas of European interest—such as North Africa, for example—where the United States might eschew involvement. Had the Europeans landed such a force in the Persian Gulf late last year but conditioned its eventual engagement on multilateral authorization, some analysts believe the United States would have been compelled to compromise.

A robust European force of this kind would certainly help matters. But does the Bush administration value European military participation so much that it would moderate its behavior to secure it? Unlikely. Neither NATO nor the United States itself really needs more high-intensity military forces, and the United States, seeking to deflect political pressure and prevent a repetition of the interallied "war by committee" in Kosovo, will not permit itself to become dependent on others for essential materiel. In sum, a high-intensity European force, inside or outside NATO, may make for evocative (albeit expensive) symbolic politics, give the Europeans a more glamorous NATO role, and dampen U.S. complaints about burden-sharing, but it would not change the underlying strategic calculus on either side of the Atlantic.

EXPLOITING ADVANTAGES

Is EUROPE then doomed to play second fiddle, with the only question being how gracefully it accepts its subordinate status? No. Ultimately, proposals to remilitarize Europe are unproductive, because they presume that military force is the predominant instrument of interstate power. This neoconservative nostrum is a poor guide to modern world politics, as well as being sharply at odds with the values most Europeans profess.

A better approach to rebuilding the transatlantic relationship would aim at reconceiving it on the basis of comparative advantage, recognizing that what both parties do is essential and complementary. Europe may possess weaker military forces than does the United States, but on almost every other dimension of global influence it is stronger. Meshing the two sets of capabilities would be the surest path to long-term global peace and security. Each side would profit from being responsible for what it does best. Complementarity is the key to transatlantic reconciliation.

The United States has already demonstrated in Iraq that military force can be remarkably effective. Yet the war's aim was not just to drive Saddam from power but also to establish a much better regime in his place. Some in Washington still believe that doing so will be easy; they assume that a two-year occupation, modest aid, a quick handoff to an interim government, and a postwar economic boom based on sales of privatized oil will spark a rapid economic miracle, similar to that which occurred in West Germany after World War II. Democracy, reconstruction, and development will be self-fulfilling, self-financing, and self-legitimating—and will make Iraq into a new reliable ally.

Few outside the White House, the Pentagon, and the American Enterprise Institute share this optimism, however. Even the postwar German miracle was based on massive, long-term U.S. assistance, and Iraq is less promising terrain. Skeptics point to Afghanistan as a cautionary tale. Indeed, its example is chastening: warlords have reasserted themselves, government ministers have been assassinated, internal security has collapsed to the point where humanitarian aid no longer reaches many regions, the country has reemerged as the world's largest exporter of opium, the battle against al Qaeda has stalled, and Taliban forces are resurfacing in a half-dozen provinces.

If rosy forecasts for Iraq prove incorrect, will the United States match its devastating military force with equally efficacious civilian engagement? Unlikely. Not since the wake of World War II has the United States forged civilian and military means into a coherent geopolitical strategy. In Afghanistan, the United States pursued a "fire and forget" policy: few peacekeepers, no trade concessions, and meager foreign assistance. A recent Carnegie Endowment study reveals that of 16 U.S. efforts at nation building over the past century, only four of them resulted in sustained democracy: Germany, Grenada, Japan, and Panama. The odds are against Iraq's becoming the fifth.

The best way to buck those odds would be for the Bush administration to reverse course and encourage far greater European participation in Iraq and for the Europeans to rise to the challenge. Why? Because with regard to each of the key policy instruments that could make a difference—trade, aid, peacekeeping, monitoring, and multilateral legitimation—Europeans are better prepared than Americans to do what has to be done. Here the central institution is the EU as much as NATO.

Arguably the single most powerful policy instrument for promoting peace and security in the world today, for example, is the ultimate in market access: admission to or association with the EU trading bloc. New EU applicants and associated nations perform well economically, and in country after country, authoritarian, ethnically intolerant, or corrupt governments have lost elections to democratic, market-oriented coalitions held together by the promise of EU membership. Although actually joining the union is an immediate option only for those nations in closest proximity, association with the EU remains an option for many. Association agreements already encompass Russia, much of the rest of the former Soviet Union, Israel, and many Arab states in the Middle East and North Africa—all of which trade more with Europe than with the United States. Holding out such a carrot to postwar Iraq would create a strong incentive for good behavior.

Foreign assistance, meanwhile—whether in the form of humanitarian aid, technical expertise, or support for nation building—reduces immediate human suffering and bolsters peaceful development. Here, too, Europe is the civilian superpower, dispensing 70 percent of global foreign aid and spreading its largess far more widely than the United States. How much aid will ultimately be needed to rebuild and stabilize Iraq is unclear, but oil revenues and U.S. aid will cover only a fraction of the costs, which include basic reconstruction, essential subsistence and infrastructure support, debt payments and reparations, and handouts to the nearly 50 percent of the population previously dependent on the public sector.

If European officials, nongovernmental organizations, and citizens are not given some direct stake in the success of Iraqi reconstruction, however, much less aid will be forthcoming. This is one of the reasons why it is so important to bring the UN into the process, having it endorse the establishment of a civilian administration, authorize participation of UN relief and reconstruction agencies, and support the deployment of a multilateral security and stabilization force. Recent Anglo-American proposals to the Security Council represent a good start. Involving prominent Europeans in the everyday management—people such as Bernard Kouchner, the pro-war French humanitarian activist who served as chief administrator of Kosovo from 1999 to 2001—would further help invest Europe's prestige (and its unmatched expertise) in Iraqi reconstruction.

Maintaining order and internal security will be a crucial challenge in Iraq, and here again Europe is the dominant player. Current and prospective EU members contribute ten times as many soldiers to peacekeeping and policing operations as does the United States. In trouble spots around the globe, European nations take the lead, as did the United Kingdom in Sierra Leone, France in Côte d'Ivoire, Italy in Albania, and Germany in Afghanistan. In Kosovo, 84 percent of the peacekeepers are non-American, as are over half of those in Afghanistan. Even optimistic scenarios estimate that two to three years will be required to establish an Iraqi army, and the U.S. leadership manifestly lacks enthusiasm for being tied down to costly and perhaps dangerous peacekeeping. The United States should thus dust off a German proposal made back in February to have NATO formally take over peacekeeping duties in Afghanistan, and throw in Iraq as well. In expanding these peacekeeping capabilities, much more so than in high-intensity missions, EU proposals for greater coordination of military procurement and deployments will be helpful.

Multilateral monitoring of disarmament and human rights, furthermore, is generally more effective and more legitimate than unilateral efforts. Multilateral measures are also less sensitive politically, for the monitored party has less reason to suspect the inspectors' motives. There is now a considerable bipartisan consensus in the United States on the desirability of a lead role for NATO or the UN in securing and destroying Iraq's weapons of mass destruction and production facilities. The policing of human rights in transitional Iraq is important as well. Europe has extensive regional experience at conditioning aid on monitoring and is the major supporter of the multilateral institutions with serious inspection capability.

The most reliable evidence of Iraq's weapons programs came from the years of UN-sponsored inspections, and even the Bush administration now concedes that the inspectors forced Saddam to dismantle, destroy, or displace many, and perhaps nearly all, of his WMD. One of the unexpected implications of the Iraq crisis is that although neither UN inspections nor American coercive diplomacy work very well alone, they can be extremely effective as complementary elements of a "good cop, bad cop" routine. This tactic would have been more effective had Europe been willing to sponsor thousands of "coercive" inspectors, a promising avenue for future EU collaboration.

Postconflict monitoring under appropriate multilateral auspices will be equally important, since American credibility has been undermined by prewar errors and exaggerations. Most important of all, the transatlantic commitment to strict controls over the use of nuclear, biological, and chemical materials might be harnessed to promote a stronger peacetime counterproliferation regime focused particularly on trafficking in WMD materials.

Finally, in gathering international legitimacy—the persuasive influence Harvard's Joseph Nye terms "soft power"—for confrontations with rogue states, European involvement is crucial. In 1991, President George H.W. Bush was initially disinclined to move against Iraq through the UN, but he was advised that European countries would not back his efforts without a Security Council resolution. The result of his administration's careful diplomacy was near unanimous Western support for the war, the unlocking of $50 billion to $60 billion in cofinancing, and near universal logistical cooperation from neighboring countries. The second Gulf war, by contrast, was opposed by large majorities throughout the world, and the most important reason for that appears to have been the lack of final, explicit UN authorization. Absent such approval, the allies offered no financial contributions, and important regional actors such as Turkey withheld vital support for military operations.

Gaining international legitimacy now for the postwar occupation will be just as crucial, and the participation of the UN and Europe remains the best way to achieve it. By laundering its power through various multilateral mechanisms, the United States would minimize the potential for violent popular backlash directed at it while still maintaining critical behind-the-scenes influence (as in Afghanistan). From this perspective, the gravest danger to coalition policy in Iraq now is not European opposition but European apathy, for without multilateral legitimation, national parliaments are likely to be stingy, and the United States will be left holding the bag.

AFTER IRAQ

FOR ALL THESE REASONS, the reconstruction of Iraq and the reconstruction of the transatlantic alliance should proceed hand in hand, with the former serving as a template for the latter. A new transatlantic bargain based on civil-military complementarity would reflect hardheaded national interests. Europe needs American military might; America needs European civilian power. Each side has reason to value a predictable relationship that will induce moderation, self-restraint, and greater accommodation in advance of military action. If this is indeed what U.S. policymakers seek, they would do well to avoid flagrant violation of multilateral norms and instead start accumulating political capital for future crises. For their part, Europeans should acknowledge the effectiveness of U.S. military power and support ongoing efforts to establish a flexible EU foreign policy that better coordinates civilian, peacekeeping, and military decision-making. Now is the time to commit to this realistic goal.

If things go smoothly—Iraq improves, Europe invests in civilian and peacekeeping instruments, and the United States prefaces future military interventions with measured consultation—a new transatlantic consensus could swiftly be reestablished.

Should Iraqi reconstruction falter, however, with Europeans staying on the sidelines and Americans sticking to their uncompromising and impatient military unilateralism, Western interests in the Middle East could be threatened. Even so, the transatlantic partners could grasp the least bad option of agreeing to disagree on controversial issues while deflecting possible collateral damage to other common interests. Either way, the diplomacy of the last year stands as a guide for what to avoid—and what to seek—the next time around.◈

E
840
.A6235
2003